Editions SR / 22

EDITIONS SR

Volume 22

# Clinical Pastoral Supervision and the Theology of Charles Gerkin

Thomas St. James O'Connor

Published for the Canadian Corporation for Studies in
Religion / Corporation Canadienne des Sciences Religieuses
by Wilfrid Laurier University Press

1998

We acknowledge the financial support of the Government of Canada through the Book Publishing Industry Development Program for our publishing activities.

## Canadian Cataloguing in Publication Data

O'Connor, Thomas St. James, 1950-
  Clinical pastoral supervision and the theology of Charles Gerkin

(Editions SR ; 22)
Includes bibliographical references and index.
ISBN 0-88920-310-5

1. Gerkin, Charles V., 1922- . 2. Pastoral counseling –
Study and teaching – Supervision. 3. Theology, Practical.
I. Canadian Corporation for Studies in Religion. II. Title.
III. Series.

BV4012.2.O36 1998     253'.5     C98-930433-7


© 1998 Canadian Corporation for Studies in Religion /
    Corporation Canadienne des Sciences Religieuses


Cover design by Leslie Macredie using a photograph by W. Glenn Empey

Printed in Canada

*Clinical Pastoral Supervision and the Theology of Charles Gerkin* has been produced from a manuscript supplied in camera-ready form by the author.

All rights reserved. No part of this work covered by the copyrights hereon may be reproduced or used in any form or by any means—graphic, electronic or mechanical—without the prior written permission of the publisher. Any request for photocopying, recording, taping or reproducing in information storage and retrieval systems of any part of this book shall be directed in writing to the Canadian Reprography Collective, 214 King Street West, Suite 312, Toronto, Ontario   M5H 3S6.


Order from:
WILFRID LAURIER UNIVERSITY PRESS
Waterloo, Ontario, Canada   N2L 3C5

*To*

***Elizabeth Ann Marie Meakes***

*wife, colleague and friend*
*and*
*Angel-Marie (Xiao-Xi), our new daughter,*
*a gift from God and China*

# Contents

| | |
|---|---:|
| **Acknowledgements** | ix |
| **Introduction** | 1 |
| Chapter 1<br>**The Field of Clinical Pastoral Supervision** | 7 |
| Chapter 2<br>**Three Approaches in the Praxis of<br>Clinical Pastoral Supervision** | 23 |
| Chapter 3<br>**Gerkin's Incarnational Theology** | 41 |
| Chapter 4<br>**Gerkin's Theological Anthropology** | 60 |
| Chapter 5<br>**Gerkin's Incarnational Theology and the<br>Praxis of Clinical Pastoral Supervision** | 72 |
| Chapter 6<br>**An Adequate Transformed Praxis** | 88 |
| Chapter 7<br>**Conclusion** | 97 |
| **Glossary of Key Terms** | 103 |
| **Notes** | 106 |
| **Bibliography** | 117 |
| **Index** | 147 |

# Acknowledgements

This book has received the help of many people in its evolution into its present form. First and foremost is Elizabeth Ann Marie Meakes. She has been a continual dialogue partner, supporter and cheerleader for me, especially in moments when the task seemed too onerous. This work is dedicated to her and to our new daughter, Angel-Marie from China. Also thank you to my thesis advisers, Dr. James Reed and Dr. Gary Redcliffe, who read, edited and commented on the original manuscript. This book has evolved from my doctoral dissertation at the Toronto School of Theology. The book also received editorial help from Pam McCarroll-Butler, Michael Meakes, Helen Federau, Karen-Anne Fox and Andrea Davis. My mother, Rosemary O'Connor, supported the work through her prayers and careful reading. May she rest in peace. Special thanks to the staff at Wilfrid Laurier University Press: Sandra Woolfrey, Carroll Klein, Doreen Armbruster and Leslie Macredie. Thank you to Charles Gerkin, James Poling and George Fitchett who offered their ideas and comments about my research. I appreciated especially my time with Dr. Gerkin in Atlanta. I thank my colleague, John O'Connor, manager of chaplaincy services, The Hamilton Health Sciences Corporation, for his continual support, insightful comments and friendship and thank you to chaplaincy services for the grant money to finish and publish the work. Thank you to my colleague Glenn Empey, for his help with the cover of the book. Also, I am appreciative of the supervisory group in the Hamilton Regional Supervised Pastoral Education (SPE) Program that has been a forum to discuss some of these ideas: Kathleen O'Neill, Jim Sandilands, George Van Arragon, Raj Hathiramani and Lori Edey. A special thank you to my colleagues in the pastoral department at Waterloo Lutheran Seminary–Dr. Delton Glebe and Dr. Peter VanKatwyk under whom I trained as a supervisor. Special thanks to Kitchener Interfaith Pastoral Counselling Centre where I did my early training in clinical pastoral supervision. Finally, I thank all my students in clinical pastoral supervision. My experience of these students with the many insights offered to me in the praxis is the basis of this book.

Thomas St. James O'Connor, ThD

# Introduction

The written texts of clinical pastoral supervision are the area of research for this book. A study of the research field raises questions about the praxis of clinical pastoral supervision which this book addresses. First, what is distinctive about the praxis of clinical pastoral supervision? Second, what is an appropriate method in theology for the praxis of clinical pastoral supervision? Third, what is an adequate praxis of clinical pastoral supervision? This book addresses these three questions through a careful examination of the writing in the field and an intensive study of Charles Gerkin's theological contribution to the field.

Praxis is the critical reflection on the practice of ministry with the belief that all practice is theory laden.[1] Praxis is different from practice in that praxis involves a critical reflection and awareness that is not necessarily present in practice. David Tracy divides theology into fundamental, systematic and practical. Fundamental theology is rooted in the academy and deals with the philosophical concerns of theology in conversation with the university. Systematic theology is rooted in the church and seeks to systematize faith into a coherent system of belief for the church community. Practical theology is concerned about praxis and converses with society. In clinical pastoral supervision, the conversation partners in society are the other professions that utilize supervision. Practical theology is different from systematic and fundamental theology in that practical theology focuses on the praxis of ministry.[2]

A key element of praxis is transformation. The conversation between theory and practice leads to a praxis that is changed. Theory offers to practice a critical, reasoned reflection that outlines various interpretations of the practice. Theory challenges the practices of ministry to act and think in new ways. Practice offers to theory various ways of acting. Practice is theology in the concrete, whereas theory is theology in the abstract. Practical theology does not seek to systematize theology into a coherent system. Rather, practical theology has its own method of theology, which is manifested in the critical reflection on praxis.

Contrary to the classical interpretation, practical theology is not the application of theory. Practical theology is constructed from the conversation between practice and theory. This constructed theology is circular and systemic in that practice and theory impact on each other in a continuous interactive process. The resulting conversation is not a monologue or a linear conversation. Theory is built from practice and practice is built from theory. Practical theology offers to fundamental and systematic theology new ways of thinking about theology based on critical reflection on the practices of ministry. In the twentieth century, practical theology has come of age and moved beyond being applied theology. Contemporary practical theology offers the theological community a way of theologizing based on praxis. As such, practical theology stands on the boundary between thinking and doing in theology. From this position, practical theology utilizes both action and thinking in its theological method.

The praxis of clinical pastoral supervision is a division of practical theology. Clinical pastoral supervision has developed as a branch of the pastoral care and counselling movement begun by Clinical Pastoral Education (CPE) in the 1920s.[3] Clinical Pastoral Education has its roots in the Emanuel Movement, which began around the turn of the century. Some of the recognized founders of CPE are Anton Boisen, Richard Cabot, William Keller and Helen Flanders Dunbar.[4] These people used the clinical method in training students for ministry.[5] Initially, clinical training in ministry focused on the lives of the patients in developing psycho-spiritual health. The life of the patient became known as the "living human document."[6] Later, the notion of the living human document also included the narrative of the supervisees. CPE borrowed heavily from the social sciences and medicine using a case study approach in its theological method. Clinical pastoral supervision is part of the CPE movement in the training of students (supervisees) in the clinical method in theology.

Clinical pastoral supervision emerges from two sources. One source is pastoral supervision, an essential part of the Christian church. Pastoral supervision has been part of the ministry of the church since its inception. Pastoral supervision is an important tool used by the church in handing down the traditions of the faith community and guiding those engaged in ministry. The second source for the praxis of clinical pastoral supervision is the clinical supervision present in disciplines other than theology. Medicine, psychiatry, psychology, social work, marriage and family therapy and education all utilize clinical supervision in training persons in their respective disciplines.[7] Clinical supervision is one of the primary ways that a person is socialized into a discipline and is trained and certified to carry on the work of the profession.

In the search for answers to the three questions about the praxis of clinical pastoral supervision, the work of Charles V. Gerkin is helpful. Gerkin is an academic, clinical pastoral supervisor and pastoral psychotherapist. He is the Franklin Parker Professor of Practical Theology (Emeritus) at the Candler School of Theology, Emory University, Atlanta, Georgia. Gerkin is a clinical pastoral supervisor and Diplomat in the American Association of Pastoral Counselors (AAPC). He is also a clinical member of the American Association of Marriage and Family Therapy (AAMFT). Gerkin has published four books and numerous articles on pastoral care and counselling, praxis and theory, narrative and hermeneutics, practical theology and clinical pastoral supervision. He has worked as a chaplain and pastoral counselor in a detention home for adolescent boys, acted as a chaplain and clinical pastoral supervisor in a large hospital and worked full time teaching graduate courses in practical theology. He is a minister in the United Methodist Church and views himself as a pastor.

Gerkin's theology, based in praxis, is described as incarnational. Gerkin developed his theology over a span of forty years. The notion of the fusion of horizons is the best description of this incarnational theology. While this notion undergirds his theology from the beginning, Gerkin articulated the fusion of horizons most fully in his third book, *Widening the Horizons*.[8] He borrowed the metaphor from the philosophical hermeneutics of Hans-Georg Gadamer. Gadamer believes that a text has a horizon of meaning, a standpoint. The person interpreting the text has a horizon of meaning as well. Interpretation involves the various horizons of text and interpreter interacting in a mutual give-and-take dialogue. Interaction between text and interpreter produces a fusion of horizons, that is, a new meaning. The person interprets the text and the text interprets the person. The fusion of horizons is an explanation of the interactive process between text and interpreter.

The fusion of horizons is key to understanding the incarnational theology of Charles Gerkin. The thesis of this book is that the fusion of horizons as developed by Charles Gerkin in his incarnational theology answers the research questions about the praxis of clinical pastoral supervision. Gerkin's incarnational theology, with its own horizons, fuses with the various horizons of the written texts on clinical pastoral supervision in developing a transformed praxis, a new horizon. Gerkin's incarnational theology articulated in the fusion of horizons has four essential characteristics. First, his incarnational theology is constructed from a standpoint based in Christian interpretations. He uses theological language and concepts to describe his incarnational theology; he is clear about his identity as a practical theologian and pastor. Second, this incarnational theology is interdisciplinary. It utilizes interpretations and languages of various disciplines inside and outside theology. There is a fusion of horizons between these various interpretations within a theological framework. Third, Gerkin's methodology is rooted in practical theology. He presents many case studies, vignettes and verbatims in developing a critical reflection on the practice of ministry. Here, there is a fusion of horizons between practice and theory. His method in practical theology is praxis/theory/praxis.[9] His incarnational theology begins with praxis and through critical conversation using many interpretations ends in a transformed praxis. Fourth, Gerkin's incarnational theology utilizes a narrative hermeneutical theory. A postmodern understanding of narrative and hermeneutics is part of his theology. This means that Gerkin believes that facts and interpretation are woven together in a narrative. He refuses to absolutize any set of meanings. Bringing Gerkin's incarnational theology into contact with the texts of clinical pastoral supervision outlines the distinctiveness of clinical pastoral supervision and offers a method of theologizing in the praxis. The fusion of horizons offers an explanation for supervision and a way of developing a praxis that is adequate and yet not absolute.

The fusion of horizons is a helpful idea in understanding and explaining the praxis of clinical pastoral supervision. In the supervisory relationship, both supervisor and supervisee have various horizons of meaning interacting. In the relationship between supervisee and patient (client/parishioner) there are various horizons that interact. The supervisee also interacts with the institutional context of training, the legacies of the supervisee's family-of-origin as well as the supervisee's denominational context. The horizons are many. In the analysis of texts and of clinical pastoral supervision, and the work of Charles Gerkin, the horizons are also many. The horizons from Gerkin and the texts are brought together in an interactive, critical dialogue.

In the fusion of different horizons, there are three possible outcomes.[10] First, there is an identical fusion. In the identical fusion, there are more similarities than differences between the narratives of the horizons. A second outcome is the absence of a fusion. The absence of fusion means that there are more differences than similarities and there is more separation than unity. There is a dialectical relationship between the narratives present in the horizons. Confrontation and challenge are key elements here. Finally, there are fusions that are both similar and different. Here the fusion is analogical. The analogical is midway between the identical fusion and the dialectical fusion. In Gerkin's incarnational theology, all three fusions are present, depending on the horizons encountered.

One discovery in analyzing the various texts of Gerkin and clinical pastoral supervision is that an author can change standpoints depending on what is being addressed. For example, Gerkin utilizes an object relations theory in pastoral counselling. Here, the fusion between object relations theory and pastoral counselling is identical. At the same time, he also utilizes a theological hermeneutical approach when discussing the soul in terms of ego and self. Here, his fusion is analogical. Finally, Gerkin focuses on contextual issues such as "race" and gender, and challenges the norms of the church. In this instance, the fusion is dialectical, emphasizing difference. Gerkin's fusion of horizons can be identical, analogical and dialectical.

The three questions are important to me because they arise from critical reflection on my practice as a clinical pastoral supervisor. I am involved in clinical supervision, pastoral supervision and clinical pastoral supervision. Professionally, I am an associate supervisor in the Canadian Association for Pastoral Practice and Education (CAPPE) and an approved supervisor in AAMFT. There are similarities and differences among the three kinds of supervision. My three questions arise from reflections on the practice of supervision in the three different contexts. I find supervision to be exciting, challenging and a learning experience. Supervision is complex and mysterious, incarnating the divine presence, and I am continually amazed at its process.

My horizon as an interpreter contains many narratives. I am a Roman Catholic pastoral theologian who has been educated in a Lutheran context, an ecumenical context and a Roman Catholic context. I have worked in pastoral counselling centres, hospitals and parishes. In theological method, I stand within my Catholic heritage and incorporate interpretations of the social sciences and other denominations. In supervision, I value competency and service. The realities of sin, grace and redemption are present in my praxis. I do believe that there are differences between social science concepts and some theological concepts. For me, the goal of supervision is to respond to the invitation of grace. The great commandment is the norm for evaluating the presence of grace. My passion for these questions arises from my experience of transformation and call to be a minister of transformation for others.

The three questions also arise from many of the texts in the field of clinical pastoral supervision. In the last fifteen years in this field, there has been a movement to increase the use of theological language and concepts in describing the praxis of clinical pastoral supervision. Some authors ask what makes clinical pastoral supervision distinctive from clinical supervision in other disciplines. Others wonder about a theological method specific to the practice of ministry. Most often, the theological method of practical theology has been borrowed from systematic theology. Does the emphasis on practice and the transformation of practice create a different method? How is praxis incorporated into theological method? These are important issues in the field of clinical pastoral supervision. Finally, an adequate transformed praxis benefits the field by offering an understanding of clinical pastoral supervision rooted in the incarnational theology of Gerkin. There is no such explanation of the praxis in the field today.

Chapter 1 describes the field of clinical pastoral supervision. This chapter explores how clinical pastoral supervision is similar to and different from clinical supervision and pastoral supervision. The chapter includes a history of clinical pastoral supervision beginning in the 1920s and traces the influences of pastoral and clinical supervision on clinical pastoral supervision. Chapter 2 analyzes the texts written on the praxis of clinical pastoral supervision. The texts are drawn from numerous journal articles and four books on the subject. I reviewed four journals for articles on clinical pastoral supervision: *Journal of Supervision and Training in Ministry, Pastoral Psychology, Pastoral Sciences* and *The Journal of Pastoral Care*. Forty-five years (1952-1997) of articles on clinical pastoral supervision were reviewed (298 articles and four books in total). My analysis produced three approaches. These three approaches are called the social science approach, the hermeneutical approach and the special interest approach.

Chapter 3 focuses on Gerkin's incarnational theology. The fusion of horizons is explained in terms of the underlying notion of his incarnational theology. The incarnational theology is described through four characteristics. Chapter 4 focuses on Gerkin's theological anthropology. His theological anthropology embodies his incarnational theology. Gerkin utilizes a narrative hermeneutical understanding of creation, sin and redemption present in the life of the soul. His understanding of the narrative of the soul in relation to "ego" and "self" demonstrates the fusion of horizons. Gerkin also emphasizes the theological virtues of faith, hope and care within his theological anthropology.

Chapter 5 presents the fusion of horizons between texts on clinical pastoral supervision and the incarnational theology of Gerkin. Each horizon, with its many narratives, presents what it has to offer the other horizon. The conversation is systemic and circular. Similarities and differences between the narratives are noted. Chapter 6 describes an adequate transformed praxis which responds to the third question outlined at the beginning of this introduction. This chapter outlines the various elements of such a praxis and presents a case in which the adequate transformed praxis is demonstrated. The case is based on work with a supervisee named Mary, and there is a conversation between the elements of an adequate transformed praxis and the needs of this case. Chapter 7 is the conclusion. This conclusion answers the first two questions about the praxis of clinical pastoral supervision. It also describes the limitations of this research in terms of the texts, the contexts and the interpreter.

The book employs Gerkin's methodology of praxis/theory/praxis. The first two chapters describe and analyze the praxis of clinical pastoral supervision. Then, Gerkin's incarnational theology is examined for its underlying theory. Gerkin's theory interacts with the praxis of clinical pastoral supervision to produce a transformed praxis. Also, the methodology is employed in the structure of each chapter. Each chapter begins with a case (praxis) from supervision. The chapter then takes a hermeneutical detour in discussing theoretical issues. There is a return to the case part way through the chapter and at the end of the chapter. The theoretical issues discussed in the chapter facilitate change in the case. The cases are composite clinical scenarios and do not refer to any specific individual. Any connection to a specific individual is coincidental.

# Chapter 1
# The Field of Clinical Pastoral Supervision

Bill has completed one year of a MDiv program. He has a bachelor's degree in social work and has worked for a number of social agencies in child welfare and family therapy. He is in his early thirties and seeking ordination in his denomination. Bill is doing a field work placement in a health care institution. In his professional work, Bill has received various kinds of clinical supervision. He begins his first session in clinical pastoral supervision by asking the supervisor how this will be different from his previous experiences of clinical supervision. "Does clinical pastoral supervision involve adding theology to clinical supervision and stirring?"

Bill's question evolved from his practice of social work and his studies in theology. The question is a central concern of clinical pastoral supervision. The number of written texts in the field of clinical pastoral supervision has increased considerably in the last twenty years. The *Journal of Supervision and Training in Ministry* has since 1978 offered the field a forum devoted to the issues of clinical pastoral supervision and the training for ministry. Other journals have presented related articles. There have also been a number of books published on the topic. The number of texts on clinical pastoral supervision has expanded the field.

Clinical pastoral supervision has evolved to its present praxis from a combination of three movements. First, there is pastoral supervision, which is the general ministry of supervision that has been part of training persons for ministry in every Christian denomination. This began in the Old Testament period. Second, there is the development in the twentieth century of clinical supervision in the professional disciplines of psychiatry, psychology, education, social work and family therapy. Third, there is the development in the 1920s of the Clinical Pastoral Education (CPE) movement. Clinical pastoral supervision evolved as an essential part of CPE, adopting its values and assumptions. Clinical pastoral supervision then has developed from the conversation between pastoral supervision and clinical supervision in the context of CPE. It is both similar to and different from pastoral supervision and clinical supervision.

## Definition of Clinical Pastoral Supervision

Clinical pastoral supervision is a complex phenomenon with many levels of involvement and diverse definitions.[1] Although there is a plurality of interpretations of clinical pastoral supervision, it can be viewed as an educational process that involves a pastoral relationship between a qualified supervisor and a group of supervisees for the purpose of developing skills for ministry integrated within a pastoral identity. The goal of such supervision is to transform and empower supervisees and supervisors to be more effective ministers of the gospel. Clinical pastoral supervision is accountable to a professional association for its praxis and can take place in an institutional setting, a pastoral counselling centre or a congregation.

As an educational process, clinical pastoral supervision focuses both on training the supervisee for praxis and learning from praxis. Praxis is a prime teacher for the supervisee in education for ministry. This educational focus works within a model of adult learning theory and thereby respects a diversity of learning styles, in developmental tasks, in gender and ethnicity, in personality and in learning goals. This adult educational model requires a learning contract.[2] The learning contract emerges from the interaction between supervisor and supervisee and the various institutions involved in the process. This pastoral education involves self-awareness and exploration of the personal dynamics[3] of the supervisee in the praxis of ministry. Supervision is, nevertheless, education and not therapy. The process of supervision includes facilitating the supervisee to become more self-aware of personal values and assumptions and how these impact on the way that the supervisee practises ministry.

As a pastoral relationship, clinical pastoral supervision involves an intentional and directed conversation between a supervisor and a supervisee. In this conversation, there is individual and group supervision in which supervisees present the practice of ministry as well as their values, assumptions and operational theology. Feedback is an essential component of this conversation on both the individual and group levels. Supervisors and peers offer the student feedback. The pastoral conversation between supervisor and supervisee offers a learning opportunity for ministry through the use of critical reflection. Clinical pastoral supervision emphasizes the development of skills for the practice of ministry. The word "clinical" comes from the Greek word *kline*, which means "at the bedside" and originated in a medical context. In the clinical component of medical education, the doctor deals with illness not in theory but in the concrete, i.e., the way that illness manifests itself in a particular sick patient. The doctor is literally at the bedside. The clinical method in pastoral supervision means dealing with the pastoral needs of specific patients/clients/parishioners and specific supervisees that the supervisor encounters in the practice of ministry. Such an approach examines the "living human document," the person in need, from the standpoint of practical theology.

The concept of the living human document is one of the key ideas of clinical pastoral supervision. This interpretation views the human person as a document or text that contains elements of sin and grace in need of redemption. Anton Boisen believed that the living human document was the focus of pastoral care. For Boisen, the living human document was a source of theology, just as scripture is a source of theology. Charles Gerkin used the idea of the living human document as the cornerstone of his book on pastoral counselling. From the standpoint of practical theology, the clinical method in pastoral supervision deals with the question: What should I do in this particular situation with this particular person in order to facilitate a response to the gospel?

Clinical pastoral supervision seeks to integrate pastoral skills with the supervisee's self-concept. This is designed to develop pastoral identity in the supervisee. Clinical pastoral supervision addresses the professional and personal self-concept of the supervisee. Training deals with two issues: 1) What I do as a minister; and 2) Who I am as a minister.[4] Ideally these two are integrated in the supervisee's practice of ministry. The awareness of one's professional and personal identity includes the awareness of the impact of self on others. This means some knowledge by the supervisee of his/her personality dynamics, values, beliefs and theology. The understanding of identity is rooted in interpretations and symbols from Christianity.

The beginning and ending points of clinical pastoral supervision are transformed practices of Christian ministry. Clinical pastoral supervision begins with the supervisee presenting some practice of ministry. This could be a verbatim, a visit, an audiotape or a videotape or a case report. In this practice, the feelings, motivations and personal dynamics of the supervisee are uncovered. The practice of the supervisee is viewed in terms of the self of the supervisee, the person(s) receiving care and the contextual elements present in the practice. An essential part of this supervision focuses on what needs to be done with the parishioner/patient/client. The conversation about all the elements in the situation transforms the practice into praxis. This transformation of the practice includes a change in the supervisee. The goal is to empower and transform both supervisor and supervisee for service to the gospel. Interpretations and practices from the social sciences and other disciplines can and must be used. However, these interpretations are not the norms for, or the goal of, ministry. Interpretations from the social sciences are a help in the practice of ministry. Clinical pastoral supervision is ultimately a theological task, a ministry of the Church, organized to help ministers serve the People of God.[5]

Clinical pastoral supervision has been embedded in the clinical pastoral education movement in the United States since the mid-1920s. This movement became standardized in various professional associations. In the USA, there are the Association for Clinical Pastoral Education (ACPE) and the American Association for Pastoral Counselors (AAPC). In Canada, there is one professional association named the Canadian Association for Pastoral Practice and Education (CAPPE). All three of these associations have standards that govern the praxis of clinical pastoral supervision.

Clinical pastoral supervision has three branches. One branch is institutionally based in hospitals, prisons, psychiatric facilities and nursing homes. Clinical pastoral supervision in this institutional setting is shaped by the multidisciplinary team approach and the demands of the institution. Another branch is pastoral counselling, which often takes place in a pastoral counselling centre. In this case, supervision requires knowledge of theories from pastoral counselling and other related disciplines. A third branch is the congregation. Supervision in this instance is shaped by the context of the congregation, with its varied roles for the supervisee. Clinical pastoral supervision is influenced by the context of each of these three branches.

## The History of Clinical Pastoral Supervision

Clinical pastoral supervision is an essential part of the clinical pastoral education (CPE) movement. Clinical pastoral supervision developed within the CPE movement. CPE originated in the Emanuel Movement, especially in the ideas and practices of its main proponent, Rev. Dr. Elwood Worcester. In 1904, Worcester, rector of Emanuel Episcopal Church in Boston, opened a clinic, in cooperation with several physicians in New England, for spiritual healing in his church. The combination of medicine and religion with a clinical focus became known as the Emanuel Movement.[6] While initially very popular, the movement ended by 1940.

The Emanuel Movement set the stage for the formal beginning of Clinical Pastoral Education in the 1920s. The founders of CPE are Rev. Anton Boisen, William S. Keller, MD, Helen Flanders Dunbar, MD, and Richard C. Cabot, MD.[7] Boisen and Cabot began training theological students in the clinical method at a mental hospital in Worcester, Massachusetts, in 1925. Keller began a similar training program in Cincinnati, Ohio, in 1927. While the movement started in different geographical locations, the emphasis on developing clinical methods in theological training was the same. For Boisen and Cabot, the focus was on the "living human document", which is the people that they met in the hospital wards, rather than on Scripture and Tradition. All the early practitioners of CPE believed that theological education needed a clinical component as well as an academic component. Like the Emanuel Movement, there was a strong connection between religion and medicine.

Allison Stokes, in her book *Ministry after Freud*, describes the first training sessions with Boisen and his students at Worcester in 1925:

> During the day they worked on the wards as attendants, conducting recreational and social programs, writing letters for patients, walking and singing with them, observing them and keeping records. During the evening they read books on psychology, psychiatry, and religion and held seminars with Boisen and the medical staff.[8]

In the first summer, four students trained with Boisen. In 1926, there were also four students. Seven students trained with Boisen in 1927. Eleven students trained in 1928 and fifteen in 1929.[9] In 1930, the Council for Clinical Training was formed and it "developed standards for training and for the pastoral supervision of trainees in CPE."[10] The first chairperson of the Council for Clinical Training was Dr. Helen Flanders Dunbar, who had been one of Boisen's students. Early in the CPE movement, there were differences in theoretical orientation between people like Cabot, Boisen, Dicks, Dunbar and Guiles. Some of the differences resulted in a split in the movement. Soon after forming the Council for Clinical Training, there was a major disagreement between the chairperson, Dunbar, and a member of the council, Philip Guiles. Their differences resulted in Dunbar moving the Council to New York. In 1944, the Boston group was incorporated as The Institute for Pastoral Care.[11] The Institute for Pastoral Care (Boston) and the Council for Clinical Training (New York) were rivals. Other groups such as the Southern Baptists and the Lutherans formed their own CPE training programs. In 1967, the Institute for Pastoral Care, the Council for Clinical Training and the CPE movement within the Southern Baptist and Lutheran traditions amalgamated to form the Association of Clinical Pastoral Education (ACPE).

Thornton noted that the theoretical differences between the Boston and New York groups were manifested in the view of the self, which has shaped many of the issues in the praxis of clinical pastoral supervision.

> The Boston group (IPC) drew from Scottish common sense with a reliance on rationality and self-control. Ethical formation meant stability and growth: facing the facts, overcoming self-deceptions, conforming to the real. Supervisors focused on finding the 'growing edge' and trusting the immanent divinity to carry one to health and meaning in life.[12]

The Boston approach had a more optimistic view of human nature while the New York group had a more pessimistic view. The New York group prized autonomy and freedom and the insights of depth psychology. They saw the self in "images of conflict, non-rational feelings and inner chaos."[13] They pursued freedom from the destructive impulses of the self in their ministry with persons. Insight was highly valued in the New York approach. Differences in values and assumptions between the Boston and New York groups have affected the entire history of the CPE movement.

In 1964, the CPE movement experienced a split. A number of pastoral counselling specialists within the CPE movement formed their own association. The association is called the American Association of Pastoral Counselors (AAPC).[14] This association formed a distinct group with its own Board of Governors separate from the rest of the CPE movement. AAPC came under instant criticism from pastoral theologians like Seward Hiltner and Wayne Oates. Hiltner and Oates argued that pastoral counselling and the supervision of pastoral counselling was a ministry connected to the church in its worship, preaching, education and pastoral care. As such, the training and supervision of pastoral counselling should not be disconnected from the church by forming its own association.

The split of AAPC from the CPE movement underlines an ongoing tension present in the praxis of supervision in the CPE movement. Supervision in CPE is connected to the ministry of pastoral supervision in the church. At the same time, supervision in CPE has been greatly informed by clinical supervision in the other disciplines. This influence has caused many supervisors to adopt the concepts and praxis of clinical supervision and to let go of the theological and pastoral roots of CPE. While supervision in CPE started as a ministry of the church, some aspects of clinical pastoral supervision are more identical to clinical supervision. Professional pastoral associations have many similarities to professional associations in others disciplines.

In Canada, Clinical Pastoral Education began as an offshoot of the American experience. The early Canadian supervisors such as Earle MacKnight, Charles Fielding, Archie MacLachlan and Jack Breckenridge were all trained in the USA.[15] In Canada, CPE became known as Supervised Pastoral Education (SPE). One of the first units of Supervised Pastoral Education (SPE) was offered in 1952 at the Mountain Sanitorium in Hamilton, now known as the Chedoke Division of The Hamilton Health Sciences Corporation.[16]

The developing SPE movement in Canada was guided by the Canadian Council for Supervised Pastoral Education (CCSPE). This organization was formed in Toronto in 1965 and, in 1974, changed its name to the Canadian Association of Pastoral Education (CAPE). Twenty years later, in 1994, CAPE became the Canadian Association for Pastoral Practice and Education (CAPPE). CAPPE, much like its American counterparts, trains, certifies and establishes standards and a code of ethics for supervisees and supervisors. Unlike the American experience, however, pastoral counselling education and clinical pastoral education in Canada remains under the same umbrella group (CAPPE), which allows for some differences in their training procedures.[17] Like the American experience, clinical pastoral supervision is a vital part of SPE.

**Standards of Clinical Pastoral Supervision in Professional Associations**

The professional organizations of ACPE, AAPC and CAPPE articulate standards for training, education and practice within the association. The standards in CAPPE focus on three areas of competence in the supervisor. First, clinical pastoral supervision requires conceptual competence in the area of pastoral supervision. This means a knowledge and integration of theories of supervision using conceptual models from theory and practice involving "education, theology, psychology, sociology and ethics."[18]

Second, the standards involve competence in the praxis of clinical pastoral supervision. Initially, the supervisor-in-training needs to practise the ministry of pastoral supervision under the direction of a qualified CAPPE supervisor. This includes using video-audio tapes, observations, interviews, administrative meetings, clinical seminars, didactic seminars, case conferences and supervisor-student sessions. The clinical pastoral supervisor also needs to be competent in the practice of individual and group supervision and the use of an adult educational approach in supervision.[19] Such supervisory competence must include the ability to assist students "in achieving their own learning goals."[20] Third, the clinical pastoral supervisor needs to develop a professional identity as a supervisor which identifies "one's personal strengths and weaknesses in order to safeguard the student's personal and pastoral integrity."[21] The supervisor is also accountable to a Code of Ethics.

**Pastoral Supervision in the Church**

Pastoral supervision is oversight of ministry. The Latin words "super" and "videre" mean to "see above." Pastoral supervision means seeing above or overseeing the pastoral work of a supervisee. As part of a ministry of the community of believers, the notion of pastoral supervision is present in the Old Testament. This is evidenced in the Old Testament account of Moses choosing elders to supervise the settling of issues of practical justice and fairness within the life of the community of Israel (Ex. 18:17-26). The term "supervision" is not used specifically in either the Old or New Testament, but various understandings of pastoral supervision are present.[22] Kenneth Pohly roots the practice of oversight in the Old Testament in faithfulness to the covenant. The core of God's relationship with Israel is articulated in the covenant. Oversight of this covenant was given to a series of charismatic leaders, priests, prophets, kings and judges. These leaders challenged the people of Israel when the people failed to fulfill their part of the covenant. The leaders pointed out specific ways to return to a faithful practice of the covenant. Supervision also included the administrative tasks of overseeing the life of the community.

In the New Testament churches, oversight was exercised by three offices: bishop, elder (presbyter) and deacon. Pohly argues that pastoring and supervision were also to be done by the laity, i.e., nonordained individuals. He draws on the Pauline image of the whole body participating in ministry (1 Cor. 12) and the Petrine image of the whole church as a royal priesthood (1 Pet. 2:5-9). Pastoring and supervision belong to the whole church. The tasks of supervision "are to be exercised by both clergy and laity.[23] The whole community of believers, through the presence of the resurrected Jesus, exercises the duty of supervision.

David Steere points out that supervision as a ministry of the church existed in the Middle Ages in an apprenticeship model. This model of apprenticeship was used in the United States during the colonial period. Pohly notes that various denominations have struggled with the theory and practice of supervision by clergy and laity. In some denominations, the use of lay supervisors was discontinued and supervision became focused on training clergy to oversee the life of the congregation or parish. In the last fifty years, however, there has been a renewal in lay involvement in many denominations, which has included a resurgence of supervision by laity and indeed by the whole community of believers.

Most theological schools now have a field education division. The training of persons for ordained and lay ministry within a particular denomination requires some experience in the practices of ministry with the oversight of a suitable supervisor. The theology student may find supervision in congregational, institutional or other settings as a way of integrating theory and practice. Schools of theology have made pastoral supervision of the student's work a requirement for the basic degree in theology. Field education departments work with off-site supervisors to provide pastoral supervision for theological students.

Much of the discussion regarding pastoral supervision as a ministry of the church focuses on the theological dimensions of supervision. Pastoral supervision has not emphasized the clinical method that uses an interdisciplinary approach with a group of supervisees. Rather, the major concern has been spiritual and theological formation in a particular denomination. John Patton describes four images of pastoral supervision that focus on the theological aspects of pastoral supervision. These images are in "continuity with the ministry of Christ,"[24] and relate to New Testament images.

One image of pastoral supervision is the "unity of person and work in Christ."[25] The pastoral supervisor oversees the supervisee's quest for unity between action and being, between what the supervisee does and is in ministry. This unity is exemplified by Jesus, who was congruent in his words and actions. This unity is sought by the supervisee through a deeper connection to Christ. This image of pastoral supervision emphasizes integration and pastoral identity in the person of the supervisee so that the being and action of the supervisee are united.

A second theological image of pastoral supervision drawn from the New Testament is the parabolic teacher. The pastoral supervisor uses parables in the same way Jesus used parables, to challenge the assumptions and world view of the listeners. The supervisor points to the unexpected and overlooked in ordinary events. The pastoral supervisor uncovers aspects of ministry that the supervisee did not notice in the practice of ministry. In this image, the unexpected and unseen in the supervisee's practice of ministry is opened up, supported and/or challenged. The goal of this approach is the transformation of the supervisee's praxis in developing a wider range of pastoral ability.

A third image of pastoral supervision is the equipper of saints. This image draws on the practical ways that the Apostle Paul dealt with concrete issues in the life of the church. Examples include Paul's advice on dealing with issues of marriage, divorce and food offered to idols. The pastoral supervisor enables the supervisee to focus on the concrete material of ministry and struggle for practical solutions. These solutions always are viewed from the standpoint of strengthening faith in Jesus Christ.

The fourth image of pastoral supervision is deacon, shepherd and overseer. This image, taken from 1 Peter, stresses the role of oversight in relation to Church structure. Shepherd and overseer combine the administrative and pastoral functions of supervision. In this understanding of pastoral supervision, oversight focuses on the context and structure of the community of believers as well as the needs of persons receiving care. Such an approach is more systemic in nature in that it facilitates the supervisee becoming more aware of the wider contextual issues.

Patton's theological images imply that theology in pastoral supervision is more than an afterthought or embellishment. Bill, the supervisee presented at the beginning of the chapter, wonders if theology is an afterthought in clinical pastoral supervision. Sometimes, theology *is* an afterthought. In these instances, however, theology is the conclusion that accommodated the central argument. Bill's concern and Patton's theological images beg further questions. How does theology become the basis for clinical pastoral supervision? How do these theological images shape the whole process and content of supervision?

Some similarities between clinical pastoral supervision and pastoral supervision have emerged. In both, the supervisee receives the authority for training in ministry from the authority of the supervisor. The supervisor is ultimately responsible for the ministry being performed and, as part of his or her professional function, is required to oversee the student's ministry. In this regard, clinical pastoral supervision and pastoral supervision are different from pastoral consultation. In pastoral consultation, the person consulting is not necessarily accountable to the person being consulted. In pastoral supervision and clinical pastoral supervision, the supervisee is accountable to the supervisor. Both clinical pastoral supervision and pastoral supervision deal with the practices of ministry. Supervisors observe in some form the supervisee's practice of ministry and give relevant feedback to the supervisee on that practice. Both clinical pastoral supervision and pastoral supervision exist in a pastoral relationship between supervisor and supervisee that operates within a theological framework.

Clinical pastoral supervision is distinct from pastoral supervision in a variety of ways. Clinical pastoral supervision includes a group of supervisees (three to six persons) with a certified supervisor. The supervisee receives feedback from both the supervisor and peers. Pastoral supervision does not necessarily require a peer group. Often, pastoral supervision works in an apprenticeship model where a supervisee works under an experienced pastor without a peer group. Second, the context of clinical pastoral supervision is interdisciplinary. The supervisees interact and receive input and feedback from these other disciplines. Supervisees are also part of interdisciplinary didactic seminars. According to the standards of the Canadian Association for Pastoral Practice and Education (CAPPE), the supervisee must become aware of the pastoral presence in interdisciplinary relationships. The supervisee is also required to combine theology with the psychological sciences in grappling with the human condition.

Third, the clinical method stresses direct observation of the supervisee's practice of ministry by the supervisor. This includes access to the supervisee's practices of ministry through audiotapes, videotapes, live supervision, verbatim reports and case studies.[26] Pastoral supervision does not always require such a clinical method.

Fourth, pastoral supervision most often takes place in a congregational setting. While the congregation has developed as a site for clinical pastoral supervision, the origins of clinical pastoral supervision are in institutions, and later, pastoral counselling centres. Both the institutional setting and the pastoral counselling centre are some distance both physically and emotionally from the local congregation.[27]

Fifth, clinical pastoral supervision emphasizes self-awareness on the part of the supervisee. The supervisee becomes aware of the manner in which their personal dynamics, values and theological assumptions affect their ministry to others. The self-in-ministry is a key concept. Pastoral supervision does not necessarily have this emphasis. Finally, pastoral supervision and clinical pastoral supervision train their supervisors differently. Supervisors in clinical pastoral supervision receive special training and are certified by the association for their ministry as supervisors. This certification includes the praxis of supervision under supervision, theoretical competence, supervisory integration and peer review. Pastoral supervisors in congregations most often are not officially certified by the denomination for this ministry of supervision. They are appointed by the denomination without formal clinical training.

## The Clinical Supervision Movement in Other Disciplines

Another important influence on clinical pastoral supervision in the twentieth century has been the development of clinical supervision in other professional disciplines. Psychiatry, social work, psychology, education and family therapy have offered many ideas and skills to clinical pastoral supervision. Supervision in psychiatry and psychotherapy has had the greatest impact on clinical pastoral supervision. George Fitchett researched influences in a study of forty-five philosophies of clinical pastoral supervision.[28] In his study, he noted that the text *The Teaching and Learning of Psychotherapy*[29] by Rudolph Ekstein and Robert Wallerstein is most often cited. In fact, in the CPE literature, this text is cited often. Ekstein and Wallerstein focus on the process of supervision. They present the clinical rhombus as a way of explaining the process of supervision. The clinical rhombus uses four elements in the process of supervision: 1) the supervisor, 2) the supervisee, 3) the patient and 4) the institution in which supervision and therapy are practised.[30] The process of supervision is shaped by the interaction of these four external elements. Supervision is also shaped by the internal psychic dynamics of the persons involved in the practice.

Ekstein and Wallerstein see two kinds of learning difficulties in the process of supervision. The learning difficulties that the supervisee has with clients are termed learning problems. The difficulties that supervisees have in the supervisory relationship are called problems about learning. These two areas form much of the supervisory agenda. Another idea of Ekstein and Wallerstein that has influenced clinical pastoral supervision is parallel process. This is the idea that the strengths and weaknesses of the relationship between the supervisee and the client are mirrored or paralleled in the relationship between supervisor and supervisee. Therefore, resolving problems about learning in the supervisory relationship influences a change in the learning problems in the therapeutic relationship.

Other ideas from the psychodynamic tradition have greatly influenced clinical pastoral supervision. One of these is the belief that supervision can be therapy. In this view, the supervisor becomes a therapist for the supervisee by sorting out the supervisee's issues of transference and countertransference. The idea is based on the belief that as supervisees work on their therapeutic issues, their work with clients is improved. Daniel V. Papero, in his experience as a supervisor in the psychodynamic tradition, drew from Bowen's theory and noted that the supervisee can bring forward both personal issues and professional issues.[31] Other views in the field disagree with this.

Other texts from the psychodynamic tradition have influenced the praxis of clinical pastoral supervision. In Table 2, titled "Twelve Authors Cited Most Frequently in CPE Supervisors' Theory Papers,"[32] Fitchett notes that the book *Coping with Conflict: Supervising Counselors and Psychotherapists* by William S. Mueller and Bill L. Kell[33] rates fifth in terms of the number of times cited by a writer. Eighth on the list is the book by Irvin D. Yalom, *The Theory and Practice of Group Psychotherapy*.[34] In the top eight books of Fitchett's list, three are from the psychodynamic tradition.

Closely connected to the psychodynamic tradition is supervision in clinical psychology. In his study, Fitchett combines the psychodynamic and psychological traditions in reviewing the texts used in clinical pastoral supervision. Steere separates these two traditions in his analysis of supervision from various disciplines.[35] Fitchett notes that the authors in his study most often cite texts from the combined field of psychology and psychodynamic theory. Second on the list are texts from the field of theology and third on the list are texts from education theory. In the area of psychology, Carl Rogers is second on Fitchett's list of most cited authors. Rogers is cited less often than Ekstein and Wallerstein and more often than the Bible. Eleven different works by Rogers are cited in various texts outlining the praxis of clinical pastoral supervision.

In the field of clinical supervision in psychology, Steere notes two streams, the behaviouralist and the humanistic.[36] Behaviouralists focus on teaching new behaviours or new skills to the supervisee in their work with clients. The humanistic approach, based on Rogers, is person-centred. The person-centred approach in supervision focuses on developing empathy, unconditional regard and congruent communication in the supervisee. In this approach, the supervisee has extensive responsibility for the agenda of supervision. According to Fitchett, the humanistic field of supervision in psychology has more influence on clinical pastoral supervision than the behaviouralist field.

The developmental psychology of Erik Erikson is fourth on the list of most cited texts. According to Fitchett, many supervisors use Erikson's developmental perspective in their philosophy of clinical pastoral supervision. The developmental work of Piaget is also frequently cited. A developmental perspective in supervision means seeing the supervisory process as various stages. Also, this developmental perspective is used in examining the developmental tasks of the supervisee and the client.

In the field of education, Fitchett notes that a number of writers of adult educational theory have been incorporated into the philosophies of clinical pastoral supervision. These authors are found at the ten and twelve mark of Fitchett's list. Most often cited in this educational literature is *Theories of Learning* by Gordon Bower and Ernest Hilgard.[37] The works of Malcolm Knowles, Jerome Bruner and John Dewey are also used. Adult learning from these educational perspectives is supervisee-centred, pragmatic and self-directed, with a learning contract outlining goals and responsibilities of both supervisor and supervisee.

Pohly, in his analysis of supervision in education, notes two streams: scientific and democratic.[38] Scientific supervision stresses research in administrative and teaching methods and implementing the research in the practice of teaching. Democratic supervision focuses more on the professional development of the teacher. This means releasing the talents of the teacher, supporting the person of the teacher and protecting the teacher's integrity. Scientific and democratic supervision are similar to behaviouralist and humanistic supervision in clinical psychology. Live supervision is used most often in the supervision of teachers in education. Live supervision means that the supervisor is present when the supervisee is teaching. The supervisor can intervene during the session or wait until later to give feedback to the supervisee.

Social work supervision has also developed in the twentieth century and impacted on the praxis of clinical pastoral supervision. In his study, Fitchett notes that the book *Supervision, Consultation and Staff Training in the Helping Professions* by Florence W. Kaslow[39] is cited occasionally. Supervision in social work began in the nineteenth century, with volunteers assisting troubled families. Paid supervisors trained these volunteers and oversaw their work.

At the beginning of the twentieth century, social work borrowed from the psychodynamic tradition.[40] Social work supervision has evolved and now focuses on teaching and administration. Skill development in a systems perspective is emphasized in training family therapists. A clear boundary is made between supervision and therapy, and supervision is not therapy. Another text important to social work supervision is Alfred Kadushin's *Supervision in Social Work*.[41] Besides teaching and administration, Kadushin added support as another essential ingredient in supervision. Pohly notes that a variety of forms of supervision have evolved in this discipline: tutorial, case consultation, supervisory group, peer-group supervision, tandem and team.

Other disciplines that developed various models of clinical supervision are in the field of business and family therapy. Fitchett does not note any texts from these areas in his study. Nevertheless, these two areas have added to the field of clinical supervision. Clinical supervision in the field of family therapy has mushroomed in the last ten years and has impacted greatly on clinical pastoral supervision. The standards of the American Association of Marriage and Family Therapists (AAMFT) indicate that supervision of family therapists should focus on a number of issues. One issue is the development of supervision theory for family therapists. Liddle, Breunlin and Schwartz note that clinical supervision is usually based on a particular theoretical orientation in family therapy. They outline seven approaches in family therapy that form the basis for different theories of clinical supervision.[42] All of these approaches share a common systemic view of supervision. In the understandings of Liddle, Breunlin and Schwartz, the supervisor views the supervisee's relationship with the family as a system. Supervision then is not supervision of the supervisee but the supervisee's relationship with the family. One of the tasks of the supervisor is to educate the relationship between supervisee and family.

Clinical supervision in family therapy under AAMFT has made a clear distinction between therapy and education.[43] Clinical supervision is education and not therapy. Abuses have taken place in supervision when it has become therapy instead of education. In AAMFT, supervisors and clinicians are subject to a Code of Ethics that affirms a principle forbidding dual relationships between supervisors and supervisees.[44] A supervisor is just a supervisor for the supervisee. For example, the supervisor cannot be a business partner, lover, family member or in any other relationship with the supervisee. Supervisors and clinicians in AAMFT are dismissed for breaking the Code of Ethics.

Clinical supervision in family therapy has developed methods that have impacted upon clinical pastoral supervision. Live supervision is practised,[45] where the supervisor watches behind a one-way mirror while the supervisee works with a family. With live supervision, the supervisee gets on-the-job supervision in the areas of skills and interventions. The supervisor intervenes when necessary. Family therapy supervision also uses the concept of isomorphism. This notion maintains that the supervisor-supervisee relationship is the same (isomorphic) as the supervisee-client relationship.[46] The supervisor has some understanding of the supervisee-family system by examining the supervisor-supervisee system. Supervisors have begun to use reflecting and consulting teams behind the one-way mirror to supervise the work of supervisees.

The differences between clinical pastoral supervision and clinical supervision have begun to emerge. Clinical pastoral supervision is distinguished from clinical supervision in that it is a ministry of the Church. The clinical pastoral supervisor, in this understanding, represents a particular denomination in the ministry of supervision. The supervisees act in ministry on the pastoral authority of the supervisor and are subject to the supervisor's oversight. Clinical supervision has no official connection to the Church nor are the supervisors mandated by the Church for service in this area.

Clinical pastoral supervision also utilizes theological language and concepts in its work, in that it employs the language and concepts of the discipline in which it is embedded. The starting and ending points are different between these two. Clinical pastoral supervision arises from standpoints with the Christian fact. Its goal is to transform the practice of the supervisee in order to create more effective ministers of the gospel. Clinical supervision does not arise from the Christian fact, nor does it seek to create more effective ministers of the gospel. There are also many similarities between clinical pastoral supervision and clinical supervision. The research of Fitchett points out the enormous influence that clinical supervision has had on clinical pastoral supervision.

**Distinctive Elements of Clinical Pastoral Supervision**

Clinical pastoral supervision is distinct from pastoral supervision and from clinical supervision in the combination of a number of elements. The clinical method, the interdisciplinary approach, the peer group of supervisees, the theological language and concepts, the connection to the church, the focus on the self-awareness of the supervisee, the development of skills in pastoral ministry, the training and certification of the supervisor and the pastoral identity of the supervisee are all elements of clinical pastoral supervision. While these elements exist in pastoral supervision and clinical supervision, they are combined in clinical pastoral supervision in a way that is distinctive. Neither clinical supervision nor pastoral supervision combine these various elements in the manner of clinical pastoral supervision.

Clinical pastoral supervision exists on the border between pastoral supervision and clinical supervision. In terms of its characteristics, clinical pastoral supervision draws from both sources. In many ways, clinical pastoral supervision is the outcome of the conversation between pastoral supervision and clinical supervision. Clinical pastoral supervision has a foot in each of these phenomenon.

The case of Bill, which began this chapter, opened up the question of the uniqueness of clinical pastoral supervision. Bill and his supervisor faced this issue throughout Bill's training and education. Bill discovered that there are many similarities between the clinical supervision that he experienced in his social work praxis and clinical pastoral supervision that he experienced as a student-chaplain.

Bill noticed some differences. One was the use of term "chaplain." That identity created a different relationship with patients than the term "social worker." The identity of chaplain has a different set of meanings than the identity of social worker. Patients and staff responded differently. Bill found it easier to adopt the identity of social worker than chaplain. There was some discomfort to the title "chaplain." Bill did not understand all the reasons for this internal discomfort. Chaplain and minister seemed lofty to him, a call from God, that went beyond his natural ability. Bill also realized that some patients were deferential to him because of the title. He learned in supervision to deal with this respect. The respect could be helpful and unhelpful.

Another difference for Bill was the use of theological language and the practice of prayer. Initially, he was uncertain about praying with patients. He struggled with what to say in prayer and when to pray. He prayed with a few patients and found the experience to be beneficial to the patient and himself. He became more at ease with asking a patient if they wanted prayer. The practice of praying and the willingness to discuss theological issues became more central to his ministry.

Besides the use of theological language and prayer, clinical pastoral supervision is founded on theological concepts and assumptions. Rodney Hunter and John Patton maintain that the clinical pastoral education movement is founded on a number of beliefs. These include a belief in divine immanence in the world and God's desire to save all, a basic hope that the world is redeemable, a view that science in cooperation with the divine can help in the salvation of the world and that religious experience is a source of theology as well as the truths of science.[47] In his first experience in SPE, Bill did not see the theological underpinnings that guide the praxis.

Bill's experience of supervision also invited him to examine his personality dynamics and their impact on his ministry. He kept a journal, reflecting on how his values, assumptions and theology affected others. Both his supervisor and peer group offered him feedback on his dynamics. He became more aware of his effect on others in ministry. Bill began to see that theology undergirded the practice of ministry and the praxis of clinical pastoral supervision. Theology was not an afterthought to clinical supervision.

The issues of an adequate transformed praxis of clinical pastoral supervision have not yet been addressed. Also, the issue of theological method in clinical pastoral supervision has not been addressed. The next chapter analyzes the texts in this field, describing three approaches in clinical pastoral supervision. Methods in theology are a key concern in this analysis.

# Chapter 2
# Three Approaches in the Praxis of Clinical Pastoral Supervision

Sally has been working in congregational ministry for eight years. She is an ordained minister in her denomination. In her seminary training, Sally did one unit of Clinical Pastoral Education and found it helpful. She has sought out a clinical pastoral supervisor to help her with some pastoral situations. In her congregational ministry, Sally inherited a program to train lay persons for visitation with the sick. These lay visitors are over sixty years old and want help from Sally about what to say and do in their visits. Sally feels adept at helping these lay visitors with theological issues. She feels inadequate with supervision theory and helping the lay visitors with intervention skills. Her praxis of ministry has taught her much and yet she is not able to develop it into a coherent theological theory. Sally wonders how she can develop the skills and theory of supervision and integrate these into her praxis of supervision of lay visitors. She also wonders about her theological method.

Sally's questions about how to supervise in a theological context relate to the focus of this chapter. It analyzes the texts written on the praxis of clinical pastoral supervision and seeks their theological method. This analysis produces three approaches: the social sciences approach, the hermeneutical approach and the special interest approach. Approach is used rather than model or paradigm because these three do not have a well-defined theoretical base. The concept of approach connotes a clinical orientation with some conceptual understanding.

In this research, 298 texts are examined. While this number is comprehensive, it is not exhaustive. The texts are analyzed using the following criteria: a) the standpoint of the text as it is expressed in the dominant language and concepts, including assumptions and values; b) the method of theology used in the text; c) the outcome of the text regarding what it advocates for an adequate praxis of clinical pastoral supervision and what it says about the distinctiveness of the praxis of clinical pastoral supervision. Investigating and analyzing these texts is similar to a building inspector investigating a building once it is completed. A building inspector prefers to be present as the building is being constructed. If a building is complete, however, the inspector has a more difficult task. In such a case, the building investigator must look at the site selection, the foundation, the design of the building, the materials used in the construction, the plumbing and electrical work embedded in the walls and compare it to other buildings in the area. These texts were not written to specifically answer the three questions raised in the introduction. Yet, these texts do have something to say about these questions. This chapter is interested in how the text is constructed in terms of its method in theology. Unfortunately, only the finished product is available. Much time, therefore, is spent in examining footnotes, the authors' other works, sources for the texts and the assumptions, values and standpoint of the text, and comparing it to other texts on the same topic.

The social sciences approach appears most often in the texts analyzed. It appears in 144 texts, or 48 percent. The hermeneutical approach is present in ninety-eight texts, or 34 percent of the total. Last is the special interest approach which appears in forty-five texts, or 12 percent. There are eleven texts, or 6 percent, that could not be classified with these categories. Distribution of texts in the three approaches is contained in Table 1:

**Table 1**
**Three Approaches in the Texts of Clinical Pastoral Supervision**
**N=298**

| Approach | Number of Texts | Percentage |
| --- | --- | --- |
| Social Sciences | 144 | 48.00 |
| Hermeneutical | 98 | 34.00 |
| Special Interest | 45 | 12.00 |
| Uncertain | 11 | 6.00 |

This review also shows that in the last fifteen years, texts with the hermeneutical and special interest approaches have increased greatly. These three approaches to theological method are presented with a critical analysis of six texts or more. The analysis is based on the criteria outlined at the beginning of the chapter.

**Social Sciences Approach**

The greatest number of texts on the praxis of clinical pastoral supervision use the social sciences approach. This approach utilizes interpretations based in psychiatry, psychology, social work, education and marriage and family therapy. The concepts and language of the social sciences approach interpret from a different standpoint than those from the hermeneutical and special interest approaches. Assumptions are also different.

A number of characteristics are present in the social sciences approach. This approach stresses the personal and professional identity of the supervisee in terms of their personal functioning. It requires an in-depth exploration of the supervisee's intrapsychic and interpersonal functioning as they are manifested in ministry. Many of the texts in this approach focus on the personal development of the supervisee in supervision. For example, Bruce Hartung, in an article entitled "The Capacity to Enter Latency in Learning Pastoral Psychotherapy,"[1] argues that the key element in a supervisee learning pastoral psychotherapy is the ability to reenter the latency period of development (ages 5-12). During the latency period, the task is to develop industry or competency as opposed to inferiority. Hartung draws on Erikson's theory of development as well as Freud's. Supervision must focus on competency, for pastoral psychotherapists cannot work effectively with clients if they cannot assume the tasks of this latency period. Hartung argues that the issues of personal competency and inferiority need to be explored by the supervisee and that supervision must provide a safe environment for this. Supervision can become psychotherapy in order to facilitate growth in the supervisee in the latency period. Hartung assumes that the personal functioning of the supervisee is crucial in training as a pastoral psychotherapist. Entering the latency period is the dominant metaphor of Hartung's interpretation of the praxis of clinical pastoral supervision.

Theological language and concepts are used in this approach to supervision. The sources for theological method are interpretations from the social sciences as well as interpretations from the Christian fact. The Christian fact includes the texts of Scripture as well as the beliefs and practices from the various Christian traditions. This two-source theological method involves the interpretations of pastoral supervision and clinical supervision. Theological ideas are developed in this conversation between the interpretations from the two sources. These theological ideas, however, accommodate the standpoint in the social sciences.[2] There is an identical correlation between the concepts and language drawn from the social sciences and the concepts and language drawn from the Christian fact. The interpretations from the Christian fact do not critique the social sciences interpretations and do not point out differences in viewpoint. The dominant language is from the social sciences.

Peter VanKatwyk utilizes this social science approach in theology in "The Helping Styles Inventory: An Update."[3] VanKatwyk presents a revision of his Helping Styles Inventory (HSI). This is a tool to be used in clinical pastoral supervision to facilitate authentic and competent ministry. The article draws on the McMaster family systems theory, Kolb's adult educational ideas and the sociolinguistic theory of Deborah Tannen. In his tool, VanKatwyk utilizes images from business, science and theology. They dominate the article. VanKatwyk also employs theological language. He presents ideas such as the cure of souls, the elements of pastoral care and the work of John Patton. These theological ideas accommodate the concepts of the social sciences and are interwoven with them.

The supervision theory of Ekstein and Wallerstein is present in many of the texts that employ a social sciences approach. Two examples demonstrate this. First, Carole Somers-Clark and Logan Jones use the clinical rhombus to facilitate learning in supervision.[4] The standpoint of the text is found within the theory of Ekstein and Wallerstein. The clinical rhombus is used to teach pastoral care, especially in the area of resistance and change. A second example is the response of the Georgia Association for Pastoral Counselling, Inc., to a supervisory case gone wrong.[5] The writers from the

Georgia Association for Pastoral Counselling, Inc., utilize many of the theories of Ekstein and Wallerstein, such as learning problems, problems about learning, parallel process and structure to critique the case. The interpretations of Ekstein and Wallerstein dominate and pastoral reflections accommodate these ideas.

Richard Voss' supervisory philosophy of family therapy is entitled "Family Counselling."[6] Voss argues that the family therapist beginning therapy with a family experiences the same reality as a person being baptized. Similar to the person being plunged into the baptismal waters, the therapist is being "plunged" into the family system. He notes that the experience of beginning therapy with a family is identical to the experience of the baptismal liturgy. In his reflection, Voss does not offer any differences between the concepts of joining a family system in therapy and the baptismal liturgy. The language and concepts of systemic family therapy dominate and are applied to explaining baptismal liturgy. Are the two interpretations the same?

In the social sciences approach, one assumption is that one does not have to use theological language or concepts in order to discuss God's presence in supervision and ministry. Grace appears whether one names it or not. All of reality, including the social sciences, manifests grace and sin. The theories of the social sciences can be revelations of God's work in the world. It is an immanent view of God, a Christology from below. The concept of joining a family system then can be a manifestation of grace, like being plunged into the waters of baptism.

Another example of this social sciences approach is the article by Alfred A. Merwald entitled "Supervision of the Psychological Self."[7] Merwald draws upon the work of Heinz Kohut to offer an explanation of clinical pastoral supervision. Kohut's psychological theory dominates the article and is the lens that Merwald uses to explain the praxis of clinical pastoral supervision. Clinical pastoral supervision has an essential task in developing the psychological self. The focus is on the person of the supervisee. This interpretation of clinical pastoral supervision stands within the social sciences with an emphasis on the personality theory of Kohut.

Merwald's interpretation does not depend heavily on the language and concepts of theology. The dominant discourse is shaped by the psychological ideas of Kohut. Merwald does mention that the pastoral supervisor is the means of grace for the supervisee. That is the only theological term used in the article. Grace is understood from the standpoint of the psychological theory of Kohut. Kohut maintains that the empathy of the therapist in a therapeutic relationship or the empathy of the parent in a parent-child relationship is crucial in the development of the psychological self. In supervision, then, the empathy of the supervisor is crucial in the development of the identity and personal integration of the supervisee. Merwald equates the notion of grace with empathy. This understanding of grace is grounded in the psychological standpoint of Kohut. Merwald does not include the notion of judgment, which is also part of the theological understanding of grace.[8]

Another example of the social sciences approach to clinical pastoral supervision is an article entitled "A Theory of Education Relevant for CPE," by Jack L. Thomas.[9] Thomas's standpoint grows out of the educational theories of David Kolb and Malcolm Knowles. He uses Kolb's Learning Styles Inventory (LSI) in facilitating the supervisee's learning. Thomas also adopts Knowles's concept of andragogy in learning as well as the adult developmental theories of Erik Erikson, Carl Jung and Daniel Levinson. The identity of the supervisee is an important focus in supervision. Thomas employs some theological language and concepts from Paul Tillich. He uses Tillich's notions of incarnation, self-transcendence and the ambiguity of human experience.[10] These ideas, however, are not the dominant discourse of his text. The adult educational theory of Kolb and Knowles dominate Thomas's philosophy. The dominant metaphor for the praxis of clinical pastoral supervision is andragogy. Tillich's theological ideas are used to endorse the educational and psychological standpoints.

Both Thomas and Merwald have focused little on the content of clinical pastoral supervision. Both Thomas and Merwald stress the person in supervision. Thomas focuses on how the supervisee learns and integrates theory and practice in ministry. The content of theology is not mentioned nor is there any discussion of what is said in clinical pastoral supervision. Merwald focuses on the supervisee's process of healing the psychological self. Again, there is no mention of the content of the Christian message. For Merwald, the person in ministry is the essential issue. Neither Thomas nor Merwald addresses the contextual issues of gender, "race" or economics. Their philosophies assume that these are not issues that shape clinical pastoral supervision. In the social sciences approach, there is little mention of pastoral supervision being connected to the Christian community. The focus is on the relationship between supervisor and supervisee and supervisee and patient. The local Christian community is not mentioned in these philosophies of supervision. Neither Thomas nor Merwald mentions the connection of clinical pastoral supervision to the worshipping community, the place of the Bible or the sacraments in the training of the supervisee.

In the social sciences approach described in the foregoing texts, attention is given to the development of skills, especially those offered by the social sciences. The stress on skills is offered both to clergy and laity . There is no delineation between clergy and laity in this approach. In these texts, clergy are not given a special voice or place. This is not an issue in the social sciences approach. Rather, the focus of education is on the particular interpretations from the social sciences, including the related skills. The clergy-lay hierarchy is reconstituted not on the basis of ordination but on the basis of competence in the clinical approach to ministry.

Competence in ministry is one of the important values in the social sciences approach. This includes theological and pastoral competence as well as skill. Competence is not determined by ordination. The social sciences approach to clinical pastoral supervision determines competence in a practitioner according to skill, relevant academic accreditation, professional certification and experience. The social sciences approach to clinical pastoral supervision has allowed many trained lay persons to become chaplains and pastoral counselors as well as administrators in health care institutions and pastoral care centres.

The social sciences approach is one category for understanding the theological method of the texts on the praxis of clinical pastoral supervision. This perspective starts with interpretations of the human person(s) from the social sciences standpoint. These interpretations describe the person of the supervisee, supervisor and client. They also explain the supervisory relationship. This approach values competence in skills and knowledge of theory as well as personal integration. In some instances, little distinction is made between supervision and therapy. Theological interpretations accommodate the social sciences interpretations. Theological method in this praxis uses two sources in correlating the interpretations from the Christian fact and the social sciences. The outcomes of this correlation are often identical. This approach assumes God is present in all reality and in the interpretations from the social sciences. The ecclesiology is based on competent training as opposed to ordination.

Sally's concern about developing skills for supervision as well as supervisory theory fits the contributions of the social sciences approach. Much of supervision in CAPPE, ACPE and AAPC has benefited from this approach. The social sciences offer many interventions that are helpful in specific situations. Such help is necessary for practical theology which is located in the concrete. The attraction of the social sciences is due in part to the belief that the social sciences are more helpful in the practice of ministry than some theological ideas. Competence utilizes practical interventions.

Sally appreciates competence and finds the theory and skills helpful. At the same time, she questions competence as the most important value. Ministry in the Bible is not just based on competence. Rather, ministry is based on God's call and the desire to serve God's people. Call and service are different from competence. Jeremiah and Peter the Apostle were not the most competent in Israel. Has competence become a modern idol?

## Hermeneutical Approach

The hermeneutical approach is concerned with the reinterpretation of the Christian message in the praxis of clinical pastoral supervision. As Table 1 shows, there are ninety-eight texts out of 298, or 34 percent, in this particular category. Similar to the social sciences approach, the hermeneutical approach focuses on the person in clinical pastoral supervision. Unlike the social sciences approach, however, the hermeneutical approach gives more attention to the Christian message as it pertains to the praxis of clinical pastoral supervision. The message is given a new understanding and meaning, which produces a variety of interpretations that are influenced by both the contemporary practice of ministry and the practice of supervision in other disciplines. The emphasis on Christian interpretation defines the hermeneutical approach. The hermeneutical aspect of clinical pastoral supervision is part of a wider movement in practical theology.

The use of hermeneutics in practical theology has developed over the last twenty-five years. Practical theologians like Charles Winquist, Donald Capps, Charles Gerkin, Don Browning and others have begun to employ some of the ideas from hermeneutics in understanding and explaining practical theology. Donald Capps in his book *Pastoral Care and Hermeneutics* argues that some of the hermeneutical principles and tools that have been used to interpret written texts can be used in understanding and explaining the practices and events of ministry.[11] Capps describes and utilizes the hermeneutical ideas of Paul Ricoeur in developing a schema for interpreting pastoral practices and events.

Pastoral hermeneutics is interdisciplinary. The interpretation of pastoral events and practices must involve interpretations from the Bible, the ongoing tradition of the church, theologians, other practices of ministry as well as contemporary ideas drawn from the social sciences. This understanding of hermeneutics is not reductionistic. An interdisciplinary stance does not reduce the interpretations of a practice/event to one perspective. This pastoral hermeneutic believes that the practices and events of ministry form a complex phenomena that cannot be explained by one interpretation or the language and ideas from one discipline. Rather, multiple perspectives offer various ways of interpreting practices or events by utilizing a variety of languages and ideas.

The interpretations that are drawn from a variety of sources dialogue with each other to understand and explain a pastoral situation. One of the assumptions of contemporary pastoral hermeneutics is that there is a plurality of claims to truth.[12] A text or event can be interpreted in more than one way depending on one's standpoint. In pastoral hermeneutics, the norm for judging whether a particular interpretation ought to be used in practice is based not on orthodoxy but on orthopraxis.[13] Orthopraxis is praxis that builds God's reign and is in communion with other praxis of the Church. In the field of clinical pastoral supervision, the hermeneutical approach begins with interpretations from the Christian fact. These interpretations form the lens through which the human person is viewed. Like the social sciences approach, the hermeneutical approach places a major emphasis on understanding and explaining the supervisee, the supervisor, the supervisory relationship, the client and the pastoral relationship. One of the differences between the two approaches is that the hermeneutical approach starts with Christian symbols, ideas and praxis, whereas the social sciences approach begins with interpretations from the social sciences.

There are many examples that demonstrate the hermeneutical approach. One is presented by Tjaard G. Hommes in an article entitled "Supervision as Theological Method."[14] Hommes begins his explanation of supervision from a standpoint in the Christian fact. One of his fundamental assumptions is that the supervisor is a theologian who reflects on the living human document of the supervisee and the living human documents of the supervisee's practice. Hommes argues that the supervisor has four tasks with the supervisee. The supervisor needs to enable the supervisee to 1) gain greater personal development; 2) develop professional skills; 3) gain the ability to diagnose clients; 4) develop spiritually. Underlying these four tasks of supervision, there is a theological method that is correlational. This correlational method links the individual experience of the supervisee with the experience of the Christian community. Hommes places his view of the supervisory experience within the corporate experience of the Christian community. He relates his theological method to narrative. He argues that in supervision the apprentice-minister reflects on their own narrative and the narrative of the client. The narrative of the supervisee and client are in conversation with the narrative of the Christian community.

In this hermeneutical approach, there are two dominant concerns. One concern focuses on interpreting the supervisee and client from a theological perspective. This is understood as theological anthropology. The other concern emphasizes ethics in practical theology and how it is embodied in praxis. This concern deals with issues of power, justice, fairness, appropriate roles and boundaries in the supervisory relationship as well as in the supervisee-client relationship.

Theological anthropology is an understanding of the human person (*anthropos*) from a theological standpoint (*theos*).[15] From a Christian perspective, theological anthropology involves explaining the nature and destiny of the human person using the notions of creation, sin and redemption.[16] Currently, theological anthropology involves both social science explanations of personality and Christian metaphors of the human person. The conversation between the interpretations from these two different standpoints constructs a particular theological anthropology.

In the hermeneutical approach to clinical pastoral supervision, theological anthropology is often presented in narrative form.[17] The narrative approach understands the Christian message as a story that manifests the themes of creation, sin and redemption. In this kind of theological anthropology, the human person is made in God's image and experiences sin in a variety of ways. Redemption is also experienced in a variety of ways through the inbreaking of God's reign. The focus of the narrative understanding of theological anthropology is to help the supervisee connect their narrative with the Christian narrative in the ministry context.

An example of this narrative approach to theological anthropology is found in Mark Jensen's article entitled "Life Histories and Narrative Theology."[18] Jensen uses narrative theology in understanding and explaining clinical pastoral supervision. He uses case studies of two supervisees: Mrs. R. and John. One is a chaplain in a hospital and the other is a pastor in a parish. In understanding the personalities of these people, Jensen draws on biblical texts and the ideas of various contemporary practical theologians. As well, he utilizes the life histories of John Bunyan, St. Augustine, St. Theresa and Jonathan Edwards to develop his narrative theological anthropology. For Jensen, the key metaphors of creation, sin and redemption are operative in the lives of these two supervisees. His goal as a supervisor is to explore the history of the supervisee while believing that all history is religious. In this case, supervision involves the intersection of personal stories. The intersection includes the meeting of the stories of supervisor and supervisee with stories from the living human documents encountered in ministry. In the midst of these various narratives, the Christian story emerges. Both supervisor and supervisee are engaged in the interpretation of the living human document as it is encountered in the self and in others. Jensen's approach involves a theological anthropology that expresses itself as narrative. The Christian themes of creation, sin and redemption are central to that story and receive interpretation through conversation with the supervisor.

Kenneth Pohly demonstrates a narrative understanding of theological anthropology in his praxis of clinical pastoral supervision.[19] He has developed a complex notion of the many narratives that impact upon the supervisee's emerging narrative. Pohly believes that a narrative approach is the most beneficial lens for theological reflection in supervision. He outlines three areas that impact upon the emerging narrative of the supervisee under supervision. First, in supervision, the supervisee presents both their person as well as the ministry in which they are engaged. There is an overlap between the person and the ministry. At the intersection of both the ministry and the person of the supervisee, there is the emerging story. This emerging story is central to the identity of the supervisee and to the ministry of the supervisee. The emerging story is impacted by the personal identity of the supervisee as well as the faith community.

A second area that impacts upon the emerging story is the lived experience of the supervisee. This story is also formed by the received narrative of the Christian community. The received narrative is the sum of all Christian tradition and praxis. The third component that impacts upon the emerging story is self-deception in the supervisee. Pohly believes that all persons have ways of remembering and telling the emerging narrative that can be self-deceiving. These ways can distort the narrative, especially in avoiding the painful and sinful aspects of the story. This self-deception can be both conscious and unconscious. The supervisee's narrative is also impacted by the supervisor's narrative. The emerging story is formed by lived experience, received narrative and self-deception. In Pohly's narrative approach to supervision, a theological anthropology undergirds his conceptual framework. This is evidenced in his case study.

The other area of concern for the hermeneutical approach is ethics in supervision. According to Don Browning and David Tracy, ethics is the prime concern of practical theology.[20] Ethics deals with the question of what ought to be done in a given situation. This means making a choice and acting on it according to moral reasoning. Practical theology is concerned with doing. Ethics has an important place in that doing. In the field of clinical pastoral supervision, ethics is an important issue because supervision deals with what ought to be done by the supervisor and the supervisee in a specific situation. Marie McCarthy and David B. McCurdy, in the introduction to "Symposium: Supervision and Training as an Ethical Endeavour," argue that supervision is an ethical endeavour in which many choices are made in the midst of doing.[21] For them, the key ethical issues in clinical pastoral supervision are power, competency and character. Included in power, competency and character are issues of gender, intimacy and sexual dynamics in supervision.

Chris Schlauch, in his article "Functioning as an Ethicist in Pastoral Supervision: Casting the Questions,"[22] argues that pastoral care, pastoral counselling and pastoral supervision are ethical activities. One's ethical approach is outlined in the answers to three questions:

> What is the place from which we interpret?
> What do we regard as salient "facts" for interpretation?
> How do we interpret?[23]

The answers to these questions expose the way the supervisor or supervisee decides about ethical issues.

Schlauch uses a narrative approach in his ethical decision making. He locates his ethical principles within the Christian fact. He uses a clinical vignette of a client who wants the phone number of the supervisee who is training as a pastoral counselor. The client is considering suicide and out of a concern for personal safety for self asks for the home phone number of the supervisee. Schlauch uses his three questions to explore the issue with the supervisee.

In the discussion of this supervision issue, Schlauch outlines two general norms that he uses in ethics: the principles of beneficence and justice. These norms are used in a variety of ways depending on the context, the salient facts and the persons involved. Schlauch stresses that ethical activity is not just a rational critical activity. There is more to ethics than the rational. He uses a flexible style that stresses the conversation about the ethical issues embedded in the situation rather than a style that is deductive, logical and rational. Schlauch exposes a host of dilemmas posed by the client's request for the supervisee's phone number. In the article, he does not provide the answer to what ought to be done. That is left for the supervisee to decide based on the supervisory conversation. Rather, he raises the questions and demonstrates that clinical pastoral supervision involves ethical issues and questions.

Ethical reflection is an important concern in supervision. In the texts that manifest a social sciences approach, ethical reflection does not occupy a central place in supervision. Seldom is ethics mentioned. In the social sciences approach, there is a fear of moralizing. The social sciences approach stresses the creation of a nonjudgmental environment that is free of moralizing. The hermeneutical approach is different. While this hermeneutical approach does not want to moralize, there is a desire to engage in moral reasoning with the supervisee. Ethical reasoning is essential to decision making and the supervisee must develop the means to rationally reflect on the ethical values embedded in any decision to act.

The hermeneutical approach uses a two-source theological method. The praxis begins with interpretations from the Christian fact. These interpretations focus on theological anthropology and ethics. The hermeneutical approach also draws on interpretations from the social sciences. Often, there is an analogical correlation between the interpretations from the Christian fact and the interpretations from the social sciences. Like the social sciences approach, the hermeneutical approach utilizes a variety of metaphors to describe its praxis.

The theology of Charles Gerkin is located in the hermeneutical approach. His writings span forty years of critical reflection on practical theology.[24] His theological contribution is in the area of practical theology and more specifically in pastoral care and counselling. He has written articles on the topic of clinical pastoral supervision, is involved in many of the issues raised in the praxis of supervision[25] and has taught pastoral theology for twenty years.[26] Gerkin defines his theology as a "narrative hermeneutical theory of practical theology."[27] Like those texts in clinical pastoral supervision that are part of the hermeneutical approach, he is concerned about the contemporary reinterpretation of the Christian message.

Gerkin is part of a group of revisionist practical theologians[28] who are interested in putting the Christian message in a more central place in the pastoral care and counselling movement. The revisionist agenda is similar to the agenda of the hermeneutical approach in clinical pastoral supervision. This agenda includes a greater emphasis on the message. Gerkin differs in some aspects from the hermeneutical approach in that he also places a lot of emphasis on contextual issues. His concern about social change, especially in terms of racism, ethnicity and the empowerment of the laity, connects him to the special interest approach.[29]

## Special Interest Approach

The special interest approach focuses on the experience of specific groups in the praxis of clinical pastoral supervision. This approach emphasizes the issues of gender, ethnicity and laity in supervision. In the texts reviewed for this study, forty-five, or 12 percent, are categorized as using the special interest approach. The special interest approach interprets from a different standpoint than the social sciences and hermeneutical approach. The special interest approach starts in the experience of a particular group in the church. That experience becomes the critical lens through which the interpretations from the social sciences and the Christian fact are viewed. This approach stresses the uniqueness of the specific group. The experience of the particular group is often marginalized in society and church. The experience of marginalization is often different from the experiences of those who interpret from the social sciences and hermeneutical approaches. The special interest approach assumes that differences in human experience are based on gender, "race", ethnicity and ecclesial status. This approach argues that the praxis of clinical pastoral supervision must take into account these contextual differences.

In this approach, there is a growing body of texts in the area of women's experience in clinical pastoral supervision. The *Journal of Supervision and Training in Ministry* devotes a special edition to women's issues in supervision.[30] Elizabeth Meakes and Thomas St. James O'Connor, in their qualitative research article entitled "Miriam Dancing and with Leprosy: Women's Experience of Supervision in CAPE,"[31] focus on the experience of women in clinical pastoral supervision. The ethnographic research found that women's experience of supervision in CAPE is both valued and negated. Their research is based on a sample of ten women from different denominational backgrounds in different SPE programs including Pastoral Counselling Education (PCE) and Clinical Pastoral Education (CPE).

These women experience both empowerment and disempowerment in clinical pastoral supervision. On the one hand, there is a sense that clinical pastoral supervision disempowers women in ministry. At the same time, these same women experience SPE supervision to be validating and empowering, especially when compared to the experience of supervision in the denominations to which they belong. Meakes and O'Connor make five recommendations for clinical pastoral supervision in CAPE to validate and empower women. First, there is a need to recognize that women's experience of ministry and supervision is different from men. Women's experience needs recognition and validation in supervision. The women interviewed preferred a more relational and less directive approach to supervision. Second, there is a preference for a learner-centred approach in supervision that includes a learning contract in which the women's goals are respected. Third, there is a need for more female supervisors in CAPPE. In the 1990 *Directory of Mem-*

*bers of CAPE*, women made up 50 percent of the membership but only 10 percent of the full teaching supervisors.[32] In the research, four of the women experienced supervision from a female. These four women found female supervisors to be validating and empowering. Fourth, the women advocated that awareness of gender issues be part of supervision. Fifth, there is the suggestion that dyadic supervision be utilized in order to minimize hierarchy when there is a male supervisor. Dyadic supervision involves two students being supervised at one time by a supervisor. Dyadic supervision puts supervision more in an educational, collaborative context and places the supervisee in a more consultative role. This research underlines some of the special interests of women in clinical pastoral supervision.

Another article, titled "The Emergence of Feminine Consciousness in Supervision,"[33] by Julia Jewett and Emily Haight, focuses on the experience of a female supervisee (Jewett) and a female supervisor (Haight) in the supervisory relationship. One of the important values that both describe in their experience of this supervision is collegiality. While there is an awareness of the difference in roles between supervisor and supervisee, there is also an awareness and experience of collegiality. Emily Haight, the supervisor, explains an image that she had of the supervisory relationship during a session with Jewett. Their experience of supervision is imaged as a *Kaffee Klatsch*, i.e., coffee cups in hand. Haight argues that this image might not fit the traditional notions of supervision that stress competency, professionalism and personal growth. Yet, the *Kaffee Klatsch* produced some important insights and support. The experience of both Jewett and Haight in this supervisory relationship is one of collegiality and mutual support that led to greater competency. This was achieved through the informality of discussing counselling cases while both had their coffee cups in hand.

Another concern of this special interest approach is ethnicity and "race." Clinical pastoral supervision with white males and females in the United States is not the same as supervision with people of colour in Kenya, Japan and Indonesia. "Race" and ethnicity are important contextual elements. The special interest approach includes the divergent experiences of different ethnic groups in the praxis of clinical pastoral supervision. Frances Randall identifies the uniqueness of training and supervising pastoral counselors in Kenya.[34] Kenya has become westernized in the last fifteen years and the people are experiencing problems "in alcoholism, family violence, robbery, rape, unwanted pregnancies, and suicides."[35] The rise in these problems has required therapists, especially clinical pastoral therapists. Randall notes that in training people from Kenya for ministry as pastoral counselors, there is a need to include the values and assumptions of their Kenyan heritage, which include the interpretation of dreams, intuition and other images. Randall finds it a challenge to include both Western and African approaches to healing in training and supervision. Kenyans have a more social notion of illness than westerners and believe that illness is tied to ancestors and witch craft. The training program designed by Randall and the team at the counselling centre focuses more on group supervision than on individual supervision. There is also a lot of time spent on the analysis of dreams and symbols. For Kenyans, dreams and fantasies are fragments of reality and they utilize dreams to guide their decisions. Randall admits that training and supervision that incorporates the values and assumptions of the Kenyan culture is at the beginning stage.

Another example of ethnicity and "race" in the special interest approach to supervision is discussed in an article by Russell F. Seabright.[36] Seabright notes the difference in attitudes and expectations of supervision in an Indonesian setting. For Indonesian supervisees, there is a mistrust of their own experience and its authority. Those training for ministry in Indonesia assume that revelation is present in Scripture, tradition and hierarchical authority. Personal experience is not a source of revelation or learning. The ministry of the Indonesian church reflects a social structure that is hierarchical and authoritarian. Women are not included or considered equal to men. The focus of training for ministry is on patterns of correct performance, and imitation of the supervisor is important. The notion of exploration and testing common to CPE approaches to clinical pastoral supervision in the United States and Canada is not prevalent in Indonesia. Supervisees in Indonesia begin their clinical training in a service role during the early years of seminary formation. They are supervised in placements in poor villages working under a pastor. Supervisees have little formal knowledge or training before they begin formal theological training. In this apprenticeship program, the supervisee trains for ministry in the church and also trains and serves other social agencies present in the village. From the beginning, the supervisee is part of an interdisciplinary approach.

These examples from Indonesia and Kenya demonstrate that ethnicity and "race" are important elements in the special interest approach. This approach challenges the assumption that clinical pastoral supervision is the same for all. Rather, this approach emphasizes that each group in the church has its own special needs, values, assumptions and theology in terms of supervision. This approach incorporates the special interests of the particular group.

The special interest approach also appears in the texts that discuss lay supervision. Lay supervision involves supervision of lay persons and the role of the whole congregation in the ministry of pastoral care. Lay supervision also includes clinical pastoral supervision by lay persons. Pohly believes that the various Christian denominations are experiencing a revival of lay ministry and lay supervision.[37]

Charles A. Van Wagner discusses this idea in his article "Supervision of Lay Pastoral Care."[38] Van Wagner has experienced CPE training and supervision. He decided to use the CPE model in a congregational setting with lay persons that he trained for visitation of the sick and shut-ins. These lay persons were older retired persons who were committed to the local congregation. Van Wagner discovered that the CPE model needed to be adapted to these people who were not ordained and who lived in a different context than clergy. They were not interested in the personal growth emphasis or in frequent meetings. Since most lacked formal academic theological education, they desired skills training and time to talk with the minister about their particular visit. They saw themselves as representing the congregation in their visits. For lay pastoral care, the connection to the Christian community was essential. Much of the lay ministry to the sick was expressed through ordinary conversations and activities.

The emphasis on the supervision of lay persons engaged in ministry is present in two other articles. One article, by Louis B. Weeks, deals with Christian education teachers.[39] The other article is by Grayson L. Tucker, who trains church volunteers.[40] Both these authors demonstrate that clinical pastoral supervision changes when the persons receiving training are lay persons. Differences in theological education, time, commitment and expertise as well as pastoral identity are key items in these different approaches. In the case of church leaders and Christian education teachers, the lay persons see their connection with the community to be essential. They are acting on behalf of the Christian community.

The special interest approach focuses on the contextual issues of gender, "race," ethnicity and empowerment of the laity. This approach assumes that clinical pastoral supervision has been dominated by ordained white males in the United States and Canada. Clinical supervision changes when the supervisor and/or the supervisee is female, black and/or lay from Kenya.

The special interest approach to clinical pastoral supervision adds another source to the method of theologizing to the praxis of clinical pastoral supervision. This is human experience. The special interest approach emphasizes the experience of the specific group as a source for theology. The group's experience is the lens through which interpretations from the Christian fact and the social sciences are viewed. Crucial to this method is the belief that the value and interpretation of the experience of the specific group must be enhanced by interpretations from the Christian fact and the social sciences. If the experience of the group is not enhanced, interpretations from the other sources are viewed with the hermeneutic of suspicion. For the special interest approach, there are three sources of theology: Christian fact, social sciences and, most importantly, the experience of the specific group.

## Theological Method in the Three Approaches

The analysis of the three approaches within the texts on the praxis of clinical pastoral supervision presents some answers to the question of theological method. The social sciences approach and the hermeneutical approach use a two source correlation method. Both approaches draw upon interpretations from within the social sciences, particularly supervisory theory, educational theory and personality theory. In their theological method, both approaches draw upon interpretations from the Christian fact. This includes understandings of grace, sin, redemption, hope, ecclesiology and pastoral supervision in the ministry of the Church. The two are different in starting point and outcome.

The works of Ekstein and Wallerstein, Kolb, Knowles, Kohut, Erikson, Rogers, Myers-Briggs and other theorists dominate the social sciences theological method. Interpretations from the Christian fact accommodate the interpretations from the social sciences. There is little difference between the various interpretations. Most often, the interpretations are identical. The outcome of this theological method is an endorsement of interpretations from the social sciences in the area of clinical pastoral supervision.

The hermeneutical approach includes the Bible and theologians like Tillich, Hiltner, Moltmann, Browning, Richard Niebuhr and Capps. Interpretations from the social sciences are accommodated with interpretations from the Christian fact. Often, the interpretations from the social sciences are critiqued. The outcome of this theological method is more analogical, noting both similarities and differences between the interpretations from the two different sources.

The special interest approach draws on a third source. This is the experience of the specific group. The special interest approach questions and critiques the interpretations from the other two sources. In this theological method, the experience of women or people of colour or lay persons confronts and challenges the interpretations of the Christian fact and of the social sciences. The outcome is dialectical, with tensions underscoring differences rather than similarities.

While there is much to be applauded in the theological methods of the three approaches to the praxis of clinical pastoral supervision, there are some missing elements. One missing element is an incarnated notion of God's presence in the praxis of clinical pastoral supervision. Such a notion is expressed in Anton Boisen's "living human document," in which he seeks to utilize the spiritual dynamics present in the person to facilitate health and redemption. Such a notion places God in practice as well as interpretation. God is not just present in interpretations found in written texts. God is also present in the living human document that is continually changing. Gerkin addresses this missing element in his incarnational theology that utilizes the notion of the fusion of horizons in understanding and explaining the living human document.

In texts on the praxis of clinical pastoral supervision, there is little use of cases and vignettes. A few texts utilize cases but most do not. What is the place of case and practice in theological method? Does a case study approach not focus on the living human document? Most of the texts on clinical pastoral supervision use a theory/praxis method. Does the actual case not play a role in method? If not, what is the difference between practical and systematic theology? The use of case studies concretizes the presence of God in a manner similar to the living human document. Case studies add a new element. Case studies make the theologizing practical. Gerkin has much to offer here.

Referring back to the case of Sally mentioned at the beginning of the chapter, her theological method belongs to the hermeneutical approach. Sally's task is to incorporate some of the elements from other approaches. She found that clinical pastoral supervision opened new understanding about supervision. The notion of parallel process helped her to see parallels between her relationship with lay visitors and the lay visitors' relationships with the sick. Sally's understanding of parallel process made her less anxious about the lay visitors' visits. She saw the supervisory relationship as offering some insight into the praxis of the particular lay visitor. With this insight, Sally felt she could better deal with problems.

Sally also did live supervision with the lay visitors. This meant that she accompanied the lay visitors on some pastoral visits. Initially, the lay visitors were nervous about being observed by their pastor in their pastoral ministry. They had some experience of such observation through the role plays in the supervisory group. Once into the visit, however, the lay visitor forgot the anxiety and was able to engage the sick person. Sally encouraged the lay visitor to conduct the visit and she played the role of observer with minimal contact with the sick person. The sick person appreciated the presence of the pastor and often told Sally about the importance of the lay visitor's presence. Afterwards, Sally discussed with the lay visitor some of the dynamics of the visit. Most often, the lay visitor found the discussions of the visit to be beneficial.

Sally also focused on helping the lay visitors to develop and pursue a goal in the pastoral visit. Initially, many of her supervisees could not distinguish between a friendly chat and a pastoral visit. Developing a goal for the visit moved the conversation from a friendly chat to a pastoral visit. Sometimes, the goal was to be a loving presence. Other times, the goal was to help with some concrete problem. Focusing on the goal of the visit proved to be helpful. It gave a structure to the pastoral conversation and also provided a way of evaluating the effectiveness of the visit.

In Sally's supervision, there was also some emphasis on developing skills for ministry. This included active listening, summarizing, structuring a conversation, and being able to talk about spiritual issues. Prayer, reading the bible, reminiscing, telling stories and acts of kindness were a few of the interventions. Time was spent in the supervisory group practising these skills. The supervisees also shared their experiences in visiting the sick and shut-ins and received helpful feedback from both their peers and Sally.

Sally became more aware of the theory present in her praxis of pastoral supervision. She began to understand that any pastoral situation can be viewed from a number of standpoints, including family systems theory, developmental psychology and narrative theology. With her supervisor, Sally reflected on her praxis and saw the many ideas and possibilities embedded in it. Her praxis was laden with theory, even though she was not aware of all of it. The reflections and conversations about her supervision praxis stimulated Sally to make some changes in her ministry. Praxis was an important teacher for her.

# Chapter 3
# Gerkin's Incarnational Theology

Mike is working as a chaplain in a long-term care facility under supervision. He has been there for over four months and has developed a good rapport with many of the residents of the facility as well as many of the staff. He has studied various theories from both theology and the social sciences and has begun to integrate them into his ministry. One is the structural systems theory of Salvatore Minuchin. Another is the hermeneutical theory of Ricoeur and Gadamer. Mike is having some difficulty in using these theories together in his ministry. He has a tendency to focus on one theory when visiting a resident and ignore the other. One resident in the long-term care facility especially posed a problem for Mike. Mike realized that the situation with this person could be easily interpreted from multiple standpoints. Each of the interpretations produces different interventions with different possible outcomes. Mike feels overwhelmed by the variety of interventions and the complexity of the case. He is confused and asks his supervisor: "Which is the right interpretation for this case?"

Mike is struggling with the plurality of interpretations. This challenges his assumption that there is one right way of intervening in the case. As a chaplain, he needs to be aware of the various interpretations and to recognize God's invitation incarnated in the midst of many possible interventions. An incarnational theology assumes God is present and invites response. This response could be in many different ways. Incarnational theology has many dimensions. In systematic theology, it includes an investigation of the person of Jesus, which is also known as Christology. He is both the Jesus of history and the Christ of faith. Systematic theology examines the humanity and divinity of Jesus, the place of Jesus in salvation history, revelation, eschatology, the church, Word and Sacrament and the life of the Christian. Today, this investigation also includes the place of the Incarnation within various Christian denominations and the relationship of the Incarnation to the other world religions. The Incarnation is also a central concern for practical theology. Practical theology is concerned with the practices of the church. It focuses on how the incarnation takes place in the practices of ministry. Specifically, this understanding of the incarnation shapes how one does ministry in the name of Christ. The different understandings of how Jesus as the Christ becomes incarnated in reality often follows denominational lines.

In Roman Catholic practice, the ministry of the sacraments is an essential part of incarnational theology. Christ is incarnated in the ministry of Word and Sacraments.[1] Based on the doctrine of the Incarnation promulgated at Chalcedon (451), Roman Catholic pastoral care understands ministry as an embodied experience of grace. God becomes present in the temporal in order to heal, sustain, guide and reconcile humankind.[2] The importance of the pastoral relationship in the embodiment of the presence of Christ has become more central to the Roman Catholic Church since Vatican II. In the Roman Catholic tradition, the Sacraments and the connection to the church community are necessary elements of pastoral care and counselling and embody Christ. The Eucharist, the Sacrament of Reconciliation and the Sacrament of the Sick are especially important in pastoral care.[3] These sacraments embody the presence of Christ and are part of their practices. In Roman Catholic incarnational pastoral care, Christ becomes present in the practices of the Sacraments, in the person of the priest and lay persons called to ministry and in the ministry of the Church as a whole.[4]

Protestant practical theology has some similarities to and differences from Roman Catholic practical theology in the area of incarnational theology. Martin Luther believed that the Christian was to be "a little Christ to the neighbour."[5] In the practice of ministry, pastoral care must incarnate the presence of Christ in the person of the pastor or lay visitor as they minister to those in need. In this understanding of incarnational theology, the pastor or lay person embodies the love of God manifest in Jesus in the work of pastoral care and counselling. The pastoral relationship becomes the place where Christ is incarnated. In this case, the emphasis is on the pastoral relationship as incarnating the risen Christ rather than on the sacraments.

Carroll Wise, a United Methodist practical theologian, argues that the ministry of pastoral care is different from preaching, teaching and administration. The context of pastoral care requires that God in Christ become embodied (in an imperfect way) in the pastor's care for the person in need. This embodiment, according to Wise, includes the qualities of listening, empathy and identification. As the pastor listens, empathizes and identifies with the struggles of the person in need, Wise believes that the Spirit of Christ comes alive. In Wise's understanding, the I-Thou relationship described by Martin Buber is the prime model for pastoral care. This I-Thou relationship is the incarnation of God in Christ.

Charles Gerkin's incarnational theology has been greatly influenced by the legacy of Carroll Wise.[6] Gerkin agrees with Wise that the pastoral relationship is an essential way that Christ becomes incarnated in reality.[7] Empathy, listening and identification are important. Gerkin's theology, however, goes beyond Wise's theology in arguing that Christ becomes incarnated not just in the pastoral relationship but in events and in other relationships. God is not just limited to the pastoral relationship. Pastoral care involves helping both pastor and parishioner to discern God's activity in a variety of events. In Gerkin's notion of incarnational theology, *everyone,* including the pastor, experiences the inbreaking of the reign of God. This understanding of incarnational theology widens the practices of ministry beyond the pastoral relationship to events, crisis experiences and other manifestations of Christ.

Gerkin defines a crisis experience as "an extreme or boundary situation in which the fundamental contradiction between human aspirations and finite possibilities becomes visible in such a way as to demand attention."[8] Building on the work of Anton Boisen, Gerkin understands these moments of crisis as offering a possibility of greater vulnerability and trust "in the power and care of God coming out of the change and contingency of the unknown."[9] In Gerkin's incarnational theology, crisis moments mysteriously incarnate Jesus as the Christ. In the tradition of Boisen, Gerkin believes that there is an offer given by God in these crisis moments for greater spiritual and ethical integration. In his book, *Crisis Experience in Modern Life,* Gerkin outlines a number of moments where there is a contradiction between human aspirations and finite possibilities: death, bereavement, loss, suicide, hopelessness, identity crisis, and broken relationships in family.

In the ministry of crisis, Gerkin articulates a pastoral care methodology that is incarnational. He sees the Incarnation to be continuing through God's appearance within a human, limited existence in the ongoing process of history. God appeared definitively in the life, death and resurrection of Jesus. God continues to be present in crisis events, in relationships, in both ordinary and unexpected events and experiences that are part of each person's life. This understanding of Christ being present in pastoral relationships, events, and crises can be explained in Gerkin's incarnational theology as the fusion of horizons, articulated in his book, *Widening the Horizons.* Borrowing from Hans-Georg Gadamer, Gerkin develops this notion in analyzing the interpretation process present in reading texts.

The interpreter approaches a text with a horizon of meaning. As the interpreter begins to interpret the text, the text's horizon of meaning impacts upon the interpreter. The hermeneutical process is a dialogue wherein the interpreter asks questions of the text and the texts ask questions of the interpreter. The horizons impact upon each other and a fusion begins. If the fusion is complete, the meanings of text and interpreter are identical. If there is no fusion, then there is tension. The relationship between the two horizons is dialectical. If there is some similarity and some difference, the fusion is analogical.

In Gerkin's theology, the Incarnation can be understood as a fusion of horizons. God's horizon connects with human horizons in an analogical fusion. Such a fusion transforms humankind and possibly even God.[10] This fusion of horizons takes place through the experience of events, especially crisis events. God's presence hidden in the event fuses with the interpreter's horizon in creating new meaning and transformation. The horizon of meaning has a narrative aspect. To describe a text's horizon or an interpreter's horizon is to tell a story about the text or the interpreter. One describes a horizon of meaning through narrative. The fusion of horizons, then, takes place between various narratives. God's horizon is articulated in narratives. The goal of ministry is to connect our narratives with God's narrative in order to produce new meaning and new life. For Gerkin, too, the fusion of human narratives with God's narrative also offers eschatological identity.

The fusion of horizons is a notion that undergirds much of Gerkin's incarnational theology. This understanding is indirectly present in his earlier works (1952-1980), and becomes more explicit in his later writings (1984-1992). The fusion of horizons reveals that new meaning surfaces through the interaction of various horizons. The goal of this fusion is transformation and it is described as the inbreaking of God's reign. Gerkin's incarnational theology prescribes meaning making as a fundamental human activity. Rodney Hunter and James Poling argue that meaning is the central concern of Gerkin's theology.[11] According to Poling, Gerkin uses meaning in a cognitive way, valuing insight and critical reflection simultaneously. With emphasis on meaning, Gerkin is part of the tradition of apologetic theology developed by Tillich and Tracy. Apologetic theology strives to provide cognitive claims for Christianity in contemporary culture.[12]

**Four Characteristics of Gerkin's Incarnational Theology**

### a) *Rooted in the Christian Fact*

First, Gerkin's incarnational theology is rooted in the Christian fact. This includes its sacred texts, traditions, rituals, metaphors and practices. James N. Poling notes that Gerkin is fundamentally a pastor.[13] In his upbringing, training and intellectual development, Gerkin is a practical theologian. Gerkin's theological understanding of the incarnation is shaped by his Methodist heritage. Gerkin is a third-generation minister in the United Methodist Church of America. His father and grandfather were ordained ministers in the United Methodist denomination. He was trained at Garrett Theological Seminary, which is a United Methodist Theological School. He has also taught for over twenty years at Candler School of Theology, which is a United Methodist Seminary at Emory University, Atlanta.

One aspect of Methodism that stands out in the theology of Gerkin is the notion of the catholicity of grace. Gerkin sees grace manifested in a variety of events, persons and experiences. His incarnational theology, rooted in the Methodist tradition, does not limit the intervention of God. He argues that crisis experiences that seem to lack any presence of God can in fact be the inbreaking of the reign of God. The conditional becomes a vehicle for the unconditional and discloses the graciousness of God that beckons for a response by all. In his article "Incarnational Pastoral Care (Protestantism)," Gerkin argues that his approach to pastoral care recognizes the presence of God in events and a variety of human relationships.

Gerkin's incarnational theology utilizes Tillich's concept of the Protestant principle.[14] Tillich believed that one of the problems of humankind was that it could absolutize the conditional and make the finite into the infinite. For Tillich, making the finite into the infinite is idol-making, just as the Israelites attempted to make God into the idol of golden calf. The Protestant principle, on the other hand, protests against this and does not seek to make the conditional into the unconditional. Tillich believes that God is disclosed in a multitude of ways in time, space and history, i.e., through the conditional. Humankind needs to respond to that manifestation and yet not make that particular manifestation into an absolute. God will reveal God's self in other ways and transcend the very way that God appears in the conditional. God is subject to the limits of the conditional and yet able to break out of those very conditions of time, space and history.

Gerkin's practice of incarnational theology follows Tillich's Protestant principle. God is incarnated in the conditional and yet this conditional should not be made an absolute. God's nature is revealed in a multitude of ways: a crisis, a relationship, the reading of Scripture, the sacraments and the ministry of the church. The unconditional becomes incarnated in the conditional. Gerkin is careful not to absolutize these moments. His theological approach is soft because it does not utilize rigid rules or norms. Gerkin's incarnational theology continually discerns God's revelation as present in the ordinary and refuses to make an absolute out of any model or theory that seeks to explain the incarnation of God's nature. Gerkin is very critical in his writing of reductionists who absolutize using a particular theory or theology. For him, such a method runs contrary to the Protestant principle and creates idols.

Gerkin is a constructivist in his theological method. He does not take principles learned in systematic theology from Scripture and Tradition and then apply them to the practice of ministry. Practical theology is not an application of theory to practice. His incarnational theology emerges from practice and finds clarity and critical dialogue with the ideas of other theologians and writers from other disciplines. His theology is continually in the process of construction. It is not static but dynamic.

The fusion of horizons is an accurate description of Gerkin's constructivist method. He synthesizes interpretations from many different sources in order to foster a theological understanding of a particular event or situation. He draws on different horizons and engages the various sources through a critical conversation which seeks the truth. Thus Gerkin believes that God's self is revealed through the social sciences. In Gerkin's incarnational theology, revelation is not limited to Scripture and Tradition. Gerkin continually draws upon insights from the social sciences in discovering revelation present in the conditional. Truth from the social sciences and human experience, however, is always in conversation with revelation from the Christian fact. Gerkin, first and foremost, is located in the Christian fact and from this standpoint he engages divine revelation present in human experience and the social sciences.

Gerkin's incarnational theology demonstrates a Christology from below. God is not so much the Wholly Other who comes from above to transform humankind. Rather, God appears in the midst and breaks open the event, the crisis or the person in order to transform them into a new Being. Grace works from below permeating our humanity from the Ground of Being rather than coming from above. Such a Christology emphasizes the humanity of Jesus in which divinity becomes manifest. This Christology is rooted in the Synoptic view of Jesus in the gospels.[15] Such a Christology is different from the Christology from above present in John's gospel.

The most frequent outcome is analogical, i.e., similarities and differences. For example, in his book *The Living Human Document*, Gerkin defines the three terms ego, self and soul. He notes the similarities and differences between these terms, each from a different field.[16] Another example of Gerkin's analogical incarnational theology is found in his understanding of time. Time is a key concept in his incarnational theology.[17] Gerkin uses different notions of time. In *The Living Human Document*, he outlines three levels of time. There is life cycle time. In this notion, time is understood as the beginning of life for the individual person and develops according to life stages in sequence. There is also socio-cultural time. Time in this dimension is structured in terms of the history of civilization and culture. Finally, there is eschatological time. In this structure of time, there is creation, redemption and final fulfillment of the Kingdom. Eschatological time has a number of polarities and tensions.[18]

Gerkin correlates these three levels of time and finds both similarities and differences. He calls the relationship between the three analogous. Each understanding views time from a different perspective and also connects at certain points. Gerkin's incarnational theology endorses the eschatological point of view while also using the other two perspectives on time.

Gerkin also describes his theology as dialectical. Dialectical means the ability to hold opposite values and positions in tension without collapsing them into one. For example, he states in one article that "power and powerlessness belong together in human life and in ministry as empowerment of human life."[19] In this article, he argues that both power and powerlessness are gospel values and both are needed in ministry. Specifically, the supervisor in a CPE program should not strive to rid the supervisee of powerlessness, for that is part of the Christian narrative and a necessary part of ministry. At the same time, Gerkin sees the need for the supervisee in clinical pastoral supervision to exert his/her sense of power in the service of the patient. Power, then, is important and must be used. Gerkin's interpretation of power in CPE supervision is dialectical, involving elements of both power and powerlessness. Both power and powerlessness ought to be used by both supervisor and supervisee in their praxis. Context and timing are key items in this dialectical relationship.

In Gerkin's incarnational theology, transformation is a key item. God became human in order to transform humanity into God's image and likeness. Incarnational pastoral care, in Gerkin's understanding, means using theological constructs to understand and explain reality as well as taking action in order to be transformed through the power of grace. Incarnation, then, includes transformation or conversion.

Gerkin's standpoint in the Christian fact also produces identical outcomes with some social science interpretations. The Bible has a privileged place, although in his earlier writings he does not cite the Bible as much as he does in his later writings. Gerkin draws on the interpretations of a number of systematic theologians. Most important are Tillich, Moltmann, H. Richard Neibuhr and Tracy. He also uses the ideas of narrative theologians, including Sallie McFague, John Dominic Crossan and Walter Breuggemann. Also important for Gerkin's incarnational theology are the interpretations of practical theologians, especially in the area of pastoral care and counselling. Anton Boisen, Thomas Oden, Seward Hiltner, Thomas Klink, Carroll Wise and Don Browning are theologians whom he cites. He also disagrees with some of the interpretations that the practical theologians employ. These theologians, however, are concerned with many of the same issues in the field of practical theology. Gerkin draws on their thought in his constructed theology.

**b)** *Multidisciplinary and Multilingual*

The second aspect of Gerkin's incarnational theology is that it is multilingual and multidisciplinary. As noted above, Gerkin roots himself in Christian concepts and interpretations in describing his theological approach. At the same time, his theology uses ideas and concepts from other disciplines. Just as the Incarnation took place in a different culture from our own around two thousand years ago, God's truth can be revealed in disciplines outside of theology. Gerkin endorses this understanding of Incarnation which finds truth in the theories of object relations, neo-Freudianism, philosophical hermeneutics and family systems theory.

In Gerkin's early writings (1954-1979), ideas from psychology, psychiatry and family systems theory dominate. In his first published article, written with psychologist George Weber, Gerkin develops a projective test using ambiguous religious pictures.[20] This test is designed for teenage boys who are in a detention home. The pictures are given to a boy and the boy is asked to tell a story about what is happening in the pictures. He argues that these pictures and stories aided the boys in their psychosocial and religious development. In a subsequent article, Gerkin uses this same projective test to measure religious growth in boys who are taking a religious education program in the detention home.[21]

Gerkin draws on the theory of John Bowlby about the notions of attachment and separation as a way to explain grief and bereavement and minister in crisis events.[22] Gerkin also uses Erik Erikson's notion of development and concept of identity throughout his early and later writings.[23] Gerkin integrates Carl Rogers and his humanistic psychology into his theology. He draws on Rogers's concept of unconditional positive regard and empathy. Gerkin's respectful approach in pastoral care and counselling bear the imprint of Rogers's ideas.

In his early writings, Gerkin was also influenced by Freud and neo-Freudianism.[24] He uses Freud's concept of the ego, id, superego and uses the structural notions of Freud that see the self as a system of interaction and exchange. He agrees with Freud that the unconscious has a desire for omnipotence while battling with the death wish. In his later writings, he adopts Ricoeur's understanding of Freud as involving the tension between the two language systems. One language system is the language of force which describes the work of the ego. The other is the language of meaning which is used by the self.[25]

In his earlier writings, Gerkin also draws upon the ideas of the neo-Freudian Eric Fromm.[26] He sees the limitations of Freud's individualism and the lack of social awareness. In Fromm, Gerkin finds interpretations that provide a marriage between the intrapsychic focus of Freud and the social need for a caring community. Gerkin adopts Fromm's argument for a change in social structure in order to facilitate human health. Fromm's emphasis on the alienation and depersonalization of modern culture is woven into Gerkin's theology.

In his early and later writings, Gerkin uses family systems theory. In working with couples in marriage therapy, Gerkin, in his book *Crisis Experience in Modern Life*,[27] draws on the ideas of Cliff Sager. He uses Eric Bermann's theory on scape-goating in dealing with families. He integrates the notions of split loyalties and boundary clarification in dealing with families in therapy. In his later writings, Gerkin uses systems theory to explain complex social interactions. His diagrams in *Widening the Horizons* show various systems with many components that interact and influence one another. These interacting systems shape ministry.[28] In *Prophetic Pastoral Practice*, Gerkin adopts the systems notions of centripetal and centrifugal family to describe the activity of the local congregation. Gerkin endorses the centrifugal model of church that reaches outward rather than the centripetal model that pulls people inward towards the pastor. Systems thinking is part of Gerkin's incarnational theology.

In his later writings (1980-1994), Gerkin emphasizes philosophical hermeneutics and narrative. He draws upon the ideas of Northrop Frye and Wesley Kort, along with Brian Wicker, regarding their notions about literary narrative.[29] Most important is the work of two philosophers, Paul Ricoeur and Hans-Georg Gadamer. Gerkin adopts Ricoeur's theory of understanding/explaining/understanding, and he uses this methodology to develop his method for practical theology; he also adopts Ricoeur's notion of the hermeneutic of suspicion and retrieval, along with his understanding of narrative. Gerkin uses Gadamer's concepts of the fusion of horizons in interpreting a text and describes interpretation as a game and prejudices. He also uses Gadamer's understanding of common sense, sound judgment and good taste in developing a way to make ethical decisions in the pastoral context. All of these ideas from Ricoeur and Gadamer are embedded in Gerkin's narrative hermeneutical theory of practical theology.

In the later writings, Gerkin moves away from Fromm and neo-Freudianism to the object relations theory[30] of Heinz Kohut. The object relations theorists are a group of thinkers who combine ideas from Freud with ideas from systems thinking. They believe that the human person's sense of self develops in the early years and is internalized by the infant and becomes the lens through which other relationships are viewed. Gerkin likes Kohut's notion of the "bi-polar" self. He sees in the self a narrative structure that holds together the view of self with the outside world.

In both the early and later writings, Gerkin uses many ideas from the social sciences disciplines to understand and explain the practice of ministry. His incarnational theology is not unilingual, but multidisciplinary and multilingual. Although he incorporates these other disciplines, Gerkin firmly takes the Christian fact as his fundamental standpoint; interpretations from other sources are part of different horizons. He appreciates different horizons and converses with these different standpoints. His theology is a fusion of interpretations from the Christian fact and interpretations from the social sciences. The purpose of this fusion is to understand, explain and transform the practice of ministry.

## c) *Method in Practical Theology*

A third characteristic of Gerkin's incarnational theology is his methodology in practical theology. This is one of his primary concerns in the later writings. He does not want to use the classical method–learning principles from Scripture and Tradition and then applying these principles to the practice of ministry. He regards the classical theological method to be reductionist. Rather, practical theology needs its own method of theology based on practice. From his experience as a practitioner and supervisor in pastoral care and counselling and with his adoption of Ricoeur's hermeneutical method, Gerkin developed a methodology described as "praxis/theory/praxis."[31]

For Gerkin, practical theology begins and ends in praxis. All praxis is theory-laden. The practical theologian first needs to develop an initial understanding of some practice or situation in ministry. Then, the theologian begins to reflect critically on the theory present in the praxis by using multiple interpretations from various standpoints. At this point, a hermeneutical play emerges, allowing a conversation to develop between various interpretations that critique the practice. For Gerkin, this second moment involves theology, hermeneutics, object relations, narrative therapy and systems. This critical conversation then transforms the first practice to produce a transformed praxis, or second praxis.

This method is similar to Ricoeur's method of text interpretation described as understanding/explanation/understanding. Ricoeur says that the interpreter begins with a naive understanding of the text. Then, the interpreter begins a critical dialogue with the text, bringing various explanations, theories and concepts in an interactive, dialogical approach. This critical reflection, then, gives the interpreter a new understanding of the text, different from the first naive understanding. In this process, the text also poses questions and issues for the interpreter. The text questions the meaning of the interpreter. Gerkin borrows from Anton Boisen the idea that the text is a living human document, or living praxis. This living human document can be a person, as in a case study, or an event, as in a critical incident report. This case or event becomes the object of study and interpretation.

Gerkin most often demonstrates the praxis/theory/praxis method through the presentation of case studies, critical incidents and verbatims. Case study is an extensive description of persons in need. Critical incident is a shorter description of an event and/or case. Verbatim is the actual words of a caregiver and client/patient/parishioner. Case studies, critical incidents and verbatims also involve critical reflection along with the interventions. His books and articles contain 23 case studies, 26 critical incidents, 13 verbatims and 23 schemata and figures.

Throughout his texts, Gerkin also develops a number of schemata and figures to facilitate the multiple interpretations and perspectives possible within a case or event. In his four books, there are twenty-three of these figures. These schemata are an aid in practical theological thinking and demonstrate the way that the fusion of horizons takes place in his incarnational theology. The schemata are open-ended and flexible and are adapted to each particular concrete situation. Gerkin does not produce a rigid theory in which reality is forced to conform to a Procrustean bed. Rather, his schemata are meant to explain and open up critical conversation on the reality presented.

An example of Gerkin's praxis/theory/praxis method in theology is the case of Susan Clark, presented in *The Living Human Document.* Gerkin initially describes his own bias and preunderstandings of the case after he received his first phone call from Susan Clark. The interpretation of the case begins even before face-to-face contact with the client. Gerkin then tells the story of Susan Clark. He notes themes, values and her process of interpretation that slowly emerges as a fragmented narrative. Gerkin makes several hermeneutical detours in discussing this case. He develops a theoretical conversation with the relationship between facts and interpretations in the case. For Gerkin, facts are part of an interpretive process. He uses Paul Ricoeur's explanation of the language of force and the language of meaning to interpret this case. The commentary on the case of Susan Clark moves between the language of force and the language of meaning in explaining the life of her soul.

Besides the theory on the languages of force and meaning, Gerkin presents a schema to aid in the interpretation process. Figure 1, "The Dialectics of the Life of the Soul,"[32] examines the various systems that impact on Susan's life. There are the social situations in which Susan lives, the faith and culture that are part of her life and the self/ego nexus. All three influence the life of Susan's soul. There are a variety of experiences of time within Susan's life. In figure 2,[33] Gerkin points out three experiences of time: life-cycle time, socio-cultural time and eschatological time. Each of these is part of Susan's life and offers a different explanation of what is happening to her.

Gerkin also explains the notion of the hermeneutical circle. This circle emerges out of his praxis; he sees it as a useful tool to explain some of the process of the case. The hermeneutical circle offers a method of interpreting the case in order to transform it. Gerkin leaves the case and comes back to it later in the book. Using theory from psychoanalysis, hermeneutics and theology, Gerkin offers some directions for change in Susan's narrative.

Gerkin does not report all the changes in Susan's life. Rather, the case demonstrates the complexity that arises when utilizing interpretations from different disciplines to understand and explain a case. The soul of Susan Clark is indeed complex. Gerkin refuses to use only one theory. Rather, he draws on a variety of interpretations. Gerkin offers a different horizon to Susan so that she might understand her narrative in a new way. Gerkin's horizon of meaning fuses with Susan's horizon of meaning to facilitate transformation.

In *Prophetic Pastoral Practice,* Gerkin articulates one of his major concerns in dealing with praxis. He asks the question: "What is God doing here?" For Gerkin, God is manifest in the concrete. Critical theological thinking informed by other disciplines discerns that presence and initiates a response to God's grace through faith, hope and love. This methodology describes an incarnational theology. The method starts not with theory or theology but with a particular case or event. It then seeks to discover God's presence, God's revelation embedded in the case. His assumption is that God's horizon is somewhere present in the situation. The various interpretations are meant to aid this task. The goal is always transformation of the concrete in response to God's inbreaking reign.

Gerkin's praxis/theory/praxis methodology proceeds with a question-and-answer approach. Gerkin's cases, critical incidents and verbatims raise questions about the practice and theory of pastoral practice in both the concrete and abstract. In the case of Susan Clark, Gerkin asks twenty-six questions. The majority of these questions are direct. Gerkin answers some of the questions; others are left unanswered or are answered by implication. Some of the questions are specific to the case of Susan Clark. Other questions are more theoretical in nature. The praxis is questioned by the interpreter and the interpreter is questioned by the praxis.

At the beginning of the chapter, Mike wondered about the right interpretation for the case. The discussion of Gerkin's notion of praxis shows that there is more to a pastoral situation or case than any one theory can grasp. In fact, God's presence incarnated in the situation defies total understanding. God's presence can't be controlled. Theories give some provisional understanding, but theories are limited. There is more to the case than what is seen and understood. Mike's concern to use the right theory and interventions assumes that there is a right theory. At best, chaplains and pastoral practitioners have partial knowledge of a situation. There is always more to it than what a practitioner knows. As a result, most chaplains and pastors utilize a more eclectic approach. This eclectic approach draws on various theories, clinical experience, evidence from research and intuition. Interventions, then, are provisional and not absolute.

### d) *Narrative and Hermeneutics*

A fourth characteristic of Gerkin's incarnational theology is his use of hermeneutics and narrative. Gerkin's narrative hermeneutical theory has evolved over time. In his early writings, Gerkin does not deal explicitly with hermeneutics and narrative. Though the ideas are implicitly present in his early theology, they reach an explicit development in the later writings. The practice of hermeneutics and narrative in Gerkin's theology is undergirded by his incarnational understanding of ministry.

In the books and articles from his later writings, Gerkin argues that human life is structured by narrative. Humans think, feel, interpret and make ethical decisions based on a narrative understanding of life. Reality is viewed through the narrative lens. Gerkin draws on the work of Stanley Hauerwas, Stephen Crites, Brian Wicker, Northrop Frye and Paul Ricoeur in developing this argument.[34] Humans make sense of life through stories. In the story of a person's life, deep within the soul, the dynamic forces of id and superego challenge the ego. This is the language of force. In this story of the self, there are also the interpretations and meaning that the self places on significant persons and events. This is the language of meaning. There is also the life of God which is incarnate in the human person. This interacts with the language of force and meaning and points beyond to a transcendent reality that has become incarnate. The interaction of the ego, self and soul develops a narrative quality to human existence. This narrative also exists for families, groups, Church communities, societies. Through narrative, identity develops.

In the case of Susan Clark, narrative is Gerkin's fundamental approach in pastoral counselling. Susan Clark is presented as a middle-aged, married woman who is having an affair and dealing with family-of-origin issues. In his therapy with her, Gerkin slowly identifies a narrative structure to her life which includes many subplots. He offers, in the course of therapy, alternate interpretations for her narratives. The goal is to transform the interpretation in order to open space for her in developing a new direction. In *Widening the Horizons*, Gerkin widens the horizon of narrative from individuals to communities. He outlines fragments of the narrative structure of the town of Centreton and the narrative structure of one of the Church communities in that town.[35]

Gerkin connects narrative to identity. In doing this, he draws on interpretations from Erikson and Moltmann. Using Erikson, Gerkin argues that identity arises from context. Family, society, culture, gender and class form one's identity and create a narrative. Borrowing from Moltmann, Gerkin argues that identity is also conferred by God. The human receives an eschatological identity through participation in the life of God. Identity arises from context and also from conferral by God. Humans develop a narrative about their identity. For some people, the dominant narrative might be life as a tragedy; for others, life might be a comedy; for others, it might be a romance or saga or documentary.

Gerkin also makes a strong connection between narrative and time. Drawing on the work of Paul Ricoeur, Gerkin argues that humans only understand past, present and future in a narrative structure. Gerkin views the revelation of God in Christianity as a narrative. He argues that the biblical witness is a narrative with many subnarratives. This biblical account provides a "somehow unified narrative account between God and the world."[36] For Gerkin, the central story line of the Christian narrative is "that our activities are permeated and given redemptive coherence and direction by the activity of God."[37]

Narrative, then, is linked to incarnational theology. Narrative is the way to understand the incarnation in one's life and in the practice of ministry. In Gerkin's incarnational perspective, the Christian narrative aids the soul in understanding the relationship between self and world. The Christian narrative facilitates the development of meaning and connects the self to a larger narrative. For Gerkin, the role of world religions is to offer the wider narrative for interpreting experience. The Christian narrative is, for Gerkin, the larger narrative through which the soul interprets, integrates and has a sense of continuity and identity. One of Gerkin's concerns is the deconstruction of these wider, larger narratives in contemporary society. This deconstruction leaves the self lost, aimless and without direction. A person who is grounded in a larger narrative, especially the Christian narrative, can live and thrive in a world of pluralism and ambiguity.

Gerkin also ties ethics to narrative. He disagrees with Don Browning who develops a rational process to practical moral reasoning.[38] Gerkin does not believe that the soul makes ethical decisions based on practical moral reasoning alone. Instead, Gerkin draws on the work of Hans-Georg Gadamer in developing an ethical process based on narrative. Narrative and imagination are closely linked in this ethical approach. Gerkin uses Gadamer's three notions of common sense, sound judgment and good taste.

Common sense, as Gerkin interprets Gadamer, is the commonly held views within a particular culture of what life should or should not be. These views are not the result of universal principles that are developed from reason and argument. Rather, they develop from a cultural narrative and are part of the cultural imagination. Sound judgment entails making decisions that fit the common sense of the culture. The person with sound judgment has an awareness of common sense and makes decisions that accommodate and implement that view of what life should be. Good taste or aesthetics is connected to truth. Good taste, beauty and truth fit together. A person who exercises good taste along with sound judgment has common sense in a particular context and can understand how a decision "fits" or "doesn't fit" the whole context.

Gerkin also links narrative ethics to the ethics of H. Richard Niebuhr. For Niebuhr, one first needs to discern what is going on in a particular situation. Then, one needs to discern what God is doing or calling people to do in the situation.[39] Gerkin grounds narrative ethics in the activity of God in each situation. Ethics is the fusion of the cultural and Christian narratives in deciding what one ought to do in a given situation. God's incarnate activity in the situation is the primary concern in his incarnational theology. Gerkin demonstrates his narrative ethics in the case of "The Neighbourhood Boundary Problem."[40]

Gerkin's understanding of Christianity as a narrative along with a narrative view of reality shapes his interpretation of how the Incarnation takes place. Incarnation is narrative in form. The Incarnation of Christ is not just one story among many, but the basis for interpretation. The Christian narrative needs to be fused with other narratives in a hermeneutical process in order to make sense of experience. This fusion is conversational and impacts both on the understanding of the Christian narrative and the meaning of other narratives. Gerkin is not interested in getting rid of the other narratives but in developing a conversation between the Christian narrative and the many other narratives present in our world. Without grounding in the narrative of the Ground of Being, humankind experiences alienation and oppression.

Gerkin's incarnational theology also takes form in his theory of hermeneutics. This theory is closely intertwined with his notion of narrative. Using the work of Paul Ricoeur and Hans-Georg Gadamer, the major focus includes his hermeneutical process of language and meaning. He is concerned with exploring how one constructs a world through language and meaning. Language and interpretation are closely linked. The young infant begins to interpret his/her world before thinking is developed. Through the acquisition of language, the child develops interpretations in a concrete form. The human person uses language to interpret experience in order to make sense out of it. For Gerkin, the strengths and limitations of language shape the interpretations. He strongly states: "Language constructs world."[41] One can only interpret experience through the language available.

Gerkin understands language to be more than words. Language includes the person's actions, feelings and body language. Gerkin uses two terms drawn from Ricoeur: the language of force and language of meaning. These different kinds of language refer to the inner psychic process of the human person. The language of force refers to the inner struggles of the ego with the id and superego. The language of meaning refers to the process of meaning-making that the self initiates. Thus, there is the language of actual words, the language of actions and the language of feeling and body, as well as the languages of force and meaning. There is also the language world of the different disciplines.

One of Gerkin's major concerns in the area of hermeneutics and language is the difference between the language worlds of psychoanalysis, psychology, family systems therapy and theology. Like other theologians in the field of pastoral care and counselling, he believes that the language world of the social sciences has become dominant. Theological ideas and language are less dominant. Gerkin is careful in his theology to note the similarities and differences between the language of the social sciences and the language of theology.

Gerkin connects interpretation to meaning. Humans use language to interpret experience and develop meaning. He sees the human as a meaning-maker. Humans interpret in order to produce meaning. This need for meaning is especially important in contemporary American life, for Gerkin believes that the crisis of meaning is the key crisis in American society. This crisis in meaning is due to the loss of the larger narrative present in the Christian story. The loss of the Christian narrative produces meaninglessness. The Christian narrative must be reinterpreted in order to develop meaning for modern people. Meaninglessness produces a fragmented identity.

Ricoeur's notion of the hermeneutic of suspicion and retrieval are also key ideas in Gerkin's hermeneutical theory. Ricoeur argues that Freud is one of the masters of the hermeneutic of suspicion. Ricoeur looks for the hidden reality beneath the rational discourse and works from the assumption that there is more to reality than is apparent.[42] Gerkin adopts the hermeneutic of suspicion. He links the hermeneutic of suspicion to the hermeneutic of retrieval. The hermeneutic of retrieval brings forward interpretations and experiences that have been overlooked. He uses the hermeneutics of retrieval and suspicion in Figure 1, entitled "A Narrative Structure of Christian Understanding of Human Activity."[43] The hermeneutic of suspicion questions and looks for more–for the vested interest–in the interpretation. It digs beneath the surface for hidden assumptions and values. The hermeneutic of retrieval brings forth the hidden and allows it to be part of the interpretation process. These are key ideas in Gerkin's hermeneutical process.

Gerkin also draws on Gadamer's hermeneutical theory of the horizon of understanding, which includes prejudices, the fusion of horizons between two subjects involved in interpretation, change as a transformation of meaning through a fusion of horizons and interpretation as a dialogical game. These concepts are central to Gerkin's practical theology. He utilizes Gadamer's horizon of understanding in his praxis of pastoral counselling. He sees clients and events as living human documents and texts. These living texts have horizons of understanding that include values and meanings, ways of seeing formed by the traditions that they embody. Gerkin, as a pastoral therapist, also mentions that his own horizon of understanding requires reflection and self-awareness. He brings these values into the therapy room with clients. This is evident in the case of Susan Clark.[44] In fact, Gerkin's hermeneutics involve the uncovering of the values and assumptions of both client and therapeutic practice. He is continually looking underneath to discover the hidden values and assumptions present in praxis.

Another aspect of Gerkin's appropriation of Gadamer's hermeneutic is how transformation or change involves a change in meanings. The fusion of horizons is a change in the horizon of understanding. This means that pastoral care and counselling is not so much a change in behaviour but a change in understanding and meaning of one's story. Gerkin is critical of the behaviouralists who are interested only in a change in behaviour of the client. He believes that interpretation, feeling and behaviour are interrelated and form a unified whole. Most of his work, however, is devoted to interpretation and its transformation. His hermeneutical praxis involves a fusion of meanings that are transformed through the dialogical and dialectical experience of the joining of various narratives.

Gerkin also appropriates Gadamer's notion of hermeneutical play. He argues that the dialogue between the horizons can create space. This space is similar to a transitional space where both parties in the dialogue can consider possibilities and options that were not previously apparent. Gerkin compares this to Winnicott's notion of transitional space,[45] and he uses Gadamer's understanding of hermeneutical play to describe it. This hermeneutical play is the point in the dialogue when both parties are able to look beyond one's own horizon and consider the horizon of the other. In pastoral counselling, hermeneutical play is necessary for change. Both therapist and client must have a space in which each can consider other options.

**Gerkin's Contribution to the Three Questions**

Gerkin's incarnational theology manifested in the four characteristics has much to offer the three questions posed in the Introduction. First, his standpoint from within the interpretations from the Christian fact underlines a distinctive quality of the praxis. Clinical pastoral supervision is a theological enterprise and therefore must be rooted in the concepts, language and methodology of that discipline. Gerkin's faithfulness to his theological tradition of Methodism, especially the notion of the catholicity of grace and the protestant principle, as well as his refinement of Wise's incarnational theology, make a contribution to the field. Clinical pastoral supervision needs to be rooted in the practice of supervision within the tradition of the Church. As well, it needs to dialogue with other disciplines. Gerkin's combination of both an analogical and dialectical theology that serves to explain and transform the praxis is helpful.

One difficulty with the social sciences approach in clinical pastoral supervision is the lack of distinction from the practice of supervision in the social sciences. The special interest approach, on the other hand, stresses the differences in experience and praxis between a particular group and the dominant praxis. Are there similarities? If there are no similarities, is conversation possible? Gerkin's incarnational theology says that there have to be both similarities and differences. Can redemption take place if Jesus is totally similar to or totally different from humanity?

At the same time, Gerkin affirms many interpretations from the social sciences. His multilingual and multidisciplinary approach is a second contribution to the distinctiveness of the praxis of clinical pastoral supervision. The social sciences have much to offer the praxis of clinical pastoral supervision. Some theologians, such as Thomas Oden, prefer a return to the Church fathers and an endorsement of their view of humanity and ministry. Gerkin disagrees, and maintains that the various interpretations from the social sciences have challenged and transformed theological thinking. His use of hermeneutical play between the various interpretations from the Christian fact and social sciences is creative and contributes to the praxis of clinical pastoral supervision. The interpretations of Eckstein and Wallerstein, Knowles, Kolb, Rogers, Kohut, Liddle and systems thinking are useful to clinical pastoral supervision. A multidisciplinary approach is necessary today.

Gerkin's work on hermeneutics and narrative also adds to the distinctiveness of the praxis of clinical pastoral supervision. The praxis of clinical pastoral supervision involves interpretation. Supervision means learning a variety of ways that praxis can be interpreted. Each of the three approaches has its own way of interpreting reality. Gerkin indicates this in his emphasis on interpretation. The social sciences, hermeneutical and special interest approaches exist within particular narratives. Each has a narrative structure to it. How do these competing narratives in the field of clinical pastoral supervision connect with the Christian narrative and the other narratives in our pluralistic society? Who is served by the narrative and who is marginalized by it? Gerkin's focus on hermeneutic and narrative opens these questions.

Gerkin's development of his praxis/theory/praxis method for practical theology offers a theological method that is specific to praxis. This is the concern of the second question. Gerkin's method employs three sources in a conversational, critical, correlational method. He draws upon the specific case, interpretations from the Christian fact and interpretations from the social sciences. Some of the philosophies of clinical pastoral supervision that have been reviewed lack such a practical theological method. These philosophies follow a theory/praxis method. In this case, one theory, whether from the social sciences, theology or special interest group, is adopted. Practice fits into that particular theory. In this view, practical theology is applied theology.

Gerkin's method starts with theory-laden practice (the specific case). He then opens up the case through critical conversation from multiple standpoints. The goal is to transform the case. Such a method elevates practice to its proper position and is not reductionistic. Gerkin demonstrates in his method that he is not a systematic theologian but a practical one. A coherent theological system is not his concern. Rather, his interest is in praxis transformed through critical conversation.

Gerkin's incarnational theology as described in the fusion of horizons offers an interpretation that deals with the process of the praxis of clinical pastoral supervision. The fusion of horizons offers an explanation for the interaction between supervisor and supervisee, between supervisee and patient/client/parishioner, between all persons involved in the situation and the various institutions and social systems. The fusion of horizons also offers an explanation for the interaction between theory and practice, between interpretations from the Christian fact and interpretations from other disciplines, between the praxis of the Christian fact and the praxis of other disciplines. The fusion of horizons also offers an explanation for the presence of God in the dynamics of the praxis of clinical pastoral supervision.

The outcomes of the fusion of horizons are identical, analogical and dialectical. This is helpful. These three outcomes explain what takes place in the various interactions between supervisee and supervisor, supervisee and patient, supervisee and institution, supervisee and family of origin, supervisee and denomination, etc. Sometimes, there is similarity; sometimes, there is similarity and difference; sometimes, there is difference.

The four characteristics of Gerkin's incarnational theology have much to contribute to the praxis of clinical pastoral supervision. Gerkin's incarnational theology is embodied in a theological anthropology. The next chapter examines Gerkin's theological anthropology and outlines its contribution to the three questions on the praxis of clinical pastoral supervision.

Returning to the case of Mike, there are some directions that could be helpful. First, Mike needs to clarify what the interpretations from the various theories say about the pastoral situation. He needs to take some time to explore the implications of each theory for the particular case. What interventions does the theory propose, and how might the resident with whom Mike is working respond to each intervention? The conversation in supervision helps in discovering the consequence of interventions suggested by an interpretation. What might be the end result of the intervention? In supervision, Mike began to see the implications of the various theories and interventions.

In using multiple theories and interventions, there is a need for a conversation between the theories and the case. First, what does each theory say about the case? The supervisor had Mike sit in different chairs, assuming the role of the particular theorist and explaining how that theory saw the case. Next, the supervisor had Mike role play how these different theories might speak to one another about this case. How are the theories similar and different? Which claims to be the best for this case?

The conversation between the various interpretations of the case requires a conversation with the case. There are elements of the case that are not sufficiently addressed by theories. Mike was asked to take the role of the resident and speak to the various theories that had interpreted the case. Did these theories sufficiently understand the situation of the resident? What does the resident want? Do the interventions of the various theories give more than what the resident desires? What does Mike want for the resident and what does the resident want for self? This conversation emphasizes the needs of the resident in relation to the various theories.

Mike found it helpful to systematically pursue each of the theories and interventions in terms of the case. He also found it helpful to engage in the conversation between the theory and the person in the case. His question of what is the best interpretation and intervention for this person ultimately rests with what is most helpful to the resident. This is client-centred pastoral care. Mike discovered that the resident had some interpretations of the situation that were disempowering and enslaving. Transformation means changing some of these disempowering ideas. The goal is to empower the resident to greater love of self, others and God.

# Chapter 4
# Gerkin's Theological Anthropology

Laura was the on-call chaplain at the hospital on the weekend. She was called to an emergency to deal with the death of a seven-year-old girl named Samantha, who was killed in a motor vehicle accident. Samantha's mother, who was driving the van, was in the hospital recovering from serious injuries. Laura spent most of the weekend with Samantha's father, older sister and mother. She was present when the husband tried to tell his wife about Samantha's death; he could not get all the words out and asked Laura to complete the task. The husband asked Laura: "Can God help us at all in this crisis?" Laura felt the pain and despair of the question. In a panic, she phoned her supervisor and asked for some way to proceed with the family. She wondered: "Where is hope here?"

Laura's wondering about hope in this crisis also raises the place of hope in human beings. Such an issue involves an understanding of theological anthropology. Theological anthropology examines the person from the standpoint of theological interpretations. Grace, sin, redemption, faith, hope, love and soul are some concepts used in theological anthropology. Gerkin's theological anthropology is a fusion of a variety of horizons, drawn from many sources. The horizons include interpretations from theology, the social sciences, narrative and hermeneutics. His understanding is rooted in practice.

**Standpoint in the Christian Fact**

In *The Living Human Document*, Gerkin describes his theological anthropology as the "life of the soul."[1] Gerkin believes that the image of soul best describes the human person. He uses the Freudian notion of ego, id and drives. Drawing on Ricouer's interpretation of Freud, he describes these Freudian terms as the language of force.[2] He also uses the concept of the self drawn from object relations theory. Gerkin describes the self in Ricouer's language of meaning.[3] The life of the soul combines the concepts of ego and self, and transcends them. The soul acknowledges the presence of God in humankind which the ego and self do not. For Gerkin, the soul roots the ego and self in the Ground of Being. Soul integrates the human being and is the gift of God and the very breath of life. Without the breath of life from God, ego and self would not exist. These are grounded in God's life.

In the life of the soul, the notions of creation, sin and redemption are present. Creation acknowledges that humans are made in God's image and likeness and that God gives humankind a soul which is the very breath of God. All created reality has its origin in God's graciousness. Sin is the radical evil present in the world and humankind's willful thoughts and actions that break the relationship with God, others, self and the environment. Redemption is enacted through Jesus who took flesh as man to redeem humankind from sin. Redemption also includes the gift of the Spirit and the formation of the church which incarnates and continues the work of the Risen Christ. Through the redemption of Jesus, humankind is saved from sin for life with God.

Gerkin's notions of creation, sin and redemption describe the life of the soul, which takes form through narrative. The narrative is interpreted in a hermeneutical manner in order to discover meaning, to make sense out of the life of the soul. Gerkin does not present doctrinal statements on creation, sin and redemption. As a practical theologian, these are woven into his many case studies, verbatims and critical incidents and are the lens through which he views reality.

In creation, God confers upon the human person an eschatological identity. This eschatological identity affirms that the person belongs to God's Kingdom and has the presence of God within. At the same time, the person lives in the world and develops an identity shaped by the contextual experiences of family, society, "race," gender, class and psycho-social development. The eschatological identity given by God at the moment of creation is the very ground upon which the person lives and moves. This is God's image and it allows the human person to be radically open to God's initiative. The eschatological identity contains the virtues of faith, hope and care, which are needed to respond to God's initiative in the world. This is God's creation. In the case of Susan Clark, Gerkin utilizes this understanding of Creation. He argues, from a theological standpoint, that part of Susan's struggle is that "she has not been able to appropriate her eschatological identity."[4] Her failure to appropriate her eschatological identity results in a distorted notion of God, who is viewed as the ultimate parental figure with the power to grant all her desires. This view of God is linked to Susan's view of her mother. The failure to see herself as created in God's image limits her freedom and sense of self. In Susan Clark's case, Gerkin utilizes a theological anthropology that sees the human person as created in God's image.

Sin for Gerkin is described in existential terms. The outcome of sin is meaninglessness.[5] Humankind has forgotten its identity in God and has lost the connection to the Christian narrative. Modern humans experience the meaninglessness of existence because they have given up their eschatological identity. Sin also manifests itself in the alienation present in our society, in racism, sexism and poverty.[6] Gerkin describes sin more often in the social sense than the personal sense. In the earlier part of his theological writings, Gerkin was influenced by Erich Fromm. Fromm combines psychoanalysis with a Marxian view of society. In Fromm, Gerkin finds interpretations that explain a social understanding of sin; his notions of alienation from self, of racism and sexism and of poverty are drawn from Fromm's critique. Gerkin does not emphasize humankind's natural depravity or the intrinsic sinfulness of humans. James Poling, in his critique of Gerkin, maintains that Gerkin does not pay sufficient attention to the destructive power of evil present in humans and in the world. Poling believes that Gerkin's theology is more Creation-centred than Redemption-centred.[7] Gerkin's response to Poling's critique is that his theology is both Creation-centred and Redemption-centred. He holds both of these theologies together in his praxis through the notion of meaning. Gerkin takes very seriously the power of evil and sin in the world. He addresses these issues in his theology of the Cross and Providence.[8] At the same time, his roots in the Methodist tradition emphasize the catholicity of grace. The focus is on God's offer, the presence of grace in all created reality and events. While sin is acknowledged in its effects, the emphasis is on God's grace and redemption. Gerkin's view of sin concentrates on the consequences of sin, especially in its social manifestations.

Redemption, like sin, is experienced existentially in Gerkin's theological anthropology. God's inbreaking reign manifests itself in the here-and-now in a realized eschatology. This realized eschatology is demonstrated in his praxis. Gerkin does not offer hope by telling people that salvation, healing and new life will be realized in heaven. Rather, he works in his cases to help people see the promise of God in the here-and-now and to pursue that promise through a life of faith, hope and care. With the case of Susan Clark, his pastoral counselling strives to facilitate her healing in the present. In his realized eschatology, the promise becomes present in a provisional way.

Grace interrupts the human order and calls for a response.[9] These redemptive experiences are manifold. They appear in ordinary events, in the pastoral relationship, in the ministry of the church and in the crisis experiences of life. For Gerkin, there is no event that cannot be redeemed and no event that cannot disclose God's redemptive activity. Gerkin believes that God continues to intervene, to sustain, to guide and to heal. For Gerkin, this redemptive activity of God is explained in his many examples. In *Widening the Horizons*, he presents the case of Centreton, a town and church in crisis.[10] Involved in this crisis are the mayor, who has been involved in corruption, a factory that has been providing employment but polluting the environment, a congregation that has become stagnant with a sense of despair and a pastor, who becomes the mediator in this crisis. Redemption in this case operates in many ways. One way redemption works is through the God of judgment, a confronting presence with the mayor about the unfaithfulness of his actions. Another redemptive moment is in the challenge to the factory about its pollution. A third redemptive moment is with the congregation's need to face the conflict in its midst and be willing to break the status quo. The fourth is the pastor's as he experiences God's risk and support in his mediating actions. Finally redemption offers to all involved in the crisis a yielding to a mysterious presence that is both powerful and caring. Redemption in Gerkin's practical theology is concrete.

In Gerkin's theological anthropology, the life of the soul also contains the theological virtues of faith, hope and care, through which the soul responds to God's inbreaking reign. His notion of faith draws on Tillich's idea of faith as trust in an ultimate concern. Tillich believed that faith is at the centre of the human being in an implicit, integrative way.[11] For Tillich, faith is a centering act that puts one in touch with one's being and with the Ground of all Being. Gerkin sees faith in a manner similar to Tillich. For Gerkin, interpretation and faith are linked. "Faith, then, is much more than a set of beliefs or even a verbal language. Faith is rather a way of seeing and of being in accordance with how we see the world."[12] This faith is both implicit and explicit. Implicit faith is a trust in the ultimate meaningfulness of life, relationships and experience. Explicit faith is able to give theological language to belief and experience. For Gerkin, both implicit and explicit faith are important for the life of the soul.[13]

In his theological anthropology, faith is at the core of the human being and is part of the eschatological identity. Faith gives the person the possibility of responding to grace. Some respond on an implicit level through trust in an ultimate concern. These persons might not know that God is making an offer and yet they are willing to respond to something that they consider meaningful. For Gerkin, a meaningful event is a graceful event. Explicit faith is the ability to articulate that invitation and response in theological language, usually in a denominational context. Gerkin also notes that a person may be able to use theological language in an explicit manner and yet be severely limited in trust.[14] In his view, faith is crucial to human existence.

Hope is an important virtue in his theological anthropology and part of the eschatological identity. Gerkin draws on both his own praxis and the work of Moltmann and Pannenberg in developing his understanding of hope.[15] Hope facilitates the response to God's grace both in the ordinary events of life and in the midst of crisis, a seeing of some possibilities. This hope is not wishful thinking but the ability to see possibilities, God's promise in the midst of suffering. The person who is lacking in hope, who is mired in the experience of despair, cannot see any possibilities present in the moment.

A key symbol for Gerkin in his understanding of hope is the cross. Gerkin draws on Moltmann's theology of the cross.[16] The cross provides a different understanding of God's Providence. This understanding is connected to hope. In the symbol of the cross, the hermeneutic of despair and hope are intertwined. In the cross, there is the terrible reality of suffering and meaninglessness and also the hope and reality of salvation. The ambiguity of the cross is especially helpful for those in crisis.

Hope is also active. The hopeful person sees God's offer and promise and then acts on it. Such a person is not like some of the inhabitants of Thessalonica in the New Testament, who believed that they could stop working because of their belief that Jesus would be returning shortly. Rather, this notion of hope responds actively to God's promise and begins to pursue it. For Gerkin as a pastoral counselor, the link is often made between hope and interpretation, what Gerkin calls the "hermeneutic of hope."[17] This hermeneutic of hope breaks through the hermeneutic of despair that enslaves the person. This hermeneutic of despair consists of feelings of self condemnation and judgment. The helping relationship strives to break the circle of despair and introduces a hermeneutic of hope. Gerkin's notion of hope is that it is necessary for the process of growth and an essential part of his theological anthropology.

In his writing, Gerkin does not use the word "love" very often. The word "care" is used more often. Gerkin describes the work of pastoral care and counselling and indeed the work of ministry in general to be one of care. In his article "On the Art of Caring," he notes that care is a root metaphor for him and includes "listening, responding, advocating and hearing."[18] Care means listening and responding to those in need. In *Crisis Experience in Modern Life*, Gerkin demonstrates care for both individuals and families in need. In *Prophetic Pastoral Practice*, he also responds to the needs of the wider culture through actively pursuing the need for transformation in people's common sense.

Care, for Gerkin, is not only responding to human needs and the need of the culture but also takes the next step of advocacy. Advocacy for the marginalized, the poor and for victims of sexism and racism is part of his approach to caring.[19] Gerkin sees the act of caring that involves responding and advocating as also hearing God's voice. For Gerkin, caring is ultimately hearing the voice of God and being sustained by that voice in acts of care. This care goes beyond all the insights and skills of the social sciences and is sustained by divine care. Care is an essential part of Gerkin's theological anthropology, along with faith and hope.

Gerkin's theological anthropology assumes that faith, hope and care are present in the family that has lost the young girl, Samantha. These theological virtues are also present in Laura, the chaplain. The crisis has dimmed the presence of faith and hope. Care, or love, has been strongly activated in the family by the crisis. Crisis often influences people to reach out and care for one another in a way that they ordinarily do not. For faith and hope to be questioned and to recede into the background is normal. One cannot predict how faith and hope will emerge from the crisis. Some people lose faith in God, and in life, from such an experience. Others experience hopelessness as the chaplain Laura did. The challenge for Laura is to remain present to this family when her hope has faltered. Later, Laura needs to reflect on the place of hopelessness within her theology of hope. Does ambiguity allow for such?

**Multidisciplinary**

Gerkin includes notions of ego and self in his theological anthropology. Besides these, he also uses Erikson's notion of identity. Erikson believes that identity develops through the psycho-social life stages[20] and conferred by the context.[21] Context includes ethnicity, gender, family, economics, geographical location, religion and historical era. This Eriksonian understanding of identity developed by the context is in dialectical tension with his theological understanding of eschatological identity conferred by God. Gerkin also uses an interpersonal systems interpretation in his theological anthropology. Much of this thought is drawn from Erich Fromm and from systems thinking in family therapy.[22] Gerkin sees the life of the soul embedded in a variety of relationships. These relationships include those in family and also those from history and culture. In many of his diagrams, Gerkin shows the impact of culture and the social situation.[23] He is not a classical Freudian in the sense that his focus is only on drives, ego and superego. He stresses the influence of the primary relationships with family and the social context in which those primary relationships are embedded. His use of object relations theory demonstrates the relational reality of interpretation.[24] The human being is embedded in an interpretation of these primary relationships, especially through mother and father.

The object relations view of the person has become more dominant in Gerkin's theological anthropology in the last number of years. In an article written for a book in honour of the thought of James Lapsely, Gerkin adopts some of the ideas of Winnicott, Fairbairn, Klein, David and Scharf.[25] He believes that in infancy the child develops a separate sense of self, and that the child's experience of separation from the parent and development of self impacts upon the child's understanding of God. The child develops three possible notions of God based on the experience of separation and self. The three notions entail a God who fulfills all needs, a God who is judgmental and rejects persons, thereby creating a sense of shame and guilt and a God who is ideal, but mysteriously abandons humans at times. He examines how these three images influence adulthood and might be changed to encourage health. Gerkin introduces his article by noting that he is working from a psychology of religion rather than a theological standpoint. He does not want to collapse the concepts and language from theology and psychology into one. Gerkin's theological anthropology includes this object relations view.

Along with the object relations view, the family receives special attention in understanding the life of the soul. Gerkin argues that Bowlby's theory of attachment and loss in the early stages of life are crucial for understanding grief and loss.[26] His emphasis on object relations theory in his later writings underlines the impact of family relationships on the life of the soul.[27] For Gerkin, a systemic view of relationships is crucial to understanding the life of the soul. The goal of ministry, in Gerkin's theological anthropology, is transformed relationships. These transformed relationships are norms for Gerkin. He argues against the individualistic norm that some psychotherapies endorse, which is founded on individual self-actualization. He advocates a norm based on transformed relationships. The life of the soul is a life-in-relationship from the moment of conception.

## Praxis and Theological Anthropology

Since Gerkin's theological anthropology is based on praxis, it emerges in the critical reflection on practice. In his early writings, Gerkin does not devote much space to articulating his theological anthropology. His later writings, especially *The Living Human Document*, give more attention to the elements of theological anthropology. His thought becomes more focused on narrative and hermeneutics and he pays more attention to the theory embedded in practice. At this later stage, critical conversation on theory present in the practices becomes more developed. Throughout his writing, Gerkin's theological anthropology evolves as his praxis changes.

In the case study of Susan Clark, Gerkin discusses certain themes that illuminate some of his theological anthropology.[28] He interprets the case from multiple standpoints. In terms of an object relations view, Gerkin highlights the conflict between Susan and her mother. From a social-cultural view, he notes the conflicting sexual values between Susan's Christian heritage and the more permissive urban attitude in which she now lives. From a theological view, he mentions the conflicting notions of God that are present in Susan's soul and her lack of understanding of her eschatological identity.

In the midst of this case, Gerkin manifests elements of his theological anthropology. He asserts that Susan has not appreciated her connection with God through creation and has not appropriated her eschatological identity. For Susan, sin is making an idol out of her relationship with a male friend with whom she is having an affair. Sin is also being locked in bondage to her past relationship with her mother and allowing that parental relationship to interpret many of her present relationships. The parental relationship has distorted Susan's relationship with her husband.

Gerkin sees redemption for Susan in a number of ways. In the pastoral counselling relationship, redemption means creating a safe environment where Susan can become aware of her experiences of bondage and idols that control her soul. This creation of a safe holding environment allows the Spirit to work. Redemption also means assisting Susan to connect with a narrative deep within her. Susan's soul has many different narratives at different levels of her being. Many of these narratives are in conflict. Gerkin believes that there is a narrative deep within her soul that can give meaning to all her stories and can make sense of them. This deep narrative is connected to the Christian story. This Christian narrative affirms her eschatological identity as a child of God. The job of the pastoral counselor is to create a safe environment where a conversation about these issues is possible. In this conversation, the pastoral counselor can explore with Susan the various narratives that impact her life. Hope develops from an awareness of the core narrative and the ability to see possibilities. Susan needs to see that redemption is possible in the journey of her soul. Gerkin's theological anthropology emerges in a praxis.

## Narrative and Hermeneutics

For Gerkin, theological anthropology takes place in narrative form wherein the notions of creation, sin and redemption are the substance of the Christian narrative. The Christian narrative is normative and the Bible provides stories and metaphors that form the basis of the Christian narrative.[29] This narrative is incarnational in that God joined God's self to the people of Israel through the Exodus event. The narrative became redemptive in the life, death and resurrection of Jesus as the Christ. The gift of the Spirit of Jesus is meant for all. For Gerkin, this theology is redemptive theology, for it involves the radical transformation of evil through grace.[30]

Gerkin argues that the Christian narrative with its biblical images is normative for identity and a sense of meaning in life. The Christian narrative is the template for the good life.[31] The loss of this narrative or the failure to make this narrative central in people's lives leads to alienation, meaninglessness and identity confusion. Sin means forsaking the narrative and thus being manipulated by the various forces both within and without the person. Forsaking the Christian narrative leaves the person lost.

Creation, sin and redemption are woven into the narrative of each person's life, the life of the soul. As the life of the soul unfolds, as in the case study of Susan Clark, the story exhibits elements of creation, sin and redemption. One can see or interpret those moments through connection with the Christian narrative. Here, Gadamer's hermeneutic of the fusion of horizons is crucial to Gerkin's theological anthropology. In the life of the soul, there are elements of creation, sin and redemption. Grace is part of human experience. A person sees these aspects of creation, sin and redemption through an understanding and connection to the Christian narrative. This Christian narrative offers a hermeneutic to interpret our individual narrative and a hermeneutic for institutional, community, family and congregational narratives.

Hermeneutics is also an important part of Gerkin's theological anthropology. In the later writings, Gerkin attributes to human beings three abilities: interpreting, feeling and acting. In *The Living Human Document*, interpreting has a central role in the life of the soul:

> I need to reemphasize that ... the life of the soul is a continuous life of interpretation: a life of attaching meanings to behavior, relationships, the self's maintenance of its line of life, and the limitations of the recurrent conflicts of the ego that press upon the soul's struggle with existence. By its hermeneutical, interpretive process the life of the soul holds together in a dynamic tension a virtual myriad of often conflicting demands, expectations, drives and desires, emo-

tions, relational commitments, meanings and values, perceptual patterns of seeing the world.[32]

In *The Living Human Document*, Gerkin acknowledges the importance of behaviour and feeling, but puts more emphasis on interpretation. He argues against a behavioural approach to pastoral counselling because its focus on behaviour is superficial and does not get to the root problem of the client/patient. Rather, the focus should be on interpretation, especially in using Ricoeur's notion of the language of force and meaning. This emphasis on interpretation rather than behavioural change is slower and less dynamic, but more fruitful in the long run.

In this phase of his theological anthropology, Gerkin maintains that if one develops a new hermeneutic, a new interpretation that facilitates the life of the soul in response to grace, then behaviour and feelings will change. Change then comes through insight in actualizing the understanding/explanation/understanding hermeneutic that is part of the interpretive process of the soul. The new understanding is a result of grace, the inbreaking of God's reign. This new hermeneutic enables a deeper understanding of one's narrative in conversation with the Christian narrative.

As such, this new understanding and new change are provisional. To make them absolute would make an idol of that particular interpretation, just as Susan Clark made an idol out of her interpretation of the relationship with her mother. The Spiritual Presence, the Ground of all Being, is continually transforming and changing the interpretations that the life of the soul develops. This is the Protestant principle that is crucial to Gerkin's incarnational theology. Gerkin does not allow any one interpretation to become absolutized. He does not attempt to reduce experience to one theory or make experience fit an interpretation. Such a methodology makes an idol of the particular theory.

Gerkin's openness to change and his refusal to absolutize a theory is demonstrated in the change in his own theological anthropology. In the course of his writings, there is a change in his understanding of the place of interpretation, feeling and behaviour in the life of the soul. He notes that in his earlier ministry he was fascinated by the place of feeling in his theological anthropology. Then, he thought, "feelings were primary,"[33] the ground for motivation, relationships, actions and self-disclosure. In his early writings, feeling was even more basic than faith. His praxis, then, was to concentrate on the feelings of the person. This view changed. In *The Living Human Document*, interpretation takes on the most significant role. He stresses interpretation over feeling and action. Subsequently, there is another change in Gerkin's thought. In a later article, entitled "Faith and Praxis: Pastoral Counselling's Hermeneutical Problem," Gerkin says that interpretation, feeling and acting are together in the life of the soul. Each influences the other. Interpretation is "one piece" with action and feeling:

> Yet, another prepositional idea that has been implicit in what I have said thus far, but which is important enough to merit specifying it separately, has to do with the connections among ways of seeing (interpretation), ways of feeling (the emotional valence attached to ways of seeing), and human actions. These three elements of being in the world are of a piece. We feel a certain way because we see or interpret things a certain way and vice versa. We also express our seeing and feeling in our actions and our ways of seeing and feeling grow out of the results of our actions and the actions of others on us. Seeing, feeling, and action go together.[34]

The life of the soul, then, is lived in the presence of God, through interpretation, feeling and action.

## Gerkin's Theological Anthropology and the Three Questions Concerning the Praxis of Clinical Pastoral Supervision

How does this theological anthropology contribute to the three questions concerning the praxis of clinical pastoral supervision? Gerkin's theological anthropology synthesizes elements from each of the social science, hermeneutical and special interest approaches. His use of the life of the soul, along with the notions of creation, sin and redemption and the importance of faith, hope and care in responding to God's initiative locates Gerkin's theory of personality within the Christian fact. Here, his approach is similar to the hermeneutical approach. Gerkin's use of the various interpretations developed by the social sciences, such as ego, self, identity, systems and object relations theory, joins his theological anthropology to the social sciences approach. He also mentions the contextual elements of "race," ethnicity, gender and the way that these shape one's understanding of the life of the soul. This awareness and use of these contextual elements join Gerkin to some aspects of the special interest approach. Gerkin synthesizes elements from the three approaches.

Also important in this contribution is the place of praxis. Gerkin's theological anthropology begins and ends in praxis. His reflections and interpretations are meant to transform the praxis. His theological anthropology emerges out of his praxis and then returns to praxis to facilitate greater response to God's inbreaking Reign, in a realized eschatology. A theological anthropology developed through critical reflection on the concrete material of cases is much needed in the field.

Gerkin's theological interpretation of human personality is important for the distinctiveness of the praxis of clinical pastoral supervision. His understanding of the eschatological identity of the soul, with the qualities of faith, hope and care, is important. Clinical pastoral supervision in its praxis needs to utilize a theological anthropology. Some texts do, but most use a theory of personality based on interpretations from the social sciences or interpretations of a specific group. Gerkin's theological anthropology developed through praxis offers much to the field.

In the quest for an adequate transformed praxis of clinical pastoral supervision, some elements have begun to emerge. The fusion of horizons between the texts on the praxis of clinical pastoral supervision and Gerkin's incarnational theology produces some elements. First, an adequate transformed praxis needs a standpoint within interpretations from the Christian fact. Second, this praxis must use interpretations from the social sciences. Of particular importance is the view that supervision is education and not therapy. Adult educational theory needs to be part of this praxis. Third, this transformed praxis must be rooted in the concrete case(s). Theory must be able to understand and explain the concrete practice. Fourth, narrative and hermeneutics need to be part of the content and process of clinical pastoral supervision. Fifth, this praxis must be seen through the lens of a theological anthropology. In some ways, his understanding of theological anthropology lends itself to developing the skills of spiritual direction in the praxis.

These are some elements of a transformed adequate praxis. The conversation between Gerkin's incarnational theology and the three approaches in the texts on clinical pastoral supervision has yielded some results. The next chapter focuses more on this fusion of horizons between Gerkin's theology and the texts, looking for similarities and differences among the different horizons and narratives. Important in this conversation are the answers that the fusion gives to the three questions.

Elizabeth, the supervisor, listened intently to Laura's pain and hopelessness on the phone. She affirmed Laura's empathy for the family and urged Laura to continue to listen and be present to them in their pain. Elizabeth also suggested that Laura facilitate some of their practical needs. These included dealing with the parking at the hospital, the need for the family to eat and rest and letting the extended family know of Samantha's death and the mother's condition.

The hermeneutic of despair has taken hold in this painful situation. The tragedy of Samantha's death has immobilized the family and the chaplain and sent the whole system into shock. From the view of theological anthropology, the situation is in need of redemption. Hopelessness has captured both the father and the chaplain. The questions of father and chaplain are authentic, fundamental theological questions. The father looks to the chaplain for a word of nourishment, bread, not stone. The chaplain, however, has entered the crisis and has no answer at this moment. What is hope here? Can God do anything?

Hope is not so much an answer as a process and promise. The process of hope means Laura sitting in the darkness with the family searching for God. The supervisor urged Laura to continue to be attentive to their pain and respond to that. She also urged Laura not to come up with quick answers but to let the questions be raised and pondered. Hope means recognizing and acknowledging the darkness. Hope also means believing that some promise or possibilities will emerge. Laura realized that this family had been permanently wounded by Samantha's death. Elizabeth urged Laura to follow up with the family. Laura attended the funeral and sent the family a note of condolence and also received a beautiful letter from the mother and father, thanking her for her support during the crisis. The husband called her a sign of hope. Laura spent a lot of time in reflection on the experience. On the one hand, she wondered how she was a sign of hope when she felt hopeless. On the other hand, she felt validated by the family and by her supervisor. In some mysterious way, she felt affirmed by God.

# Chapter 5
# Gerkin's Incarnational Theology and the Praxis of Clinical Pastoral Supervision

Alfred is a clinical pastoral supervisor who trained in Boston and Canada in the early seventies. He works in a teaching hospital as a chaplain and clinical pastoral supervisor. Alfred, trained to challenge and question students in order to facilitate personal and professional growth, has a deep loyalty to his students and the relationship with most of them lasts long after supervision and clinical training had ended. Alfred demands a great deal of his students. He expects excellence in their work and sound theory for what they do in ministry. Over many years, Alfred has become adept in the politics of the hospital. He is a strong advocate for chaplaincy and has made substantial gains for chaplaincy amongst the administration of the hospital. On reflection, Alfred notes that he is not as demanding and challenging with students as in his early years. He wonders if he has become too easygoing in his supervision. Alfred's question arises from years of experiences with students.

The fusion of horizons between Alfred and his students, Alfred and the hospital, Alfred and the changes in his own psycho-social and theological development has made an impact on him. His questioning rises from this two-way interaction. He wonders if he has been changed too much through the fusion of horizons. Utilizing the fusion of horizons, between Gerkin's theology and the praxis of clinical pastoral supervision, there are many possibilities. The incarnational theology of Charles Gerkin offers much to the praxis of clinical pastoral supervision. The texts that outline the praxis of clinical pastoral supervision offer much to the incarnational theology of Charles Gerkin. Gerkin's theology offers a critical theory to the practice. Conversely, the texts offer a critical praxis to his theory. This chapter describes the critical conversation between Gerkin's incarnational theology and the praxis of clinical pastoral supervision within the three questions.

**Gerkin's Contribution to the Praxis of Clinical Pastoral Supervision**

Gerkin contributes to the praxis of clinical pastoral supervision in five areas. First, Gerkin's standpoint in the Christian fact is not dominant in the praxis of clinical pastoral supervision. Interpretations borrowed from the social sciences and other disciplines have dominated the understanding of clinical pastoral supervision. Gerkin, as part of the revisionist critique in the field of practical theology, emphasizes interpretations that are drawn from Christian sources. These interpretations are his starting point and provide the framework for his thought.

Gerkin's theology is not a denial or an invalidation of interpretations from the other disciplines and professions. Rather, he places these interpretations within the hermeneutical framework of the Christian message. Gerkin's hermeneutical approach is different from the interpretations that accommodate Christian concepts with social science or medical concepts. In the social sciences approach, there is an identical correlation between the interpretations from the social sciences and those from the Christian message. Here, the particular social sciences discipline provides the hermeneutical framework. Like the prodigal son who returns a changed man to his father, Gerkin's incarnational theology challenges the social sciences approach to return to concepts and language within the Christian message. This return requires some social sciences interpretations.

Gerkin's standpoint within the Christian fact is also a challenge to the special interest approach. The special interest approach starts with its own experience. Their experience is the norm from which they view both the interpretations from the social sciences and Christian fact. Gerkin's incarnational theology questions how that experience is interpreted. What language and concepts describe the experience of the group? Where does that language originate? Is there any experience that can be described that is not standpoint dependent? Gerkin argues in favour of multiple perspectives, but holds that these multiple perspectives are best used within a Christian standpoint. Can human experience be the standpoint beyond all other standpoints? Gerkin confronts those texts, utilizing the special interest approach to think theologically about the human experience that they endorse.

Gerkin's incarnational theology challenges those in the hermeneutical approach who bypass the contributions of the social sciences. Thomas Oden, for example, returns to the patristics in order to discover the classical mode of pastoral care in the church.[1] His standpoint is located within Christian patristics. His theological approach, however, bypasses the contributions of the social sciences. Oden argues that contemporary pastoral care, pastoral counselling and pastoral supervision are adequately presented in the biblical texts and the texts of the Church Fathers. Contemporary social sciences add little to that contribution of the early church. In fact, Oden argues that many interpretations from the social sciences often lead ministry astray.

Gerkin's theology, contrary to Oden's, includes interpretations from standpoints outside the Christian fact. Gerkin does not dismiss the interpretations from the social sciences. Rather, Gerkin endorses many of these interpretations and uses them to develop his theology. He does believe, however, that in the field of practical theology today, the interpretations from the social sciences are given far too much weight and often outweigh in importance the interpretations from the Christian message. Gerkin's implementation of the various theories and interpretations from the Christian message and the social sciences is similar to David Tracy's revised critical correlational method in theology. In the theory dimension of the praxis/theory/praxis method, Gerkin correlates the interpretations from the social sciences with interpretations from the Christian message. Gerkin creates a conversation between these various standpoints in his theological approach and develops a hermeneutical play between the various concepts and interpretations, moving towards a fusion of horizons. Out of this conversation, praxis is transformed. Gerkin takes very seriously the contribution of the social sciences. He offers a challenge to those in the hermeneutical approach who dismiss the interpretations of the social sciences.

Gerkin's notion of narrative theology and hermeneutics is a second area of contribution to the texts on the praxis of clinical pastoral supervision. In a small number of the written texts on clinical pastoral supervision, there exists an emerging sense of narrative identity, narrative theology and narrative methodology. None of these texts, however, are identical to Gerkin's understanding of narrative. Gerkin's understanding of narrative, based on Ricoeur and Gadamer, along with his clinical experience of narrative in his praxis of ministry, is unique in the field of clinical pastoral supervision.

None of the written texts employs Gerkin's notion of hermeneutics. None of the texts uses both Ricoeur and Gadamer in understanding and explaining a method of hermeneutics. None mentions the notion of the "fusion of horizons" or argues against applying theory to practice, and none uses Ricoeur's method of understanding/explanation/understanding.The field is lacking in these elements. A small number mention the hermeneutical aspect of clinical pastoral supervision and a few mention the work of Ricoeur. These few texts, however, have not explained and understood the praxis of clinical pastoral supervision in a fashion similar to Gerkin. These texts that use Ricoeur have not developed his thought into a critical theory about the praxis.

The social sciences approach has little notion of narrative and hermeneutics as is evidenced in its texts. Most often, the social sciences approach works within an endorsement of objective truth that can be known through scientific means and is reliable and valid. That assumption is contrary to the more subjective narrative hermeneutical approach. The endorsement of objective truth implies that at the core of the human being are experiences, values and dynamics that are common to all humans, regardless of "race," gender, economics or class. With such a belief, then, one can make generalizations true of all humans.[2] Here, Gerkin's narrative hermeneutical theory confronts the social sciences objectivism underlining the differences. His theology offers an alternative epistemology emphasizing the standpoint of the interpreter.

Narrative and hermeneutics are used in small measure by the special interest groups in their texts on supervision. This special interest approach often describes experiences in terms of the group narrative. The special interest group narrative is different from the narrative of the dominant group. The interpretations of the dominant group do not serve the special interest group. In this way, there are some similarities with Gerkin's narrative hermeneutical approach. There are differences in that the special interest group has not developed a critical theory about narrative hermeneutics in the way that Gerkin has.

A third contribution of Gerkin's incarnational theology to the texts on clinical pastoral supervision is his use of praxis/theory/praxis method. He acknowledges that this view of practical theology is drawn from Ricoeur's understanding/explanation/understanding view of hermeneutics. In his understanding of praxis and theory and the play between the two, Gerkin utilizes a theology based upon concrete experience, and in particular case studies, vignettes and verbatims taken from the praxis of ministry. Central to Gerkin's methodology is a concern to develop a methodology that is specific to practical theology. Both Tillich's correlational method and Tracy's revised critical correlational method are more specifically designed for systematic theology and not practical theology.

Gerkin is also seeking in his methodology to offer an alternative to reductionism. All three approaches in the texts on clinical pastoral supervision have many examples of reductionism. In a reductionistic methodology, practice is applied theory. A text, in a reductionist method, adopts certain interpretations from theory. The practice of supervision then fits into the particular interpretations adopted from a particular theory. In the reductionistic methodology, theory comes first and practice is made to fit the theory. Gerkin believes, on the other hand, that practice is the high point, the starting point and the end point of practical theology. Theory from multiple disciplines within the framework of the Christian fact helps to explain and critique the practice. Practice questions theory just as theory questions the practice. Practice is theory laden and theory is practice laden. In Gerkin's methodology, practical theology is not applied systematic theology. Rather, practical theology questions systematic theology. There is a dialogue, a fusion of horizons between the two.

Gerkin's incarnational theology is most often expressed in both the dialectical and analogical outcomes of his thinking. This dialectical and analogical aspect of his theology is his fourth contribution to the texts on clinical pastoral supervision. This combination is not based on a systematic theory that is coherent in itself, but rather on a practical theology rooted in practice. His dialectical framework stresses the tension of opposites, ambiguity and variety. Clinical pastoral supervision does not articulate a dialectical framework in most of its written texts. Many of the writers in this field seek to present a map that offers a road with straight lines in describing the way ahead in the praxis of clinical pastoral supervision. Gerkin offers to the field, however, a map that contains roads with many forks. Growth, for Gerkin, means appreciating the tension present in the forks in the road and allowing the tension between the opposites to transform those involved in the situation. Both supervisor and supervisee have to live in this creative tension in order to discover the way ahead.

George Fitchett outlines in detail some of the tensions and dialectical elements present in the praxis of supervision in his philosophy of clinical pastoral supervision.[3] For Fitchett, these tensions in the praxis produce the double bind, or "no-win," situation and can easily produce paralysis in both supervisor and student. When these tensions are viewed as paradox, then there is a way out of the double bind. Paradox, according to Fitchett, can break the double bind, break the paralysis and produce transformation. Gerkin works within a similar paradoxical, dialectical framework. He argues, in his article on power and powerlessness in CPE supervision, that both supervisor and student need to be able to deal with power and powerlessness in clinical pastoral supervision.[4] Contrary to other perspectives, Gerkin argues that supervisor and supervisee need to use their power and powerlessness in their ministry. CPE training is not just a matter of eliminating the supervisee's experience of powerlessness. In Gerkin's theology, the experiences of power and powerlessness are held in tension. Both are validated as part of the Christian narrative and both are necessary for transformation. Gerkin's contribution to clinical pastoral supervision in the area of the dialectic of power and powerlessness is unique. Many of the written texts speak of empowerment of the supervisee and the facilitation of the constructive use of power. None speaks of the importance of powerlessness in both supervisor and supervisee. None of the texts connects to the powerlessness of Jesus. Gerkin's narrative hermeneutical theology offers a dialectical framework to the texts.

Similarly, Gerkin's use of analogy in his incarnational theology is a contribution to the field. His understanding of time from three different perspectives, as well as his interpretation of the concepts of ego, self and soul are examples of his analogical thinking. He strongly emphasizes both similarities and differences between concepts from the social sciences and those based in the Christian fact. Gerkin is unlike practitioners from the social sciences approach who develop identical correlations between the various interpretations. This analogical theology also challenges the differentness of the special interest approach. Analogy sees both similarities and differences between interpretations. With analogy, there is some similarity and some difference between the experiences of the special interest approach and the experience, of other groups. Many of the texts in the special interest approach argue that their experience is utterly different from that of the dominant group.[5] For example, the experience of poor black males being trained for ministry in Kenya is quite different from the experience of white female university graduates supervising the clinical training for ministry in Canada. An analogical theology says that there are differences and similarities between these experiences. Is it possible to have a conversation if there are not some similarities between different experiences? Can the special interest approach to clinical pastoral supervision see any similarities with the other two approaches? Gerkin's analogical incarnational theology offers a bridge between the social sciences, hermeneutical and special interest approaches. This bridge stresses both similarities and differences between the various interpretations and practices.

Gerkin's theological anthropology makes a fifth contribution to the field of clinical pastoral supervision. This is demonstrated in his understanding and explanation of the human being as living the life of the soul. For Gerkin, a person's theological identity is captured in the metaphor of the life of the soul. This identity is both conferred by the context and by God, and is mysteriously connected within the individual. The fusion of these two identities forms the basis of personal and professional selves. The life of the soul is explained in a narrative hermeneutical form. For Gerkin, the theology of hope has a special place in the life of the soul. In many of his writings, he focuses on the way that hope operates in the life of the soul and the manner in which hope actualizes the person to transformation. Being human means exercising faith, hope and care in response to God's activity in life. Faith, hope and care are not dependent on outward religious practices. Rather, Gerkin sees these operating in both religious contexts and nonreligious contexts. All of humanity experiences these qualities, for they are part of the narrative of the soul. Ministry, in his view, encourages their use in response to the inbreaking reign of God.

This theological anthropology is rooted in ideas from the contemporary age. Ego, self and system are borrowed from other disciplines. Gerkin's integration of ego, self and system into the life of the soul makes him unique. Such a view of the human is crucial for the praxis of the clinical pastoral supervision. Clinical pastoral supervision includes a focus on the person, and Gerkin's theological anthropology gives a lens through which the praxis can be interpreted. This praxis-based anthropology reinterprets the Christian message in light of the contextual issues and a developmental perspective of human personality.

## The Contribution of Clinical Pastoral Supervision to the Theology of Charles Gerkin

The praxis of clinical pastoral supervision as recorded in the written documents challenges some aspects of the incarnational theology of Charles V. Gerkin. These supervision texts question Gerkin and contribute to his theology. The contributions of these texts to Gerkin's theology are four.

The first contribution of the texts is in the area of practice. In the development of Gerkin's theology over forty years, he has moved from the practices, or doing, of pastoral care, counselling and supervision into a discussion of the theory present in the practices. In the earlier part of his theological career, as manifested in his written articles, Gerkin focused more on the practices than on the theory present in the practices. At this earlier stage, he was interested in theory, but the emphasis was on transforming the practice. The underlying question was, What must I do to help this person? As Gerkin adopted the work of Ricoeur and Gadamer, he became more interested in philosophical hermeneutical theory. This change becomes obvious in the book *The Living Human Document*, in which Gerkin focuses more on critical thinking and the hermeneutical theory present in the practice.

The focus in the later stage of Gerkin's theology is more on thinking and theory than on doing and practice. This change in Gerkin is influenced by both a change in his context as well as the development of an assumption in his thought. In his thought, Gerkin mentions that he is not a behaviouralist and he writes against the behaviouralist approach in both family systems theory and behavioural psychology. Gerkin's roots in Freudian and neo-Freudian psychiatry, as well as his later belief in object relations, support a more insight-oriented approach in therapy. His training in pastoral psychotherapy, which values insight and cognitive awareness, lends itself in the later Gerkin to focusing more on narrative and hermeneutics and less on doing and practice.

Many of the written texts on clinical pastoral supervision are more similar to the early Gerkin than the later Gerkin. Their focus is more on practice and doing than on theory and insight. Critical praxis is stressed more than critical reasoning. Certainly, pastoral supervisors are interested in the theory present in practice. Many of the texts question and challenge Gerkin's later thought and the way that Gerkin develops this methodology. His critical theory using multiple standpoints tends to dominate the praxis/theory/praxis method. This theoretical approach emphasizing insight is questioned by the texts. The texts also challenge the complexity of the insight. Gerkin shows himself to be an able academician rooted in the university in the way that he dialogues with many different interpretations drawn from the Christian fact and social sciences. In many ways, however, the later Gerkin is a far distance from the clinical setting of Grady hospital in Atlanta and the "Boys' Industrial Home" in Topeka, where he started his career.

In the later Gerkin, theory dominates, and the nature of his explanations of the praxis is complex. In many ways, he takes up the task of what Don Browning says is a "fundamental practical theology."[6] This fundamental practical theology is more interested in providing a philosophical structure for the practice of theology than in answering what needs to be done in any particular case or situation. Such theoretical complexity based on a philosophical hermeneutical narrative approach can frustrate the clinical pastoral supervisor. The complexity of Gerkin's theology and theory easily leads to paralysis for those who are interested in what to do in any given moment of supervision.

In his study, George Fitchett shows that few writers cite Gerkin. In Fitchett's analysis of forty-five philosophies of clinical pastoral supervision written between 1963 and 1982, the written texts of Charles V. Gerkin are cited by only two supervisors. These two cite one of Gerkin's written texts.[7]

The complexity of his incarnational theology is not helpful for clinicians. The case studies in his later works are more complex, and Gerkin presents longer explanations of theoretical discussion of the cases. As one reviewer noted after reading *The Living Human Document*, "This is clearly not a book for students at the Master of Divinity level."[8]

The social sciences approach in the texts on clinical pastoral supervision emphasizes the performance in ministry. The interpretations from the social sciences give the clinical supervisor direction for proceeding in supervision. Gerkin's movement to complex theory in his later writings is challenged by the social sciences approach. Is Gerkin striving to be a systematic theologian rather than a practical one in developing his theory of practical theology? Do the social sciences interpretations dominate the field of clinical pastoral supervision because these interpretations are more helpful and practical in a clinical setting? Many of the interpretations from the Christian fact are helpful in addressing the bigger issues. The interpretations from the social sciences are more helpful in dealing with the concrete situation faced by the supervisor and supervisee. The dominance of social sciences texts in the field demonstrate this.

The social sciences approach also challenges Gerkin's epistemology. Gerkin believes that there are many different interpretations of any reality. For Gerkin, truth is always interpreted truth, whether the method of interpretation is empirical, based on observation and conclusion, or through reasoned argument, based on first principles. Gerkin is keen on presenting various interpretations from different standpoints. The social sciences texts, especially those developed within a medical scientific context, seek a truth that can be verified through observation and experimentation.[9] Gerkin's complex incarnational theology challenges that epistemology. While Gerkin's challenge is vital to the field of pastoral supervision, the social sciences approach challenges Gerkin not to lapse into total subjectivism. The social sciences approach asks: Does Gerkin's incarnational theology work in clinical pastoral supervision? How would a supervisor know that it works? Can it be verified? Is it reliable and valid? The horizons of these social sciences texts challenge Gerkin's epistemology.

The training and clinical experiences of Alfred the supervisor challenges Gerkin's incarnational theology. Part of Alfred's Boston training is an emphasis on common sense and practicality. This means developing concrete interventions that solve problems. The New York approach stressed insight and an understanding of the complexity of the situation. Alfred has become a master of practicality and problem solving. His clinical experience and supervision of students have taught him well. Alfred works in a setting where the research concepts of reliability and validity are common and accepted terms. Practice is based on evidence from research. This evidence stems from both quantitative and qualitative research methodologies. Evidence-based practice needs to be reliable and valid. The reliability and validity of the evidence that shape Albert's praxis of chaplaincy is challenged by the other disciplines. One health professional asked Alfred: "What evidence do you have that demonstrates that chaplaincy helps patients?" Such a question can also be asked of Gerkin's theology.

A second issue raised by the texts on clinical pastoral supervision for Gerkin's incarnational theology is Gerkin's utilization of his own method of praxis/theory/praxis. As has been noted, Gerkin's methodology is very useful to the praxis of clinical pastoral supervision. Yet, the way that Gerkin employs the methodology in his written texts is not that helpful for practitioners of clinical pastoral supervision. Gerkin presents the case and provides a variety of standpoints for understanding and explaining the case. Most often, however, he does not present the second praxis, the transformed praxis. He does not often demonstrate the way that the critical reflection and conversation of the theory present in praxis produces a new praxis. How was Susan Clark transformed through pastoral counselling and the other experiences in her life? What is the transformed praxis in this case? Gerkin leaves this unanswered. Readers of Gerkin's incarnational theology are offered his reflections and critical thinking. The second praxis of the praxis/theory/praxis method is often missing.

For supervisors of clinical pastoral supervision, uncovering the theory present in practice is not enough. The supervisor desires critical reflection and, most importantly, transformed praxis. The later Gerkin deals more with the critical reflection and the early Gerkin focuses on the transformed praxis. As his thought develops in his incarnational theology, the critical thinking of theology becomes more complex and the transformation of theology becomes less evident. This change in Gerkin's theology could be influenced by the change in his context. In 1970, he moved from hospital chaplain and supervisor at Grady Hospital in Atlanta to university professor and academician at Emory University in Atlanta. In Gerkin's later work, a theory for practical theology receives more attention than the practices of ministry.

Along with his failure to outline the transformed praxis in his case studies, the texts on clinical pastoral supervision question how Gerkin uses the fusion of horizons. Fusion of horizons is very useful in explaining the relationship between supervisor and supervisee as well as supervisee and client/patient. Such an idea focuses on the horizon of meanings and narratives that both supervisor and supervisee bring to the supervisory relationship. In Gerkin's presentation of the fusion of horizons in his case studies, however, there is very little mention of the way in which he is transformed through the connection with the client or supervisee. How is Gerkin transformed by the fusion of horizons with Susan Clark? In his response to James Poling's critique, Gerkin mentions that he experienced transformation through dealing with the case study of Centreton. That is the only instance in which Gerkin mentions the impact of the case on his own horizon. While Gerkin endorses the fusion of horizons, there is little evidence in his writing of the transformation that has taken place in him within the process of working with the cases that he presents.

The fusion of horizons is a concept similar to the notion of advocacy which is present in the special interest approach. In the special interest approach, the helper is one of the people that he/she is helping. Ministry, in this view, is not given by a detached professional. Rather, the helper is a participant-observer in the practices of ministry. In the special interest approach, there is no such thing as a detached objective expert. Every helper belongs to a group and brings the values of that group to the process of ministry. The texts from the special interest approach endorse Gerkin's understanding of the fusion of horizons and challenge him to move out of the image of the objective, detached professional. These texts challenge Gerkin to be transformed and to utilize the very interpretations that he endorses.

An example of the change in the helper that takes place through the fusion of horizons is present in an article by Thomas O'Connor, titled "Ministry Without a Future: A Pastoral Care Approach to Patients with Senile Dementia."[10] That article was the result of eight months of full-time presence on a ward of patients with various forms of senile dementia. The author attempted to answer the research question: What is an appropriate pastoral care approach to patients with senile dementia? The research produced some findings to the research question and also led to some change in the researcher. That change is noted by the researcher.

> I can certainly speak for my own growth in working with these patients. I found that I became less task-focused and more relational. I found that I became more satisfied by the here-and-now and not so future-oriented. I found that I became less verbal and more nonverbal. I found that I gained a new wisdom from patients who appear foolish. In a real way, the sickness of these patients has helped me to be healthier. I know that I received a lot from them. The pastoral care was mutual.[11]

The praxis of clinical pastoral supervision, viewed as a fusion of horizons, involves change in the supervisee as well as in the supervisor. This change, according to Gerkin's incarnational theology, is usually first a change in meaning. This change in meaning can involve a change in all the meaning systems of the participants. This change in meaning impacts upon the participants' relational systems and skills as well as beliefs and ego development. The idea of the fusion of horizons offers some explanation of what is going on in the supervisory process. Supervisees challenge the supervisor's values, assumptions and theology. The narrative of the supervisees interprets the narrative of the supervisor in a way that offers a new meaning and understanding to the supervisor's narrative. Gerkin's practice of the fusion of horizons, however, indicates a lack of change in the supervisor.

A third area where Gerkin's incarnational theology is challenged concerns his emphasis on meaning in practical theology. The special interest group challenges Gerkin's theology here and argues that power, fairness and justice are more important than meaning. James N. Poling, in his article "A Critical Appraisal of Charles Gerkin's Pastoral Theology,"[12] maintains that the central metaphor for Gerkin's theology is the concern for meaning. The special interest approach in the praxis of clinical pastoral supervision argues that meaning lacks a focus on the issues of power, fairness and justice. The crisis of meaning is a crisis for white, middle-class males who are in positions of power. These white, middle-class males struggle with the abuses of power that exist in our society because of the positions of power that they occupy. For Poling, the crisis of meaning does not exist for those groups in our society who are not in power or who experience disenfranchisement. These marginalized groups have less power and are usually not part of the decision-making process. Their concern is not with meaning. Rather, their concern is for justice, fairness for all and the distribution of power.

Poling articulates the position of those texts in the special interest approach. These texts confront Gerkin's incarnational theology and its stress on narrative and hermeneutics. According to this critique, the desire to discover meaning glosses over the issues of power, fairness and justice. The issue for these special interest texts is not what is the meaning of this experience or event or what language system needs to be used. Rather, the more important issue is who is served by the interpretations and what does the interpretation do for the powerless. This view examines the sociology of hermeneutics rather than the content of the hermeneutics. The emphasis on hermeneutics and interpreting language and events needs to focus more on issues of power and justice than on cognitive claims and meaning. Narrative theology in the special interest approach means giving voice to those whose narrative is not heard and developing interpretations that serve these voiceless narratives. The special interest approach asks: How can our interpretations of events and narrative empower those groups that are disenfranchised? How can they be given equal access to power?

Gerkin, in his response to Poling, maintains that meaning includes power and justice.[13] The crisis of meaning also deals with the injustices that are present in our society. Gerkin argues that the approaches of liberation theology and the metaphor of meaning drawn from Ricoeur includes justice and the liberation of the oppressed. Liberation theology has to do with a change in meaning. The special interest approach in clinical pastoral supervision endorses issues of justice and fairness, especially for those in society who have less power and voice than the dominant group. This approach challenges the emphasis on meaning. The research of Meakes and O'Connor has shown that women's experience of supervision in the Canadian Association for Pastoral Practice and Education (CAPPE) is one of both liberation and enslavement.[14] The male experience is considered normative, and women are trained with that standard. From the vantage point of women in a male-dominated society, fairness, power and justice are crucial items in the experience of clinical pastoral supervision.

The special interest approach challenges the incarnational theology of Gerkin to examine its implications for praxis. These texts ask: "Who is served by Gerkin's incarnational theology in clinical pastoral supervision?" The answer is easy to imagine. To use Gerkin's incarnational theology, one needs an advanced degree in theology. Gerkin's ideas require a sophisticated understanding of theology, especially regarding hermeneutics and narrative. The person who uses Gerkin in pastoral supervision must be experienced with object relations, systems theory and the work of Ricoeur and Gadamer and the praxis of pastoral care and counselling. This person must be able to think in a dialectical way as well as be able to work analogically with the various interpretations from the different disciplines in theology and the social sciences. This person must be able to fuse horizons using various interpretations and praxis. Meaning-making must be a concern that undergirds the ability to work with both theory and practice. Besides having an advanced degree in theology, the person who uses Gerkin's theology needs extensive training in Clinical Pastoral Education. Such a person needs to be adept with the use of language and able to make subtle distinctions in a rational constructed way. Gerkin's incarnational theology does not serve well the supervisor in Brazil working with the poor, the black person in Kenya learning some pastoral counselling skills, men and women trained in theology but who are lacking the facility of multiple language systems.

The struggle between meaning on the one hand, and fairness, power and justice on the other hand, is demonstrated in Gerkin's article titled "Power and Powerlessness in CPE Supervision."[15] Here, he adopts an interpretation of power in supervision based on the work of the sociologist David McClelland. Gerkin argues that in supervision and ministry, the supervisor, supervisee and patient need to use their power and powerlessness on behalf of the Kingdom of God. In this article on power and powerlessness, Gerkin is mostly concerned with the power dynamics present in the supervisory relationship. He argues that power is a central concern of CPE supervision. However, his understanding of power lacks a sociological analysis. Which gender, class, ethnic and denominational backgrounds predominate in CPE supervision? Gerkin does not address these issues. He also does not explore the sociology and politics of power, i.e., who benefits from both power and powerlessness in the supervisory relationship. Rather, Gerkin focuses on the meaning of power in terms of gospel meaning and the meaning within the supervisory relationship. He is interested in empowering both supervisor and supervisee in this article, but his analysis lacks any notion of gender, "race" or economics. Gerkin is more concerned with the meaning of power than the sociology of power in CPE supervision.

A fourth area where the texts of clinical pastoral supervision confront Gerkin's incarnational theology is his ecclesiology. Gerkin, in *Prophetic Pastoral Practice,* endorses an ecclesiology that is centrifugal in its mission.[16] He compares this centrifugal ecclesiology to centripetal ecclesiology, of which he is very critical. The centrifugal church is one that reaches out and seeks to serve both those who are members of the Christian community and those who are not. Avery Dulles, in his book *Models of the Church* defines this centrifugal model of ecclesiology as the servant model.[17] Dulles describes this model of church as one that dialogues with the world (including the social sciences) and seeks to serve those outside of the church. Like leaven in the dough, the Christian brings to everyone the life that God gives. Such an ecclesiology does not seek to bring members into the Christian community in the manner of a centrifugal ecclesiology.

The centripetal approach, on the other hand, believes that God's activity is within both the church and the world. The mission of the church is to bring humanity into contact with the divine life given to the church. The centripetal notion of ecclesiology stresses a model of church that is communion and herald. In this view, the task of the church and ministry is to preach the *kerygma* and bring those outside the community of believers into communion with the Christian community. The centripetal notion of church stresses the church as a light to the nations, a community where health and salvation exist.

Gerkin contrasts the centrifugal model (church as servant) of ecclesiology with the centripetal (church as communion and herald) ecclesiology. He prefers the centrifugal model and sees the centripetal as enclosing and confining. Gerkin's centrifugal ecclesiology, which seeks to reach out and offer the meanings and relationships present in the Christian community, ultimately becomes the work of specialized ministers. These ministers, in Gerkin's model, can be ordained or lay, but they must have special training in theology and the social sciences. Some texts in the hermeneutical approach in clinical pastoral supervision endorse a centripetal ecclesiology. This centripetal ecclesiology stresses the connection with the local church and the sacramental life of the community of believers. The practices of Gerkin's incarnational theology lack these elements.

Gerkin's praxis lacks the supervision offered by the whole Christian community. Clinical pastoral supervision, in Gerkin's model of church, most often is limited to the one-on-one relationship between supervisor and supervisee and a small group of students. This tends to be more private and less communal. It is rational and reflective, not active and symbolic. In this absence of the communal dimension, there is also an absence of sacrament, ritual and worship.[18] The goal in Gerkin's theology is service, not communion and proclamation. There is most often an absence of connection to the worshipping community. That is not a concern for him. The case studies and vignettes within his books and articles seldom include the worshipping community. There is no mention of ritual or sacraments or their place in the ministry of pastoral care/supervision.

There is a growing body of written texts in clinical pastoral supervision within the hermeneutical approach that views clinical pastoral supervision as spiritual direction. This spiritual direction seeks to discern God's activity in the here-and-now (a concern of Gerkin) and to facilitate the response of the supervisee, supervisor and everyone in the context to that presence. Such an understanding of supervision utilizes worship, the Christian community, prayer and the help of a spiritual director. Clinical pastoral supervision in the tradition of spiritual direction is not focused on the supervisory relationship or the pastoral care relationship. Rather the focus is on the many ways that God is revealed in the church and the world. The task, then, is to connect the supervisee to the wider Christian community, which is an agent of God's presence in the world. This connection includes the use of worship, preaching and the relationships present in the whole community. The Christian community in its life becomes the agent for supervision.

Gerkin's incarnational theology could easily be adapted to this approach in clinical pastoral supervision. His emphasis on God's self-disclosure in the experiences of life, in relationships and crisis events, makes discernment of God's offer an essential item. Those texts from the hermeneutical approach that employ a centripetal ecclesiology and emphasize awareness of God's offer invite Gerkin to consider a more communal and less private approach. Cannot clinical pastoral supervision utilize the rich life of the community of believers through worship, education, homiletics and the life shared together? Is not the Risen Christ present in the community as the sustainer, healer, guider and reconciler in pastoral care and clinical pastoral supervision? These hermeneutical texts challenge Gerkin's ecclesiology.

The texts on the praxis of clinical pastoral supervision offer four challenges to Gerkin's incarnational theology. First, these texts, especially the ones from the social sciences approach, focus on critical practice in demonstrating what a supervisor *does* in clinical pastoral supervision. They challenge the later Gerkin to move back into critical practice and out of his complex theory. The social sciences approach occupies 48 percent of the texts because it offers some concrete things to do in supervision. These texts find those concrete interventions helpful in clinical pastoral supervision, providing a way ahead in supervision. The social sciences approach argues that clinical pastoral supervision is distinctive in that it focuses on critical praxis rather than critical theory.

Second, these texts challenge Gerkin to practice what he preaches. His implementation of his praxis/theory/praxis method does not follow his method. He does not offer the transformed praxis, the second praxis. Practitioners of clinical pastoral supervision want to see the transformed praxis.

Gerkin hints at it but seldom outlines it. While the metaphor of the fusion of horizons is helpful for the praxis, Gerkin seldom describes how his horizon is transformed through his interaction with patients, parishioners, clients, supervisees and/or academic colleagues. His implementation of the fusion of horizons is unidirectional. The others are changed, but there is little evidence that he is changed.

Third, the special interest texts on clinical pastoral supervision challenge Gerkin to expand his focus beyond meaning and cognitive claims. They emphasize power, fairness and justice. The awareness of these values makes one become more aware of gender, ethnicity and the struggle between the privileges of ordination and the place of laity. Meaning-making tends to serve the concerns of white, middle-class males who dominate much of the clinical pastoral supervision in Canada. The special interest approach strives to equalize power by bringing other groups into the positions of supervision with a validation of their experience.

Finally, some elements of the hermeneutical approach challenge Gerkin in his ecclesiology. His centrifugal theology of Church could benefit from a more centripetal theology of Church. A centripetal ecclesiology would shape clinical pastoral supervision in a new and different way. This would include the use of worship, spiritual direction, Christian education, homilectics, administration and, indeed, the whole Church community as the agent of supervision. Clinical pastoral supervision utilizing a centripetal ecclesiology is a less private relationship between supervisor and supervisee and a greater connection to the whole worshipping community.

In the case of the supervisor Alfred, there have been many changes in his supervision since the beginning of his praxis. In that time, he has experienced a multitude of horizons and there have been a many kinds of fusions with these various horizons. His challenging style most often creates a tension between him and the student. The horizons are dialectical in this case. Alfred has learned in his praxis that tension and challenge is not the best way for all students to learn. Some students learn better when there are similarities as well as differences between the supervisor's horizon and the student's horizon. He has become more affirming of student's work over time. The horizons now are more similar than different.

Competence in ministry is an important value for Alfred. His desire for excellence is fueled by that value of competence. His social sciences approach to supervision, based on systemic theory, has connected him to other disciplines in the hospital. His desire for competence has pushed him to change, based on the evidence that research has brought to his pastoral practice. That value of competence has helped him to remain current in his supervisory praxis. At the same time, competence has also aided him in dealing with the many changes in the praxis of clinical pastoral supervision that have taken place over the last twenty-five years.

Alfred's concern about being too easygoing in supervision now could also be viewed as accumulated wisdom from the many fusions of horizons that have taken place in his praxis. His age, the cultural context, the rise of the special interest approach as well as a renewed interest in theological issues have been some major shifts in his field. While Alfred looks back with fondness to his early years as a supervisor, was that the golden age of clinical pastoral supervision? If supervision then was so great, why did that kind of supervision change? Alfred needs to appreciate some of the gains of the hermeneutical and special interest approaches that he has actually incorporated into his style and thinking. Possibly, his easygoing attitude is a sign of wisdom and growing competence as a supervisor.

# Chapter 6
# An Adequate Transformed Praxis

Mary is an American woman in her thirties who has experienced many losses. She has a BA in psychology and is currently in a MTS program in pastoral counselling with a focus on family therapy. She is uncertain about seeking ordination in her Protestant denomination. On the Myers-Briggs test,[1] Mary scores as an INTJ. She is an introvert who prefers thinking as her dominant mode. On Kolb's Learning Styles Inventory (LSI),[2] Mary learns through assimilation, i.e., through abstract conceptualization and reflective observation. On the Helping Styles Inventory (HSI),[3] Mary tends to the consultant and celebrant styles when working with patients. In her professional life before theology, Mary worked as a research assistant in a medical facility. Mary came to the educational unit wondering if chaplaincy was an avenue that she might pursue as a career. In the initial interview, she displayed excellent communication skills, manifested a desire to learn and articulated her professional goals, but found it difficult to identify personal goals for herself. Within the first week of the unit, a learning contract between the supervisor, Mary, and the peer group was negotiated and formulated. Mary's goals for the unit were to:

1. Practise the skills of joining with patients that included summarizing, the use of positive connotation, tentative language.
2. Utilize the experience of ministering with patients with chronic illness in developing a theology of suffering.
3. Examine issues from Mary's family-of-origin, especially concerning closeness/distance that influence her ministry.
4. Describe patients in systems concepts and language from the Structural school, using her theory in family therapy.

Mary was placed as a chaplain on a unit for patients with Acquired Brain Injury (ABIP); she also worked clinically with the families of patients.

Clinical pastoral supervision is concerned with transforming Mary's praxis. What is an adequate transformed praxis? What are the components of an adequate praxis? This chapter describes five elements of an adequate transformed praxis. These are demonstrated with Mary in supervision. The chapter also outlines the five concrete areas that clinical pastoral supervision addresses in its praxis. In terms of the adequate praxis, the first element is the utilization of interpretations from the Christian fact.[4] This includes a theory of personality that is grounded in a theological anthropology described as the life of the soul. The life of the soul is a narrative of creation, sin and redemption. The soul within a systemic perspective responds to grace through the gifts of faith, hope and care.[5]

Theologically, Mary is wondering about God's call to her and where the call is leading her. This is the issue of vocation as Mary is searching for her place in ministry. Mary struggled with notions of sin in praxis. She was able to identify systemic and social sin. Personal sin was harder for her to identify. For her, it smacked of moralism. Grace and redemption were easily used by Mary, and she could quickly identify such moments in her praxis. Mary had a well-developed sense of meaning. She worked hard to use the language of meaning and make sense of her experience. The language of force (ego) was less developed. While Mary struggled with her specific vocation, she had a sense of her eschatological identity in God. This identity was informed by feminist theology.

Second, this transformed praxis also uses interpretations from the social sciences. In the case of clinical pastoral supervision, interpretations from adult education theory are especially helpful.[6] Clinical pastoral supervision is education for ministry directed at adult learners. Also important to this adequate transformed praxis is a systemic understanding of personality with a distinction between supervision and therapy.[7] As adult education, clinical pastoral supervision facilitates Mary's learning goals, the needs of patients and the institution and the goals of the supervisor, peer group and the learning context. Dialogue and negotiation are key elements in this approach to learning.[8] This adult educational model utilizes the supervisee's learning style. Mary, according to the Learning Styles Inventory (LSI), is an assimilator who learns primarily through cognitive reasoning and observation. Adult education assumes that the learner is self-directed, responsible, learns from experience and is able to evaluate learning. Mary demonstrated these characteristics. She was able to articulate a goal for a pastoral visit and evaluate the visit based on the goal. She implemented her own learning goals and asked for feedback from supervisors and peers on these goals.

Adult education also exposes the student to a variety of learning experiences. With Mary learning primarily through reasoning and observation, she liked the rational discussion of cases and critical incidents, the observation of clinicians behind the one-way mirror and the discussion of assigned readings. At the same time, Mary was able to use other styles of learning. She was able to use the action/reflection model in clinical visits. She developed an awareness in a few situations where her feelings were a source of learning. Mary benefited from the variety of supervisors as well as the connection to a regional SPE program.

Third, an adequate praxis is rooted in the concrete, especially in the specific case.[9] The transformed praxis is concrete and specific. Clinical pastoral supervision must be tailored to Mary, her learning goals and her praxis. Such an approach challenges the supervisor and the whole learning environment to tailor supervision to the learning needs of the individual student. A learning contract is especially helpful. Gerkin's theological method of praxis/theory/praxis is appropriate for the task of transformation.

Fourth, the transformed praxis emphasizes the narrative hermeneutical quality of supervision. For Mary, this narrative hermeneutical quality addresses the way that she interprets and makes sense of her experience of ABIP, the other students and her supervisor. Are her interpretations and dominant narrative helpful to her and others? The narrative hermeneutical understanding includes the contextual issues of gender, ethnicity, denomination and ecclesiological status.[10] Mary is a lay woman in ministry from a Protestant denomination, with rich legacies from her ethnic background. These contextual issues, along with the various interpretations from theology and the social sciences, identify her standpoint. These interpretations offer hints and insights as to what is happening with Mary. They do not, however, speak the whole truth about her. There is much more to Mary than all of these interpretations.

A fifth element is the fusion of horizons.[11] As a concept, the fusion of horizons captures the process of interactions that take place on many levels, in many ways, in the praxis of clinical pastoral supervision. The fusion of horizons offers an explanation of how praxis is transformed. The praxis of the supervisee is changed through the supervisee's interaction with supervisor, peers, patients, readings, family of origin and the institution, as well as other systems and the many experiences of grace that are incarnated in all of these horizons. All of the various horizons interact with the praxis of the supervisee to offer the possibility for transformation. The fusion of horizons explains the way that this praxis is transformed into a more adequate praxis.

An adequate praxis means acceptable without being perfect.[12] Any praxis can improve actions as well as theory. There is always more that could be done and said. Praxis is limited by the abilities of those involved, the nature of the issues that are being faced, the interpretations possible within a given context, and the range of interpretations and actions open to the participants at the time. An adequate transformed praxis offers change that seeks greater love of God, others and self, realizing the limitations of the situation.

These five aspects of an adequate transformed praxis take shape in a concrete way in the praxis of clinical pastoral supervision. Clinical pastoral supervision is education for ministry, and the focus is the transformation of the praxis of the supervisee. The supervisee participates in this education for ministry in order that his/her praxis will be improved. Thus, an adequate transformed praxis means that the ministry of the supervisee is transformed through the process of clinical pastoral supervision.

**Five Praxes of the Supervisee**

The first praxis of the supervisee is the supervisee's ministerial relationship with his/her patients, clients and/or parishioners.[13] Using a systemic lens, the professional relationship becomes the focus of reflection, education and transformation. This ministerial relationship requires developing a number of relational abilities. These are the ability to assess the client theologically and psycho-socially, and the ability to use basic ministerial skills such as joining, positive regard, active listening, summarizing and positive connotation.[14] In this ministerial relationship, the supervisee also develops the ability to discuss pastoral issues and use religious and spiritual resources to make various interventions that facilitate the pastoral goals of the patient. The supervisee in this ministerial relationship demonstrates appropriate professional boundaries. Clinical pastoral supervision seeks to transform the ministerial praxis of the supervisee.

In the first week of the educational unit, Mary demonstrated in her praxis with patients a professional distance. Joining seemed difficult for her with the ABIP patients. Her assessments of patients from a theological and psycho-social perspective were appropriate. Mary was assigned a number of male patients in their early twenties whose cognitive functioning was impaired. These patients had limited verbal skills and operated mainly on a feeling, metaphorical level. Mary struggled with some of these patients. Her cognitive, rational approach did not work well here. It created frustration in the helping relationship. Her work with these patients produced a number of critical incidents for Mary. On one occasion, a male patient in his twenties became very angry at Mary when she told him that he had to follow the rules of the ward. The incident upset her and created an impasse with the patient. Through supervision and the help from the social worker on the unit, Mary was able to listen to the concerns of the male patient on a feeling level. She was able to hear the needs of this male patient who had suffered many losses. This changed the relationship between her and the patient and some appropriate adaptation of the rules was made. By the end of the unit, Mary noted in her self-evaluation that she learned from these patients about developing better joining skills and a more relevant and concrete theology of suffering, as well as improving closeness and distance dynamics in ministry.

From a theological anthropology standpoint, Mary's hope was challenged by the reality of suffering that she saw on ABIP. Mary saw that some of the patients were abandoned. She also saw the severe limitations that the acquired brain injury placed on patients. She wondered if life was meaningful and hopeful for these people. How could these people hope in a God who had left them abandoned, brain injured and paralyzed? Mary's theology of Providence was challenged. This opened other questions about God's presence in her own life. Mary's questions reshaped her interpretation of faith, hope and care. Hope existed with hopelessness, faith included doubt, love included inadequacy and emptiness. This theological change suggested the inbreaking reign of God, a challenge to live in God's mystery. Rahner describes this mystery as God's Incomprehensibility and Uncontrollability,[15] which is eminently God's fullness. This experience of hopelessness, doubt and inadequacy challenged Mary's certainty and rationalism, which had become essential parts of her operational theology. The crisis precipitated by these ABIP patients offered a redemptive moment.

A second praxis to be transformed is the various relationships of the patients. Supervisees are ministers-in-training with the goal of facilitating the transformation of the pastoral goals of those in need (patients).[16] The ministry of the supervisee is to facilitate a greater living of the Great Commandment in those with whom the supervisee has developed a ministerial relationship. Clinical pastoral supervision strives to transform the praxis of the client, patient or parishioner in their many relationships. In transforming the praxis of the supervisee-patient relationship, the praxis of the patient and her/his other relationships is changed. In her work with patients on ABIP, Mary was both angered and saddened that some of the patients' families seem to abandon them. In supervision, Mary processed those feelings and discussed ways that she could change some of this. She listened to patients' concerns about their families and friends. She met with some of the family members of the patients in order to facilitate better communication and changing roles. For some patients, the relationship with family improved.

The third praxis that needs to be transformed is the relationship between the supervisor and supervisee.[17] That relationship is isomorphic to the relationship between the supervisee and the patient,[18] i.e., the supervisory relationship is a mirror of the supervisee-patient relationship. Often, in the supervisory relationship, transference and countertransference take place.[19] The praxis of the supervisory relationship like the other relationships in clinical pastoral supervision experiences change in terms of the response of the participants to God's grace. In terms of her relationship with her supervisor, Mary was an eager learner who focused on appropriate interventions with patients. She had come to learn and she wanted to maximize that learning. Mary was initially distant, rational and task orientated. Focusing on feelings and the relational component was more problematic. Supervision meant joining Mary with her goals and questions and facilitating her learning in the context of her ongoing narrative.[20]

The supervisory relationship can also be viewed developmentally.[21] There are three stages. In the first stage, the supervisee manifests dependence on the supervisor. Anxiety and compliance are high and autonomy is low. The supervisee focuses on learning what to do. In the second stage, the supervisee rebels in various ways from the authority of the supervisor, exercises high autonomy and focuses more on the pastoral relationship in helping. Here the emphasis is on being rather than doing. In the third stage, the supervisee acts independently, but still uses the supervisor to consult in terms of learning and difficulties. There is a balance between being and doing. Although this was Mary's first experience of clinical pastoral supervision in a hospital, she had experience in supervision with previous internships in ministry and in her professional life. In this context, she was in stage two, with some elements of stages one and three.

In terms of the narrative of her male supervisor, Mary posed many challenges. Their horizons were different. First, there was the difference in gender. Second, there was a difference in learning styles. Third, there was a difference in personality types, as well as ethnic and denominational backgrounds. In terms of theology, the supervisor and Mary differed. The difference in horizons produced some creative tension. There were some similarities in the narratives present in the different horizons between Mary and the supervisor. Mary drew on the supervisor's rational, left-brain approach. The supervisor found himself becoming more rational with Mary in supervision in struggling to offer intelligible answers to her questions. Mary struggled to articulate her needs in terms of peers and co-workers. The supervisor invited her to become more aware of what she needed. In weekly supervision, Mary brought an agenda, based on her learning goals. She wanted concrete help with her goals. Her eagerness increased the pace in supervision.

A fourth praxis is the supervisee's relationship to self. This includes awareness of the impact of the family-of-origin of the supervisee on the supervisee's praxis. This also involves the supervisee's values, assumptions, personality dynamics, belief systems and operational theology. Mary's learning focus is her professional goals. In the initial interview, she was anxious about focusing on her personal issues. In clinical pastoral supervision, there is some emphasis on facilitating the supervisee's awareness of personal values, assumptions and theology, as well as the intrapsychic and interpersonal dynamics that affect her ministerial functioning.[22] Supervision as education encourages the supervisee in developing a greater awareness of self and how self affects ministry.

The family-of-origin seminar was led by a female supervisor different from her individual supervisor. Mary connected well with the female supervisor, who shared a similar feminist orientation. The various conversations between Mary and the female supervisor produced some change in Mary's behaviour. She became more relaxed in the peer group and more focused on the feeling, metaphorical aspects of communication. According to *Women's Ways of Knowing*, Mary's knowledge was dominated by reason.[23] In the process of this educational unit, she utilized a knowledge that included reason and a connected knowing based on an inner voice and relationships.[24] Mary initially kept distance in both the peer group and in her relationship with patients. As the unit progressed, she became more open and vulnerable with peers and supervisors. Her sense of personal boundaries became more flexible. Her professional boundaries with patients and staff remained appropriate.

Narrative and hermeneutics are important items in this praxis of clinical pastoral supervision. Mary's narrative had many subplots to it. Using narrative within an adult educational approach requires helping Mary explore her narrative. One way is through the genogram in the family-of-origin seminar. This genogram helped Mary to become more aware of her family narrative and the legacies handed on to her by her family. The focus on hermeneutics means also examining the interpretation process present in the narrative, the living human document. How does Mary's hermeneutical process serve her and/or enslave her in competence in ministry? This hermeneutical narrative theory of practical theology also means that at an appropriate time in the learning process, Mary is offered some alternatives, some new directions to her goals. This is the process of deconstruction and co-construction of the narrative. This process is shaped by Mary's learning goals.

A fifth praxis in clinical pastoral supervision focuses on the supervisee's relationships with the various institutions and wider systems.[25] In a hospital context, this involves the politics of the particular hospital ward on which the supervisee is placed. This also includes the dynamics of the role of chaplaincy in the hospital system. In a congregational setting, the institutional praxis includes the relationship between the supervisee and the congregation as a whole, as well as the many committees and groups in the congregation. Sometimes, the relationship between the supervisee and the particular denominational administration is a focus of attention requiring some transformation. In the denominational relationship, the supervisee might need to reflect on his/her experience within the denomination and ways in which the supervisee adjusts to the denominational demands. The many wider systems and institutions that impact upon the ministry of the supervisee are part of the adequate transformed praxis. The staff on Mary's ABIP unit reported that Mary fit in well professionally.

One of the goals of learning in supervision is to facilitate competence in ministry with the belief that the whole praxis, including supervisor, supervisee and the context, learn.[26] Mary was the first student-chaplain to be placed on ABIP. Her presence educated the staff and patients about student chaplains. Some qualities and beliefs connected to competence in ministry are relational and systemic aspects involving the ethics of fairness, trustworthiness and give-and-take in striving to build the I-Thou relationship in supervision and ministry.[27] Mary exhibited some of these qualities.

The hospital institution in this case provides the learning context for the supervisee. The learning context is viewed as an essential educator for the supervisee.[28] This learning context forms the framework for many of the other relationships: the supervisee's experience, patients, peers, other supervisors, other professionals and the relationship to self. The supervisor facilitates in the supervisee a reflection on the learning that is taking place in the various relationships. The supervisory relationship encourages new behaviours and attitudes in ministry that are tested out in the learning context in order to facilitate competence. Thus the supervisory relationship is also crucial and connected to the learning context in facilitating the conversation about learning in the institution. Often the supervisory relationship becomes a safe place for the supervisee to discuss the challenges and successes in the whole learning context.

In this understanding of the context as the educator, a team approach in clinical pastoral supervision is utilized in order to facilitate transformation. This team consists of both women and men with different denominational backgrounds and different clinical, supervisory and theological orientations. Mary had a male supervisor for individual and verbatim supervision and interpersonal relations group (IPR). Mary also experienced other supervisors in the didactic seminars, the family-of-origin seminar, theological reflection and worship. In this educational approach, the supervisee receives feedback from many different supervisors as well as peers and patients in facilitating competence. Mary enjoyed the variety of supervisors and this variety facilitated her learning.

The fusion of horizons takes place in the various areas of praxis. It also takes place in other ways. There is the horizon of Mary's practice and the horizon of her theory, the horizons of her personal and professional identities, the horizon of her narrative and the horizons of the narrative of her patients, peers and supervisors. There is the ongoing conversation between Mary's narrative and the Christian narrative. Mary's experience on ABIP deconstructed some aspects of her interpretation of the Christian narrative and retrieved other hidden aspects.

## Transformation of Praxis

These five areas of praxis are the focus for transformation in clinical pastoral supervision. The transformation in the various relationships can take place in a variety of ways, in a variety of areas. Transformation is change in beliefs, values, self-awareness, feelings, behaviour, skills, theology, spirituality, relational ability and cognitive awareness and takes place within a relational context. Each person is responsible for his/her own transformation and yet is influenced to change by the relationship with others.

At the basis of the transformation of praxis, is the mystery of God's Incomprehensibility and Uncontrollability.[29] A Christian theological perspective sees that God's grace summons change in the supervisee in relationship with patients. Grace also summons change in the many other relationships. This change is towards greater love of God, neighbour and self. The call to a transformed praxis might not be recognized by the participants as a call from God. The ability to change the praxis might not be seen as God's grace. Nevertheless, the summons to change, the ability to do so and the transformed praxis are viewed as the work of grace.

This transformation of praxis includes a change in behaviour and thinking. As such, this transformation could mean a change in the various interpretations. As noted in the Introduction, practical theology deals with transformed praxis and can offer systematic and fundamental theology the benefits of truth from transformed praxis. The transformation is on many levels. It is interactive and systemic, and ultimately directed by the mystery of God's grace incarnated in the praxis. The participants have a role in this transformed praxis. They can refuse to listen to the call and proceed through the praxis of clinical pastoral supervision unchanged from the beginning. They can respond to some of the invited change. They can stop at any moment in this process of transformation. They can respond wholeheartedly in faith, hope and care to God's offer. This is the inbreaking of God's reign.

By the end of the educational experience, there was some change in Mary. She had developed her metaphorical, feeling side to a greater extent. She had learned some skills in terms of joining with people who are quite different from her. Her theology of suffering now included a sense of hopelessness and doubt, as well as faith and hope. Mary has explored family-of-origin issues around closeness and distance and has developed more ease with closeness in ministry. Concepts like boundaries, enmeshment and disengagement from the Structural school in family therapy became more concrete for Mary.

There was also a change in some institutional aspects. The nurse manager and doctor on the ABIP unit were pleased with Mary's work as a student-chaplain. They reported that she had a positive effect on the patients and their families and they requested that other student-chaplains be placed there. The supervisor experienced some change through the fusion of horizons with Mary. The supervisor found a greater facility in moving between the rational and nonrational in the praxis of clinical pastoral supervision. Mary's questions about suffering and the way that she articulated them also stayed. Does God abandon some persons?

# Chapter 7
# Conclusion

As the educational unit came to an end, the students were anxious about their evaluations. Bill, Sally, Mike, Laura and Mary had various experiences in the clinical pastoral placement. In fact, their learnings seemed so rich that they found it hard to capture all the learnings on paper. The students wondered how their supervisors–Alfred and Elizabeth–would evaluate their praxis. These students also wanted an opportunity to evaluate the praxis of their clinical pastoral supervisors. What criteria could they use in evaluating supervision?

In the Introduction, I asked three questions about the praxis of clinical pastoral supervision. First, what is distinctive about the praxis of clinical pastoral supervision? Second, what is an appropriate way of doing theology in the praxis of clinical pastoral supervision? Third, what is an adequate transformed praxis of clinical pastoral supervision? In answering these questions, I have analyzed 298 texts and examined a number of cases. I have taken a hermeneutical detour into the work of Charles V. Gerkin in examining his incarnational theology and its contribution to the praxis of clinical pastoral supervision. Chapter 6 presented the answer to the third question, which is an adequate transformed praxis. This concluding chapter summarizes and synthesizes the answers to the first two questions. This chapter also notes the limitations of this research and possible directions for future research.

**Distinctiveness of the Praxis of Clinical Pastoral Supervision**

The distinctiveness of the praxis of clinical pastoral supervision rests with a number of elements. First, clinical pastoral supervision utilizes concepts and language from the Christian fact to describe its praxis. Language is a crucial item because it both shapes and reflects experience. In this case, clinical pastoral supervision is located in language and interpretations from the Christian fact. This element has been influenced by the hermeneutical approach of Gerkin's theology. Without this standpoint, the praxis of clinical pastoral supervision loses an essential aspect of its distinctiveness.

Second, clinical pastoral supervision is grounded in the specific. That means focusing on cases, verbatims and vignettes within the practice of ministry. Essential to the clinical method is a focus on the concrete and what happens in the supervisory relationship, the supervisee and client/patient relationship, the supervisee and institutional relationship. This clinical method was developed in medicine and the social sciences. In clinical pastoral supervision, the influence of the clinical method is demonstrated in the texts from the social sciences approach. A focus on the clinical method is also a major concern of Gerkin's methodology. This method opposes reductionism. Clinical pastoral supervision utilizes the clinical method from the standpoint of practical theology. The practices of clinical pastoral supervision are faith in action.

A third distinctive aspect of clinical pastoral supervision is its ability to incorporate interpretations from other disciplines. Clinical pastoral supervision is not unilingual but multilingual, as it incorporates the insights and interpretations from medicine and the social sciences. Adult educational theory, object relations theory and systems theory are parts of this incorporation. The social sciences approach and Gerkin's theology bring out this aspect of clinical pastoral supervision.

A fourth distinctive element in the praxis of clinical pastoral supervision is its emphasis on narrative and hermeneutics. The narrative of the supervisee, the supervisor, the client/patient and the various cultural, family and institutional narratives are central items. These narratives are also embedded in a hermeneutical framework. Clinical pastoral supervision needs to focus on how these narratives are interpreted by the various people involved in the praxis of ministry. How are the people served and not served by the various interpretations? Gerkin's theology and the special interest approach emphasize this narrative hermeneutical element.

A fifth distinctive element in clinical pastoral supervision is its connection to the wider ministry of the church. Clinical pastoral supervision is education for ministry. This education for ministry can also be described as formation. As formation for ministry, the education requires connection to an ecclesial community. Supervision in a theological clinical context is understood as handing on the traditions of the ecclesial community and the traditions of Clinical Pastoral Education, as well as offering skills and interpretations from the social sciences. This connection to the church also includes the rich heritage of sacramental ministry, preaching, education, administration and spiritual direction. In some ways, the supervisor acts in an episcopal role in overseeing the supervisee in his/her formation in ministry in the clinical context. The hermeneutical approach, especially in those texts that endorse spiritual direction, have contributed in this area.

A sixth element of the distinctiveness of the praxis of clinical pastoral supervision is the emerging emphasis on gender, ethnicity and lay status. These items have contextualized theology and ministry, moving ministry and theology from universals to particulars. For example, there is a difference when the supervisee, supervisor or patient is a male or female, lay or ordained. These contextual items influence the kind of clinical pastoral supervision offered. The special interest approach has underlined these issues and noted the imbalance of power in the supervisory and helping relationships. This approach has challenged the praxis of clinical pastoral supervision to incorporate diverse experiences and also to be aware of the power differentials in the helping relationships.

## Theologizing in the Praxis of Clinical Pastoral Supervision

The use of theological language and interpretations from the Christian fact are key items in clinical pastoral supervision. Theologizing involves an interplay between praxis and theory from a multidisciplinary approach. Gerkin's praxis/theory/praxis method of practical theology is appropriate for this ministry. Theologizing begins with praxis and ends with a transformed praxis. This transformed praxis is developed through a critical conversation on the theory present in the practice. The theory embedded in practice is viewed from many disciplines and is multilingual. Such a theological method, then, requires a three-way conversation between the case, the interpretations from the Christian fact and the interpretations from the social sciences. This conversation produces a transformed praxis.

Theologizing within the praxis of clinical pastoral supervision also works within a narrative hermeneutical framework. This framework views experience in a narrative structure and interprets experience through narrative. In clinical pastoral supervision, there are a variety of narratives that are part of the theologizing: narratives of the supervisor, of the supervisee and of the client/patient with whom the supervisee ministers. This theologizing also includes all the other narratives involved in the concrete situation. For example, there are the many narratives within a particular denomination or religious belief. Institutions and communities have a plurality of narratives. Most important is the central narrative, which is the Christian narrative. The Christian narrative is the norm beyond all other norms and the basis of the praxis. The Christian narrative is the standpoint for interpreting all these other interacting narratives.

Such a theological method is correlational, expecting similarities and differences. These similarities and differences are expressed dialectically, analogically and identically in the relationship between theory and practice and the relationship among various interpretations from theory. At times, the correlation is different stressing the tension between dialectically opposite understandings. At other times, there are both similarities and differences in a more analogical fashion. Sometimes, there are legitimate similarities, identical correlations. All of these correlations, however, are meant to serve the praxis of clinical pastoral supervision in directing what must be done.

The fusion of horizons offers a relatively adequate explanation for the supervisory relationship. The narrative of the supervisor joins with the narrative of the supervisee on many levels. There is the level of professional development where the supervisor and supervisee bring their own horizons of professional development and support and challenge and transform each other through the supervisory relationship. There is also the level of personal development where the personal narrative of each connects and transforms the other. Another area is the supervisee's relationships with clients/patients and the institutions in which they operate. For the supervisee, there is a fusion of horizons in these helping relationships. The helpee is transformed by the pastoral care and counselling of the supervisee and the supervisee is transformed by the narrative of the helpee. In these helping relationships, the supervisor strives to facilitate in the supervisee a healthy interaction between the two horizons, while respecting professional boundaries.

The fusion of horizons is also an appropriate notion to describe the relationship of the supervisee with God and their own ecclesial communities. The supervisee and supervisor experience shifts in their interpretation of God's activity in the praxis. Some of this shift is due to the fusion of horizons that happens in the supervisory relationship, the helping relationship and the many examples of the supervisee's praxis. However, the inbreaking of God's horizon is not limited to this explanation. The shift can take place in many ways. Sometimes, there is also a shift in the relationship between the supervisee and the ecclesial community in which the supervisee is a member.

The fusion of horizons offers a new understanding of hermeneutics in clinical pastoral supervision. In connecting with others, the interpretation process can be altered. The facts of the narrative may remain the same, but the interpretation could change. The change in interpretation is significant for it can change the practice. The awareness of the interpretation process focuses on whether the person's interpretation of the narrative serves or enslaves the interpreter. Gerkin's use of the fusion of horizons along with the emphasis in the special interest texts draws attention to the role of hermeneutics in understanding one's narrative.

The fusion of horizons is also helpful in explaining the conversation between practice and theory. Clinical pastoral supervision develops the clinical ability of the supervisee. Along with this learning in the clinical area, there is also an awareness and discussion of theory present in the clinical praxis. Supervisees in this learning experience strive to integrate the practical and theoretical in developing an adequate praxis. The fusion of horizons is appropriate for describing the interaction between theory and practice. Theory that is completely different from practice is not helpful. Practice and theory that are completely the same are unilingual and lacking a critical edge. Theory and practice that are similar and different (analogical) offer a fusion that contains tension, critical awareness and dialogue.

## Limitations of the Research and Future Directions

This research is limited by a number of factors. First, there are the limitations of the texts that have been reviewed. These texts, which include those on the praxis of clinical pastoral supervision and the theology of Gerkin, were not written to answer the three questions. Their agendas were different. In the case of clinical pastoral supervision, some texts presented a philosophy of the praxis of clinical pastoral supervision. Other texts addressed specific issues in clinical pastoral supervision. The agenda of this book required searching underneath the text for assumptions, values and sources that might answer my questions. Some texts disclosed these answers easily. Others did not. This was also true of Gerkin's theology. While he has some written articles on the praxis of clinical pastoral supervision, he never officially addressed the three questions. The image of the building inspector inspecting a house after it is finished is an appropriate symbol for this investigative analysis. The research is limited by the disclosive power of these texts around these questions.

A second limitation of the research is the context in which the questions have been asked and the context in which the interpretations of these texts has taken place. This is a professional and academic theological context based in North America, and more particularly in Canada. One realizes the limitations of this context when one reads some of the texts from Kenya, Japan and Indonesia on clinical pastoral supervision. These texts address other issues and are involved in a different conversation about the praxis of clinical pastoral supervision. For example, dreams in Kenya play a role in directing the praxis. That is different from the context in which I work. I realize that my three questions and answers arise from this Canadian academic and professional theological context. These interpretations are also limited by the context, and the context limits the questions that are asked.

A third limitation is the ability of the interpreter. The interpreter is a white, middle-class Canadian male with an academic and clinical background. These characteristics, along with my formation as a clinical pastoral supervisor and practical theologian, shape and limit my interpretative ability. While I support many of the issues of the special interest approach, I do not share the characteristics of the group that are described. I am fascinated by the theology and clinical practice developing in these groups, especially around the issues of gender. Using the categories of this research, I locate myself with Gerkin's incarnational theology and with the hermeneutical approach. I share some of the concerns of the social sciences and special interest approaches and have incorporated some aspects of these approaches into my praxis of clinical pastoral supervision. This research has been limited by the standpoint of the interpreter.

In terms of future research, one area to pursue could be an ethnographic study of clinical pastoral supervisors regarding these three questions. These men and women who are clinical pastoral supervisors could offer their answers to the three questions, based on their clinical experience. The agenda of the three questions would be offered directly to those who practise in this field. A combination of ethnographic interviews and a Delphi study would seem to be appropriate. This is an area that I am interested in pursuing. Another area of future research could concentrate on the special interest approach. This approach had the smallest number of texts, yet this seems to be the growing interest in the field. What can the other approaches learn from this approach? If some of the issues of the special interest group are utilized, is it possible to have standardized training and norms? These are questions for future research.

At the beginning of this chapter, the students raised questions about the criteria for evaluating the praxis of clinical pastoral supervision. The five elements of an adequate praxis along with the five different praxes that need to be addressed offer some answers to their questions. In addition, the praxis of clinical pastoral supervision needs to be distinct from other forms of supervision. Clinical pastoral supervision should not be the same as pastoral supervision or clinical supervision. Otherwise, students could experience clinical pastoral supervision from the perspective of a clinical supervisor or pastoral supervisor.

Another criterion for evaluating clinical pastoral supervision is based on its method of theology. Is theologizing at the core of the praxis? If not, why not? How does one theologize using praxis? This book has offered a theological method from the work of Charles Gerkin. There are other ways of doing theology. Does the student find the theological method used in clinical pastoral supervision to be helpful?

A third criterion for evaluating the praxis of clinical pastoral supervision centres around the goal of greater love of God, others and self. Students need to ask if their experience of supervision fosters that. Clinical pastoral supervision is one aspect in the education for ministry. As such, clinical pastoral supervision offers a horizon in that educational process. Education does not end here; rather, the fusion of horizons continues.

# Glossary of Key Terms

**Analogical** is based on David Tracy's use of the term in *The Analogical Imagination: Christian Theology and the Culture of Pluralism*. Analogical refers to the similarities and differences between two interpretations. Usually, one interpretation is from theology and the other interpretation is from a non-theological source. The two interpretations are analogical when there are both similarities and differences between them.

**Applied theology** is the process where theology is developed from Scripture and/or Tradition and then applied to the pastoral situation. This is a theory/praxis methodology that is different from the practical theology utilized in this book.

**Christian Fact** refers to Scripture, Tradition, creeds, theologians and their theologies, sacraments, worship, denominational structures and teachings, administrative policies, Magisterium, lives of the saints, historic events, spiritual books, official prayers, etc., within Christianity. Christian fact is borrowed from David Tracy and is a short form to include all that is encompassed by Christianity.

**Clinical method** developed in medicine. Clinical comes from the Greek *"kline"* meaning by the bedside. In medicine, clinical refers to doctors in training moving from examining medical theory in the abstract to seeing it manifested in a particular patient. Clinical method focuses on what the practitioner needs to do in this specific moment. Skill development and feedback are important elements of the clinical method.

**Clinical pastoral supervision** developed from two sources: pastoral supervision, which has been part of the tradition of the church since its beginning, and clinical supervision, developed by the professional disciplines outside of theology in the last hundred years. Clinical pastoral supervision evolved into the Clinical Pastoral Education (CPE) movement as it drew on both these sources. Supervision involves oversight of a student's work from the Latin *super,* meaning over, and *videre,* meaning to see. Clinical pastoral supervision focuses on the clinical training of supervisees from a theological standpoint. It most often takes place in an institutional setting and/or pastoral counselling centre.

**Clinical supervision** is the training that takes place in the professions outside of theology. Clinical supervision focuses on skills and theory in dealing with the concrete person in a real situation. Clinical supervision is one of the important ways that a person is socialized into the profession.

**Dialectical** refers to interpretations that are mostly different. When interpretations are different, there is usually tension and challenge and little or no similarity between the horizons of meaning in which the interpretations are embedded. An example from Gerkin of dialectical is the tension between power and powerlessness.

**Fusion of horizons** describes the process of interpretation and interaction that takes place between text and interpreter. This concept was developed by Georg-Hans Gadamer. Gerkin uses this idea to understand and explain the process between pastoral caregiver and care receiver. The fusion of horizons can be identical, analogical or dialectical.

**Hermeneutical approach** describes certain texts in clinical pastoral supervision. These texts number 98 out of 298, or 34 percent. As such, they interpret supervision using theological concepts and language. Most often, these texts use interpretations from the social sciences but there are both similarities and differences between the theological concepts and those from the social sciences.

**Hermeneutical circle** is the interpretative process. This process involves an interaction between interpreter and text or situation. In this dissertation, Gerkin utilizes Ricoeur's understanding/explanation/understanding as well as Gadamer's fusion of horizons in interpreting pastoral praxis. The goal of the hermeneutical circle is to transform praxis.

**Horizon** is the standpoint of a particular person or text. Horizon is a term borrowed from Gadamer and refers to the meaning of a text and/or person. A text is embued with meaning and values and the interpreter also has a horizon of meaning that he/she brings to the text. One's horizon, or meanings, is often described in narrative forms.

**Identical** means similarity. Identical is one outcome of the fusion of horizons where the two horizons that meet are very similar, with little difference.

**Mystery** is drawn from the work of Karl Rahner. It underlines that to every case or praxis there is always more to be understood or explained. No one interpretation or series of interpretations grasps the full nature of what is going on in the situation. This *more* manifests God's Incomprehensibility and Uncontrollability. Every living human document demonstrates aspects of God's mystery.

**Narrative** is a means that humans utilize to make sense of experience. Narrative is often associated with story. Narrative stresses that fact and interpretation are interwoven and embedded in larger themes and stories. In narrative, events and facts are selected by the interpreter.

**Pastoral supervision** is a ministry of the church. This pastoral supervision most often takes place in a congregational setting and it focuses more on the theological than the clinical. The pastoral dimension of supervision emphasizes theology in the concrete in the living human documents as opposed to theology based only on the sacred texts of Scripture and Tradition.

**Pastoral theology** is synonymous with practical theology.

**Practical Theology** is a division within theology that focuses on the practices of ministry. According to Gerkin, practical theology has its own method, i.e., praxis/theory/praxis. Practical theology includes homiletics, liturgics, pastoral care and counselling, clinical pastoral supervision, Christian education, administration and other practices of ministry. Practical theology critically examines the various interpretations present in practice, i.e., praxis. Transformation is a key value in this praxis. Practical theology is synonymous with pastoral theology.

**Practices of ministry** are faith in action. Practice differs from praxis in that practice lacks critical reflection. For example, attending worship is a practice, an act of faith. Attending worship becomes praxis when this action of faith is critically examined. Pastoral counselling is a practice of ministry. Pastoral counselling becomes praxis when there is a critical reflection on the practice of pastoral counselling.

**Praxis** is critical reflection on the practices of ministry. The term was first developed by liberation theologians. In liberation theology, praxis involves critical social consciousness and an analysis of power interests. In this thesis, praxis is the critical awareness of theory present in practice. Praxis assumes that practice is theory-laden and is not applied theory. In this view, practice can be understood and explained from various standpoints and interpretations.

**Praxis/theory/praxis** is Gerkin's theological method. Gerkin borrowed from Ricoeur's hermeneutical method of understanding/explanation/understanding. For Gerkin, practical theology begins with a naive understanding of a case. Then, the case enters into a critical conversation with narrative theology, object relations theory, systems theory and hermeneutics. This critical conversation transforms the case into a new praxis.

**Social sciences approach** describes texts in clinical pastoral supervision that use interpretations mainly from medicine, psychiatry, psychology, family therapy and education. These texts number 144 out of 298, or 48 percent. Theological concepts are accommodated to the social science concepts, emphasizing similarities and not differences.

**Special interest approach** describes those texts in clinical pastoral supervision that emphasize the experience of a special group, e.g., females, persons of colour, lay persons, the poor, etc. The experience of the specific group is the lens for interpretation. These texts number 45 out of 298, or 12 percent. Often this special interest approach challenges the theory and theology of the dominant groups. Differences rather than similarities are emphasized.

**Understanding** is part of Ricoeur's hermeneutical method of understanding/explanation/understanding. This method is utilized in interpreting texts and actions. The interpreter develops an initial interpretation of a text. Then, critical theory is brought to the text in developing a better explanation. This leads to a second understanding of the text.

# Notes

## Introduction

1. Don Browning, *A Fundamental Practical Theology* (Philadelphia: Fortress Press, 1991, 6.
2. David Tracy, *The Analogical Imagination: Christian Theology and the Culture of Pluralism* (New York: Crossroad, 1989).
3. Allison Stokes, *Ministry After Freud* (New York: Pilgrim Press, 1985), 37-90.
4. Brooks Holifield, *A History of Pastoral Care in America* (Nashville: Abingdon Press, 1983).
5. Edward E. Thornton, *Professional Education for Ministry* (Nashville: Abingdon Press, 1970), 23-74, and "Clinical Pastoral Education (CPE)," in Rodney Hunter et al., eds., *Dictionary of Pastoral Care and Counselling* (Nashville: Abingdon Press, Press, 1991), 179-81.
6. Anton Boisen, *The Exploration of the Inner World* (New York: Harper and Brothers, 1936).
7. Kenneth Pohly, *Transforming the Rough Places: The Ministry of Supervision* (Dayton, OH: Whaleprints, 1993), 19-50; David Steere, "Supervision Among the Helping Professions," in David Steere, ed., *The Supervision of Pastoral Care* (Louisville: Westminster/John Knox Press, 1989), 39-64.
8. Charles V. Gerkin, *Widening the Horizons* (Philadelphia: Westminster Press, 1986), 61-66.
9. Charles V. Gerkin, "Faith and Praxis: Pastoral Counselling's Hermeneutical Problem," *Pastoral Psychology*, 35, 1 (Fall 1986).
10. David Tracy, "Practical Theology in the Situation of Global Pluralism," in L.S. Mudge and J.N. Poling, eds., *Formation and Reflection* (Philadelphia: Fortress Press, 1987), 139.

## Chapter 1

1. John Patton, "The 'Holy Complexity' of the Clinical: Some Reflections on Pastoral Supervision," *Journal of Supervision and Training in Ministry* 13 (1991): 243.
2. Malcolm Knowles, *The Modern Practice of Adult Education: From Pedagogy to Andragogy* (New York: Cambridge Adult Education, 1980).
3. George Fitchett, in his article on the philosophy of clinical pastoral supervision titled "The Paradoxical Nature of CPE," *Journal of Supervision and Training in Ministry* 3 (1980): 57-71, notes the tension between professional and personal growth in CPE. He argues that both are a necessary part of CPE. The joining of professional and personal growth expresses a dialectical tension articulated in the paradoxical nature of CPE training.
4. Peter VanKatwyk, "The Helping Styles Inventory: A Tool in Supervised Pastoral Education," *The Journal of Pastoral Care* 42, 4 (Winter 1988): 324.
5. Tjaard Hommes, "Supervision as Theological Method," *The Journal of Pastoral Care* 31 (September 1971): 164-71.
6. E. B. Holifield, *A History of Pastoral Care in America*, 201-209; O. Strunk, Jr., "Emanuel Movement," in *Dictionary of Pastoral Care and Counselling*, 350.
7. E. E. Thornton, *Professional Education for Ministry*, 40-75, and "Clinical Pastoral Education (CPE)," in *Dictionary of Pastoral Care and Counselling*, 178. In his list of the founders of CPE, Thornton excludes Helen Flanders Dunbar.
8. Allison Stokes, *Ministry After Freud*, 52.

9   Ibid.
10  E. E. Thornton, "Clinical Pastoral Education (CPE)," in *Dictionary of Pastoral Care and Counselling*, 178.
11  E. E. Thornton, *Professional Education for Ministry*, 99-112, and "Clinical Pastoral Education (CPE)," in *Dictionary of Pastoral Care and Counselling*, 178.
12  E. E. Thornton, "Clinical Pastoral Education (CPE)," in *Dictionary of Pastoral Counselling*, 178.
13  Ibid., 179.
14  Allison Stokes, *Ministry After Freud*, 185.
15  Archie MacLachlan, "Canadian Pastoral Care Movement," in *Dictionary of Pastoral Care and Counselling*, 118.
16  Ibid. MacLachlan notes that there is some controversy over the beginnings of SPE in Canada. The first unit was begun in Hamilton at the Sanitorium on the mountain in 1952, but in 1951, Earle MacKnight supervised one student, Charles Taylor, in Halifax, Nova Scotia, at Royal Victoria Hospital. MacKnight resided in Fredericton, New Brunswick, and did the supervision through written correspondence with Taylor. "Canadian Pastoral Care Movement," in *Dictionary of Pastoral Care and Counselling*, 118.
17  Elizabeth Kilbourn, "Canadian Association for Pastoral Education," in *Dictionary of Pastoral Care and Counselling*, 116-17.
18  *Certification Standards Procedures and Guidelines for the Canadian Association for Pastoral Practice and Education* (Toronto, ON: CAPPE, 1996), 4, 1A1.
19  Ibid., 4, 1B1-4.
20  Ibid., 4, 1B1-4.
21  *Certification Standards Procedures and Guidelines for the Canadian Association for Pastoral Practice and Education* (Toronto, ON: CAPPE, 1996), 4, 1C1.
22  Kenneth Pohly, *Transforming the Rough Places: The Ministry of Supervision*, 10-11.
23  Ibid., 10.
24  John Patton, "Pastoral Supervision and Theology," *Journal of Supervision and Training in Ministry* 8 (1986): 59-71.
25  Ibid.
26  Glen Asquith, "Case Study Method," in *Dictionary of Pastoral Care and Counselling*, 123-27.
27  Donald S. Browning, "Introduction to Pastoral Counselling," in Robert J. Wicks et al., eds., *Clinical Handbook of Pastoral Counselling* (New York: Paulist Press, 1985): 5-13.
28  "A Coherent Theory of Education Relevant for CPE," *Journal of Supervision and Training in Ministry* 6: 73-108.
29  Second Edition (New York: International Universities Press, 1972).
30  Ibid., 11-15.
31  "Training in Bowen Theory," in Howard A. Liddle et al., *Handbook of Family Therapy Training and Supervision,* (New York: Guilford Press, 1988), 62-77. Papero notes: "The single most important goal of training is to assist the learner in understanding the concept of differentiation of self and to assist each person to go as far as he or she is able toward increased personal differentiation.... Clinical skill is believed to derive directly from the effort with one's own family," 71.
32  George Fitchett, "A Coherent Theory of Education Relevant for CPE," 101.
33  (New York: Appleton-Century-Crofts, 1972).
34  (New York: Basic Books, 1975).
35  David Steere, "Supervision Among the Helping Professions," in Steere, ed., *The Supervision of Pastoral Care*. In his description of supervision in the other professions, Kenneth Pohly does not separate the psychodynamic tradition of supervision from clinical supervision and clinical psychology. In Pohly's analysis,

both traditions in clinical supervision are viewed as one. See *Transforming the Rough Places: The Ministry of Supervision*, 19-50.
36. "Supervision Among the Helping Professions," 50.
37. (Englewood Cliffs, NJ: Prentice-Hall, 1981).
38. Kenneth Pohly, *Transforming the Rough Places: The Ministry of Supervision*, 24.
39. (San Francisco: Jossey-Bass, 1977).
40. David Steere, "Supervision Among the Helping Professions," in Steere, ed., *The Supervision of Pastoral Care*, 49.
41. (New York: Columbia University Press, 1976).
42. Howard Liddle, Douglas C. Breunlin and Richard C. Schwartz, eds., *A Handbook of Family Therapy Training and Supervision* (New York: Guilford Press, 1988). Papers are presented on training and supervision from Structural, Milan, Bowen, Brief Therapy, Strategic, Psychodynamic and Functional approaches. The editors acknowledge that other approaches in family therapy are evolving and influencing clinical supervision in family therapy.
43. *The AAMFT Approved Supervisor Designation: Standards and Responsibilities*, (Washington, DC: AAMFT, 1991), 32.
44. *AAMFT Code of Ethics* (Washington, DC: AAMFT, 1991), #4.1, 5.
45. Richard C. Schwartz, Howard Liddle, and Douglas C. Breunlin, "Muddles in Live Supervision," in Liddle et al., *A Handbook of Family Therapy Training and Supervision*, 183-93.
46. Richard C. Schwartz, "The Trainer-Trainee Relationship in Family Therapy Training," in Liddle et al., *A Handbook of Family Therapy Training and Supervision*, 172-82.
47. "The Therapeutic Tradition's Theological and Ethical Commitments Viewed Through Its Pedagogical Practices: A Tradition in Transition," in Pamela Couture and Rodney Hunter, eds., *Pastoral Care and Social Conflict* (Nashville: Abingdon Press, 1995), 33.

## Chapter 2

1. Carole Somers-Clark and Logan Jones, "The Clinical Rhombus Revisited: Learning through Resistance and Change," *The Journal of Pastoral Care* 47, 3 (Fall 1993): 207-15.
2. Calvin Kropp et al., "A Critique from a Relational Perspective," *Journal of Supervision and Training in Ministry* 17 (1996): 48-58.
3. Peter VanKatwyk, "The Helping Styles Inventory: An Update," *The Journal of Pastoral Care* 49, 4 (Winter 1995): 375-82.
4. Bruce Hartung, "The Capacity to Enter Latency in Learning Pastoral Psychotherapy," in *Journal of Supervision and Training in Ministry* 17 (1996): 48-58.
5. Gary Redcliffe, "Post-Liberal Foundations for Pastoral Care," in Adrian M. Visscher, ed., *Pastoral Studies in the University Setting* (Ottawa: University of Ottawa Press, 1988), 211-21. Redcliffe argues that the liberal approach to theology accommodates the insights developed by the culture. This theological approach endorses the values of progress and personalism and sees God's presence unfolding in society and the social sciences. Here, theological interpretations endorse the interpretations from the social sciences.
6. Barry Estadt et al., *The Art of Clinical Pastoral Supervision: A Pastoral Counselling Perspective* (New York: Paulist Press, 1987), 195-211.
7. Alfred A. Merwald, "Supervision of the Psychological Self," *Journal of Supervision and Training in Ministry* 5 (1982): 167-80.

8   See Delton Glebe, "Law and Gospel in Pastoral Counselling," *Pastoral Psychology* (December 1965): 45-50. In this paper, Glebe argues that many in pastoral counselling have equated acceptance and unconditional regard with grace. He points out the difference between grace and unconditional regard in that grace includes God's acceptance and judgment. The notion of acceptance and unconditional regard is both similar and different from the theological notion of grace.
9   Jack Thomas, "A Theory of Education Relevant for CPE," *Journal of Supervision and Training in Ministry* 5 (1982): 15-23.
10  Ibid.
11  Don Capps, *Pastoral Care and Hermeneutics* (Philadelphia: Fortress Press, 1984), 37-61.
12  David Tracy, *Plurality and Ambiguity* (San Francisco: Harper and Row, 1987).
13  David Tracy, *The Analogical Imagination: Christian Theology and the Culture of Pluralism* (New York: Crossroad, 1981), 71.
14  Tjaard G. Hommes, "Supervision as Theological Method," *The Journal of Pastoral Care* 31 (September 1987): 150-57.
15  Richard McBrien, "Understanding Human Existence" and "Toward a Theology of Human Existence," in *Catholicism*, Vol. 1, 101-83. Also see C.B. Kline, "Theological Anthropology, Discipline of," *Dictionary of Pastoral Care and Counselling*, 1259.
16  Richard McBrien, "Toward a Theology of Human Existence," 141-83.
17  The 1987 edition of the *Journal of Supervision and Training in Ministry* is devoted to narrative theology and clinical pastoral supervision. In that edition, there are many articles that pertain to narrative and theological anthropology. See the following articles from that edition: Beth Burbank, "Reflecting Upon Stories as a Way of Doing Theology in CPE"; William Nelson, "A Narrative Approach to Theological Reflection"; Gerald Cowing Johnson, "Parable: The Bridge Between Theology and Psychology in Supervision." In this edition, Beth Burbank presents a clinical vignette of an interaction between supervisor and supervisee. A number of narrative theologians, such as Lauree Hersch Meyer, John Dominic Crossan and John Shea, respond to the vignette. For books on the topic, see Kenneth Pohly, *Transforming the Rough Places: The Ministry of Supervision.*
18  Mark Jensen, "Life Histories and Narrative Theology," *The Supervision of Pastoral Care*, 114-28.
19  *Transforming the Rough Places: The Ministry of Supervision.*
20  Don Browning, *The Moral Context of Pastoral Care* (Philadelphia: Fortress Press, 1976); *Religious Ethics and Pastoral Care* (Philadelphia: Fortress Press, 1983); David Tracy, *The Analogical Imagination: Christian Theology and the Culture of Pluralism.*
21  Marie McCarthy and David B. McCurdy, "Symposium: Supervision and Training as an Ethical Endeavour," *Journal of Supervision and Training in Ministry* 12 (1990): 106-10.
22  Chris Schlauch, "Functioning as an Ethicist in Supervision: Casting the Questions," *Journal of Supervision and Training in Ministry* 12 (1990): 111-31.
23  Ibid., 126.
24  Charles Gerkin's first published article, in 1953, was co-authored with George H. Weber; "A Religious Story Test: Some Findings with Delinquent Boys," *The Journal of Pastoral Care* 7, 2 (1953): 77-90.
25  "The Identity of the Pastoral Supervisor," *The Pastoral Supervisor and His Identity*, Proceedings of the National Conference on Clinical Pastoral Education (1966); "Clinical Pastoral Education and Social Change," *The Journal of Pastoral Care* (September 1971); "Power and Powerlessness in Clinical Pastoral Education," *The Journal of Pastoral Care* 34 (June 1980): 114-24.

26  Gerkin began full-time teaching at Candler School of Theology at Emory University in Atlanta, Georgia, in 1970.
27  *Widening the Horizons: Pastoral Responses to a Fragmented Society.*
28  In his address entitled "Charles V. Gerkin, Pastoral Theologian of the Year," *Pastoral Psychology* 36, 1 (Fall 1987): 3-9, Rodney Hunter describes a group of practical theologians who are small in number but have begun a "highly important revision of the clinical pastoral tradition." In this group, Hunter includes Don Browning, Thomas Oden, Donald Capps, Paul Pruyser, James Fowler and Charles Gerkin. Gerkin received the award of Pastoral Theologian of the Year from *Pastoral Psychology* for 1987.
29  Pamela Couture and Rodney Hunter, "Charles V. Gerkin," in Couture and Hunter, eds., *Pastoral Care and Social Conflict*, 7-10.
30  Vol. 6, 1983.
31  Elizabeth Meakes and Thomas St. James O'Connor, "Miriam Dancing and With Leprosy: Women's Experience of Supervision in CAPE," *Pastoral Sciences* 12 (1993): 25-40.
32  Toronto, ON: CAPPE.
33  Julia Jewett and Emily Haight, "The Emergence of Feminine Consciousness in Supervision," *Journal of Supervision and Training in Ministry* 6 (1983): 164-74.
34  "Black Africa–A Pioneer Venture," *Journal of Supervision and Training in Ministry* 12 (1990): 76-80.
35  Ibid., 76.
36  "Supervision and Training for Ministry in Indonesia," *Journal of Supervision and Training in Ministry* 12 (1990): 83-86.
37  *Transforming the Rough Places: The Ministry of Supervision*, 8-9.
38  Charles A. Van Wagner II, "Supervision of Lay Pastoral Care," *The Journal of Pastoral Care* 31, 3 (1977): 158-63.
39  Louis B.Weeks, "Supervising Teachers in a Christian Education Program," in Steere, ed., *The Supervision of Pastoral Care*, 250-61.
40  Grayson L.Tucker Jr., "Supervision of Church Volunteers in the Local Congregation," *The Supervision of Pastoral Care*, 236-49.

**Chapter 3**

1  Regis Duffy, *Roman Catholic Theology of Pastoral Care* (Philadelphia: Fortress Press, 1983); J.A. Melloh, "Incarnational Theology and Pastoral Care (Roman Catholicism)," in Hunter et al., *Dictionary of Pastoral Care and Counselling*, 573-74.
2  William A.Clebsch and Charles R. Jaekle, *Pastoral Care in Historical Perspective* (Englewood Cliffs, NJ: Prentice-Hall, 1964).
3  Karl Rahner, *Foundations of Christian Faith* (New York: Crossroad, 1989), 402-31.
4  Vatican II has underlined the ministry of all baptized persons within the Roman Catholic Church. Ministry is not limited to those who have been ordained. The Dogmatic Constitution on the Church (Lumen Gentium) and the Decree on the Apostolate of Lay People (Apostolicam Actuositatem) affirm the call of lay persons in the church to ministry. See Austin Flannery, ed., *Vatican Council II* (Collegeville, MN: Liturgical Press, 1975), 350-427, 766-99. This call to ministry by the Magisterium has meant that many lay Roman Catholics have pursued clinical training and exercised their ministry in the pastoral care field.
5  Carroll A. Wise, *The Meaning of Pastoral Care* (New York: Harper and Row, 1966), 26.

# Notes

6 For Gerkin's relationship with Carroll Wise and the connection with Wise's theology see Gerkin's book review entitled "Responding to Living Human Experience at the Point of Need: Remembering Carroll Wise," *The Journal of Pastoral Care* 42, 4 (Winter 1988). This book review is on *At the Point of Need: Living Human Experience: Essays in Honour of Carroll A. Wise* (Lanham, MD: University Press, 1988).

7 Charles V. Gerkin, "Incarnational Theology and Pastoral Care (Protestantism)," in *Dictionary of Pastoral Care and Counselling*, 573.

8 *Crisis Experience in Modern Life* (Nashville: Abingdon Press, 1979), 32.

9 Ibid., 33.

10 James Poling argues that much of Gerkin's thought is similar to process theology. In process theology, both God and humans change. See James N. Poling, "A Critical Appraisal of Charles V. Gerkin's Pastoral Theology," *Pastoral Psychology* 37, 2 (Winter 1988).

11 Both Rodney Hunter and James N. Poling argue that meaning is the central image of Gerkin's theology. I see it differently. For me, the incarnation described as the fusion of horizons is central to Gerkin's thought. Gerkin is fundamentally a pastor rooted in the interpretations from the Christian fact. While he uses meaning-making to describe the fusion of horizons, there is an underlying belief in God's presence in all reality (although also different from that reality). The divine presence is waiting to connect with human experience. All crisis experiences offer the possibility of an encounter with God. The cross, in Gerkin's theology, is the prime example of God's offer in the midst of meaninglessness. See Rodney Hunter, "Charles V. Gerkin: Pastoral Theologian of the Year," *Pastoral Psychology* 36, 1 (Fall 1987); James N. Poling, "A Critical Appraisal of Charles Gerkin's Pastoral Theology," *Pastoral Psychology* 37, 2 (Winter 1988).

In a later appraisal of Gerkin's theology, Pamela Couture and Rodney Hunter add that Gerkin is also concerned about social change. See *"Charles V. Gerkin"* in Couture and Hunter, eds., *Pastoral Care and Social Conflict*, 7-10.

12 Rebecca Chopp is critical of the cognitive claims that Tillich and Tracy provide for Christianity in the contemporary society. She claims that these cognitive claims serve the white Euro-American university males. She argues, on the other hand, for a theology of liberation that serves the oppressed. See "Practical Theology and Liberation," in Mudge and Poling, eds., *Formation and Reflection*, 120-38.

13 "A Critical Appraisal of Charles Gerkin's Pastoral Theology," *Pastoral Psychology* 37, 2 (Winter 1988): 86.

14 Paul Tillich, *The Protestant Era* (Chicago: University of Chicago Press, 1957), 161-84.

15 In Mark's gospel, the divine nature of Jesus is kept a secret and is known as the Messianic Secret. The evil spirits know this secret, but are forced to be quiet about it. Jesus' divine nature is slowly revealed in his acts. This is Christology from below. See Mk. 1:34.

16 *The Living Human Document*, 98.

17 James Poling, "A Critical Appraisal of Charles Gerkin's Pastoral Theology," *Pastoral Psychology* 37, 2 (Winter 1988): 85-96.

18 *The Living Human Document*, Figure 2, 107.

19 "Power and Powerlessness in Clinical Pastoral Education," *The Journal of Pastoral Care* 34 (1980): 122.

20 "A Religious Story Test: Some Findings with Delinquent Boys," *The Journal of Pastoral Care* 7, 2 (1953): 77-90.

21 Charles V. Gerkin and Donald Cox, "Religious Story Test as a Tool for Evaluating Religious Growth," *The Journal of Pastoral Care* 9 (Spring 1955): 8-13.

22 *Crisis Experience in Modern Life*, 110-61.

23 *Crisis Experience in Modern Life*, 208-209, 245-46, 323-24; *The Living Human Document*, 99-100, 105.
24 Charles V. Gerkin, *Prophetic Pastoral Practice: A Christian Vision of Life Together* (Nashville: Abingdon Press, 1991), 401.
25 *The Living Human Document*, 50.
26 Ibid., 80.
27 *Crisis Experience in Modern Life*, 60.
28 *Widening the Horizons*, 69.
29 *The Living Human Document*, 113-15.
30 "Implicit and Explicit Faith: Practical Theology in Dialogue with Object Relations Theory," *Pastoral Sciences* (Fall 1988).
31 "Response to James Poling's 'A Critical Appraisal of Charles V. Gerkin's Pastoral Theology,' " *Pastoral Psychology* 37 (Winter 1988): 98.
32 Ibid., 102.
33 Ibid., 106-107.
34 *The Living Human Document*, 112.
35 *Widening the Horizons*, 76-97.
36 Ibid.
37 Ibid., 71.
38 *Prophetic Pastoral Practice*, 48.
39 Ibid., 58.
40 Ibid., 50-53, 62-66.
41 *The Living Human Document*, 39.
42 Ibid., 141n5.
43 Ibid., 66.
44 *The Living Human Document*, 124-56.
45 *The Living Human Document*, 153.

## Chapter 4

1 *The Living Human Document*, 97-117. Gerkin also draws on Boisen's image of "the living human document." In his book *The Living Human Document*, Gerkin presents both the metaphors of the "living human document" and "life of the soul." In the book, he tends to concentrate, however, on the "life of the soul." Certainly "soul" is a term used for centuries in theology. The term "living human document" was coined by Boisen and it does not have any specifically theological notion about it. Boisen argues that practical theologians need to pay particular attention to human beings "living human documents" as well as attending to the written documents of faith like Scripture. In his discussion of "ego" and "self," Gerkin does not compare and contrast these terms with the "living human document," but to the "soul." Life of the soul is his dominant notion.
2 *The Living Human Document*, 50.
3 Gerkin draws on Moltmann's notion of the eschatological identity. *The Living Human Document*, 68-70. For Moltmann, eschatological identity means that the human person lives in the limitations of this world and yet realizes that they are bound in a pilgrimage towards a Kingdom that is not yet. Somehow, even in the present there are glimpses of the final promise. This eschatological identity is rooted in the here-and-now and also transcends it through the promise of God's inbreaking Reign.
4 *The Living Human Document*, 135.
5 See Rodney Hunter, "Charles Gerkin: Pastoral Theologian of the Year," *Pastoral Psychology* 36, 1 (Fall 1987); James N. Poling, "A Critical Appraisal of Charles Gerkin's Pastoral Theology," *Pastoral Psychology* 37, 2 (Winter 1988); Charles V.

Gerkin, "A Response to James Poling's 'Critical Appraisal of Charles Gerkin's Pastoral Theology,' " *Pastoral Psychology* 37, 2 (Winter 1988).
6  Many of Gerkin's case examples show these effects of racism, sexism and poverty. See *Prophetic Pastoral Practice*, 72-87, 36-39, 50-53, 62-64. See also Pamela Couture and Rodney Hunter, "Charles V. Gerkin," in Couture and Hunter, eds., *Pastoral Care and Social Conflict*, 7-10.
7  James N. Poling, "A Critical Appraisal of Charles Gerkin's Pastoral Theology," *Pastoral Psychology* 37, 2 (Winter 1988).
8  Charles V. Gerkin, "A Response to James Poling's 'A Critical Appraisal of Charles V. Gerkin's Pastoral Theology,' " *Pastoral Psychology* 37, 2 (Winter 1988).
9  Gerkin especially sees this interruption in crisis moments in life. These moments disclose in a mysterious way God's presence and upset our usual way of thinking and experiencing life. David Tracy calls these moments interruptions when the normal way of thinking, feeling and acting are not helpful in some instances. See *Plurality and Ambiguity* (San Francisco: Harper and Row, 1987).
10  *Widening the Horizons*, 76-97.
11  Paul Tillich, *Dynamics of Faith* (New York: Harper and Row, 1957), 1-30.
12  Charles Gerkin, "Faith and Praxis: Pastoral Counselling's Hermeneutical Problem," *Pastoral Psychology* 35, 1 (Fall 1986): 6.
13  *Crisis Experience in Modern Life*, 137.
14  Ibid., 136-40.
15  Ibid., 30-31, 197-201.
16  See *Crisis Experience in Modern Life*, 101-103, 322.
17  Ibid., 202.
18  "On the Art of Caring," *The Journal of Pastoral Care* 45, 4 (Winter 1991): 205.
19  Ibid., 405.
20  Erik Erikson, *Identity and the Life Cycle* (New York: W.W. Norton and Company, 1959).
21  *The Living Human Document*, 99-105.
22  Gerkin draws on a number of writers and therapists in family systems therapy. Most important are Clifford Sager, *Marriage Contracts and Couple Therapy* (New York: Bruner/Mazel, 1976); Ivan Boszormenyi-Nagy and Geraldine Sparks, *Invisible Loyalties* (New York: Harper, 1973); Salvatore Minuchin, *Families and Family Therapy* (Cambridge: Harvard University Press, 1974)
23  *Crisis Experience in Modern Life*, Figure 1, 40; Figure 14, 233; *The Living Human Document*, Figure 2, 106-107; *Widening the Horizons*, Figure 2, 69.
24  *The Living Human Document*, 77-96.
25  Charles V. Gerkin, "Projective Identification and the Image of God: Reflections on Object Relations Theory and the Psychology of Religion," in Brian H. Childs and David W. Waanders, eds., *The Treasure of Earthen Vessels: Explorations in Theological Anthropology* (Louisville: Westminster John Knox Press, 1994), 52-65.
26  *Crisis Experience in Modern Life*, 110-41.
27  *The Living Human Document*, 77-96. Also see "Implicit and Explicit Faith: Practical Theology in Dialogue with Object Relations Theory," *Pastoral Sciences* (Fall 1988).
28  *The Living Human Document*, 124f.
29  *Prophetic Pastoral Practice*, 17-19.
30  "Response to James Poling, 'A Critical Appraisal of Charles V. Gerkin's Pastoral Theology,' " *Pastoral Psychology* 37, 2 (Winter 1988).
31  *Prophetic Pastoral Practice*, 17.
32  *The Living Human Document*, 104.

33 "Faith and Praxis: Pastoral Counselling's Hermeneutical Problem," *Pastoral Psychology* 35, 1 (Fall 1986): 7.
34 Ibid., 6.

## Chapter 5

1. Thomas Oden, *The Care of Souls in the Classic Tradition* (Philadelphia: Fortress Press, 1984); *Pastoral Counselling*, Classic Pastoral Care Series 3 (New York: Crossroad Publishing,1987).
2. Rodney J. Hunter and John Patton, "The Therapeutic Tradition's Theological and Ethical Commitments Viewed Through Its Pedagogical Practices: A Tradition in Transition," in *Pastoral Care and Social Conflict*, 35-37.
3. George Fitchett, "The Paradoxical Nature of CPE," *Journal of Supervision and Training in Ministry* 3 (1980): 57-71.
4. Charles Gerkin, "Power and Powerlessness in Clinical Pastoral Education," *Journal of Pastoral Care* (Summer, 1980).
5. See Janet O. Foy, "Women in Pastoral Counselling: The Clients, the Therapist and the Supervisor," *Journal of Supervision and Training in Ministry* 6 (1983): 175-86; Julia Jewett and Emily Haight, "The Emergence of Feminine Consciousness in Supervision," *Journal of Supervision and Training in Ministry* 6 (1983): 164-74.
6. Don Browning, *A Fundamental Practical Theology*.
7. George Fitchett, "A Coherent Theory of Education Relevant for CPE," *Journal of Supervision and Training in Ministry* 6 (1983): 164-74.
8. Kenneth Mitchell, "In the Translator's House: A Book Review of *The Living Human Document*," *The Journal of Pastoral Care* 38, 1 (1984): 70.
9. See Anthony W. Seaton-Johnson and Craig Everett, "An Analysis of Clinical Pastoral Education Supervisors: Their Identities, Roles and Resources," *The Journal of Pastoral Care* 34 (September 1980): 148-58.
10. Thomas St. James O'Connor, "Ministry Without a Future: A Pastoral Care Approach with Patients with Senile Dementia," *Journal of Pastoral Care* 46, 1 (Spring 1992): 5-12.
11. Ibid., 12.
12. James Poling, "A Critical Appraisal of Charles V. Gerkin's Pastoral Theology," *Pastoral Psychology* 37, 2 (Winter 1988).
13. "Response to James Poling, 'A Critical Appraisal of Charles V. Gerkin's Pastoral Theology,' " *Pastoral Psychology* 37, 2 (Winter 1988).
14. Elizabeth Meakes and Thomas O'Connor, "Miriam Dancing and With Leprosy: Women's Experience of Supervision in CAPE," *Pastoral Sciences* 12 (1993): 25-39.
15. Charles V. Gerkin, "Power and Powerlessness in CPE Supervision," *The Journal of Pastoral Care* (Summer 1980).
16. *Prophetic Pastoral Practice*, 135.
17. Avery Dulles, *Models of the Church* (Garden City, NY: Doubleday and Co., 1974), 83-96.
18. Rodney Hunter, "The Therapeutic Tradition of Pastoral Care and Counselling," in *Pastoral Care and Social Conflict*, 17-31.

## Chapter 6

1. I. Myers-Briggs, *The Myers-Briggs Type Indicator Manual* (Princeton, NJ: Educational Testing Service, 1962).

## Notes 115

2   David Kolb, *Learning Styles Inventory; Technical Manual* (Boston: McBer and Co., 1976).
3   Peter VanKatwyk, "The Helping Styles Inventory: A Tool for Supervised Pastoral Education," *The Journal of Pastoral Care* 43, 4 (Winter 1988): 319-28.
4   Charles V. Gerkin, *The Living Human Document*, 53. See also James N. Poling and A.J. van den Blink, "Symposium: Theology and Supervision Introduction," *Dictionary of Pastoral Care and Counselling* 13 (1991): 149-53. The hermeneutical approach begins and ends in the Christian fact. That is its standpoint.
5   Charles V. Gerkin, *The Living Human Document*.
6   Don Brundage and Dorothy MacKeracher, *Adult Learning Principles and their Application to Program Planning* (Queen's Park, Toronto: Ministry of Education, 1980); Malcolm Knowles, *The Modern Practice of Adult Education* (rev.) (New York: Cambridge, 1980); Thomas St. James O'Connor "Take What You Can and Dance: Adult Education Theory and Pastoral Supervision," *Journal of Supervision and Training in Ministry* 15 (1994): 50-62.
7   Edwin A. Hoover, "Pastoral Supervision as an Interpersonal Experience," *The Journal of Pastoral Care* 31 (September 1971): 164-71.
8   Malcolm Knowles, *The Modern Practice of Adult Education*, 57.
9   G. H. Asquith, "Case Study Method," in Hunter et al., *Dictionary of Pastoral Care and Counselling*, 123-26. Gerkin is strong in rooting his theology in cases and avoiding reductionism. See Charles V. Gerkin, "Faith and Praxis: Pastoral Counselling's Hermeneutical Problem," *Pastoral Psychology* 35, 1 (Fall 1986).
10  Charles V. Gerkin, *The Living Human Document*; *Widening the Horizons*. The special interest approach values the contextual issues of gender, "race," ethnicity, denomination and ordained vs. lay. This approach advocates that these issues shape clinical pastoral supervision.
11  Charles V. Gerkin, *Widening the Horizons*.
12  I am using David Tracy's notion of relative adequacy. Tracy develops this notion in interpreting written texts. He argues that a relatively adequate interpretation of a text is acceptable. I am using the notion of adequate to describe praxis. For Tracy's understanding of relatively adequate, see *Plurality and Ambiguity*, 22-23.
13  Peter VanKatwyk, "The Helping Styles Inventory: A Tool for Supervised Pastoral Education," *The Journal of Pastoral Care* 42, 4 (Winter 1988): 319-29; Howard Liddle, "Systemic Supervision: Conceptual Overlays and Pragmatic Guidelines," in Liddle et al., *Handbook of Family Therapy Training and Supervision*, 153-71.
14  Terry H. Kriesel, "Training in Basic Pastoral Counselling Skills: A Comparison of Microtraining Approach with a Skills Practice Approach," *The Journal of Pastoral Care* 31, 2 (1977): 125-35.
15  Karl Rahner, *Foundations of Christian Faith*, 65f.
16  Carroll Wise, *The Meaning of Pastoral Care* (New York: Harper and Row, 1966).
17  Paul Sanderson, "Key Issues in the Pastoral Supervisory Relationship," *Pastoral Psychology* 26, 4 (Summer 1978): 240-52.
18  Howard Liddle, "Systemic Supervision: Conceptual Overlays and Pragmatic Guide lines," in Liddle et al., *Handbook of Family Therapy Training and Supervision*, 153-71.
19  Melvin C. Blanchette, "Transference and Countertransference," in Barry K. Estadt et al., *The Art of Clinical Supervision: A Pastoral Counselling Perspective*, 83-96.
20  Malcolm Knowles, *The Modern Practice of Adult Education*, 57.
21  Carl Stoltenberg and U. Delworth, *Supervising Counselors and Therapists: A Developmental Approach* (San Francisco: Jossey-Bass, 1987).
22  *Certification Standards Procedures and Guidelines for the Canadian Association for Pastoral Practice and Education* (Toronto, ON: CAPPE, 1996).

23 Mary Field Belenky, Blythe McVicker Clinchy, Nancy Rule Goldberger and Jill Mattuck Tarule, *Women's Ways of Knowing* (New York: Basic Books, 1986), 87-100.
24 Ibid., 100-31.
25 Joseph Heim, "The Social Justice Issues in Supervision," in Estadt et al., *The Art of Clinical Supervision: A Pastoral Counselling Perspective,* 262-74.
26 Malcolm Knowles, *The Modern Practice of Adult Education,* 57.
27 Ivan Boszormenyi-Nagy and Barbara R. Krasner, *Between Give and Take: A Clinical Guide to Contextual Therapy* (New York: Bruner/Mazel, 1986).
28 Thomas Klink, "Issues in Learning Through Supervision," *The Journal of Pastoral Care* 17, 2 (1963):61-72; "Supervision," *Journal of Supervision and Training in Ministry* 11 (1989):161-203.
29 Karl Rahner, *Foundations of Christian Faith,* 65f.

# Bibliography

**Books by Charles Gerkin**

Gerkin, Charles V. *Crisis Experience in Modern Life: Theory and Theology for Pastoral Care*. Nashville: Abingdon Press, 1979.

_____. *The Living Human Document: Re-Visioning Pastoral Counselling in a Hermeneutical Mode*. Nashville: Abingdon Press, 1984.

_____. *Widening the Horizons: Pastoral Responses to a Fragmented Society*. Philadelphia: Westminster Press, 1986.

_____. *Prophetic Pastoral Practice: A Christian Vision of Life Together*. Nashville: Abingdon Press, 1991.

**Articles by Charles Gerkin**

_____. "Helping Parents Whose Children are in Trouble." *The Christian Advocate*, (October 7, 1954): 13-20.

_____. "The Church and Juvenile Delinquency." *Pastoral Psychology* 6 (October 1955): 8-13.

_____. "A Theologian's View of Cardiac Resuscitation." In Willis M. Hurst, ed. *Cardiac Resuscitation*, New York: Charles Thomas Publishers (1960): 73-85.

_____. "Objectives of Clinical Pastoral Education." *Trends In Clinical Pastoral Education*, Proceedings on Seventh National Conference on Clinical Pastoral Education (1960): 41-50.

_____. "On Becoming a Pastor." *Pastoral Psychology* 16, 151 (February 1965): 9-14.

_____. "Interprofessional Healing and Pastoral Identity." *The St. Luke's Journal of Theology* 11, 1 (1969): 18-25.

_____. "Changing Dilemmas of a Maturing Pastor." *The Christian Advocate*, (October 2, 1969): 33-38.

_____. "Clinical Pastoral Education and Social Change." *The Journal of Pastoral Care* (September 1971): 171-81.

_____. "Is Pastoral Counselling a Credible Alternative to the Ministry?" *The Journal of Pastoral Care* (December 1972): 181-90.

_____. "On the Renewal of Ministry as Pastoral Guidance." *The Candler Review* (January 1974): 11-13.

_____. "Pastoral Ministry Between the Times." *The Journal of Pastoral Care* 30 (September 1976): 178-85.

_____. "Power and Powerlessness in Clinical Pastoral Education." *The Journal of Pastoral Care* 34 (June 1980): 114-24.

_____. "Healing as Transformation." In Barbara Brown, ed. *Ministry and Mission*. New York: Post Horn Press, 1985.

_____. "Stages in Ministerial Burnout." In Barbara Brown, ed. *Ministry and Mission*.

_____. "Faith and Praxis: Pastoral Counselling's Hermeneutical Problem." *Pastoral Psychology* 35 (Fall 1986): 3-15.

_____."Response to James Poling, A Critical Appraisal of Charles V. Gerkin's Pastoral Theology." *Pastoral Psychology* 37 (Winter 1988): 97-102.

_____."Implicit and Explicit Faith: Practical Theology in Dialogue with Object Relations Theory." *Pastoral Sciences.* Ottawa: University of Ottawa Press (1988): 13-29.

_____."Response: Klink's Theory of Supervision–Memories and Reflections." *Journal of Supervision and Training in Ministry* 11 (1989): 204-10.

_____. "Pastoral Care and Models of Aging." In Barbara Payne and Earl Brewer, eds., *Gerontology in Theological Education: Local Program Development.* New York: Hawthorn Press, 1989.

_____. "Interpretation and Hermeneutics, Pastoral." In Rodney Hunter et al., eds., *Dictionary of Pastoral Care and Counselling.* Nashville: Abingdon Press, 1990, 591-93.

_____. "Incarnational Pastoral Care (Protestantism)." In Hunter et al., eds., *Dictionary of Pastoral Care and Counselling,* 573.

_____. "Psychoanalysis and Pastoral Care." In Hunter et al., eds., *Dictionary of Pastoral Care and Counselling,* 979-84.

_____. "Crisis Ministry." In Hunter et al., *Dictionary of Pastoral Care and Counselling,* 246-48.

_____. "Practical Theology, Pastoral Theology and Pastoral Care Practice." In Adrian M. Visscher, ed., *Pastoral Studies in the University Setting,* Ottawa: University of Ottawa Press, 1990, 387-99.

_____. "On the Art of Caring." *The Journal of Pastoral Care* 45, 4 (Winter 1991): 399-408.

_____. "A Fresh Look at Our History." *The Journal of Pastoral Theology,* 3 (1993): 99-108.

_____. "Projective Identification and the Image of God: Reflections on Object Relations Theory and the Psychology of Religion." In Brian H. Childs and David W. Waanders, eds., *The Treasure of Earthen Vessels: Explorations in Theological Anthropology,* Louisville: Westminster/John Knox Press, 1994, 52-64.

_____, and Donald G. Cox. "Religious Story Test as a Tool for Evaluating Religious Growth." *The Journal of Pastoral Care* 9 (Spring 1955): 21-26.

_____, James T. Laney and Edward F. Dobihal. Monograph, *1977 APCE Conference: Association for Clinical Pastoral Education.* New York: 1977.

Gerkin, Charles V., and George H. Weber. "A Religious Story Test: Some Findings of Delinquent Boys." *The Journal of Pastoral Care* 7, 2 (1953): 77-90.

**Book Reviews by Charles Gerkin**

Gerkin, Charles V. Review of *Tongue Speaking: An Experiment in Spiritual Experience,* by Morton T. Kelsey. *Religious Life* 34, 4 (Autumn 1965): 663-64.

_____. Review of *Scapegoat: The Impact of Death–Fear of an American Family,* by Eric Bermann. *Pastoral Psychology* 24 (Summer 1976): 329-34.

_____. Review of *Pastoral Care and Hermeneutics,* by Donald E. Capps. *Theology Today* 42 (April 1985): 138-40.

_____. Review of *Pastoral Counselling: A Ministry of the Church*, by John Patton. *St. Luke's Journal of Theology* 29 (March 1986): 136-38.

_____. Review of *Spiritual Dimensions of Pastoral Care*, by Gerald L. Borchert and Andrew D. Lester, eds. *Baptist Theological Journal* 83, 1 (Winter 1986): 111-12.

_____. Review of *Christian Caring: Selections from Practical Theology*, by Frederick D. E. Schleiermacher. James O. Duke and Howard Stone, eds. *The Journal of Pastoral Care* 42 (Spring 1988): 90-92.

_____. Review of *At the Point of Need: Living Human Experience: Essays in Honour of Carroll A. Wise,* by James B. Ashbrook and John E. Hinkle, Jr., eds. *The Journal of Pastoral Care* 42 (Winter 1988): 363-72.

_____. Review of *Law, Freedom and Story: The Role of Narrative in Therapy, Society and Faith,* by John C. Hoffman. *Pastoral Psychology* 37 (Spring 1989): 208-11.

_____. Review of *The Meaning of Pastoral Care*, rev. ed., by Carroll A. Wise, ed. John E. Hinkle Jr., and Meyer Stone, eds. *Pastoral Psychology* 38 (Spring 1990): 188-91.

## Doctoral Theses on the Theology of Charles Gerkin

O'Connor, Thomas St. James, "A Critical Examination of the Praxis of Clinical Pastoral Supervision in Light of the Incarnational Theology of Charles Gerkin." ThD dissertation, Toronto School of Theology, 1995.

Raurwerda, Garrett L., Jr. "Idolatrous Myth and Hermeneutical Pastoral Counselling." DMin dissertation, Boston University Theological School, 1985.

Watson, Henry D. "Pastoral Care in a Hermeneutical Narrative Style." DMin dissertation, Emory University, 1988.

Williams, Gene M. "A Hermeneutical Approach to Crisis Ministry in the Local Church." DMin dissertation, Emory University, 1990.

## Articles on Charles Gerkin's Theology

Couture, Pamela, and Rodney Hunter. "Charles V. Gerkin," in P. Couture and R. Hunter, eds., *Pastoral Care and Social Conflict* (Nashville: Abingdon Press, 1995), 7-10.

Hunter, Rodney. "Charles V. Gerkin, Pastoral Theologian of the Year." *Pastoral Psychology* 36, 1 (Fall 1987): 3-9.

Poling, James. "A Critical Appraisal of Charles Gerkin's Pastoral Theology." *Pastoral Psychology* 37, 2 (Winter 1988): 85-96.

## Book Reviews on Charles Gerkin's Books

Aden, LeRoy. Review of *The Living Human Document: Revisioning Pastoral Counselling in a Hermeneutical Mode*, by Charles V. Gerkin. *Journal of Psychology and Christianity* 7 (Summer 1988): 90-92.

Bain, Homer A. Review of *The Living Human Document: Revisioning Pastoral Counselling in a Hermeneutical Mode,* by Charles V. Gerkin. *Pastoral Psychology* 34 (Winter 1985): 136-39.

Carr, Warren. Review of *Widening the Horizons: Responses to a Fragmented Society*, by Charles V. Gerkin. *Perspectives in Religious Studies* 16 (Fall 1989): 268-72.
Childs, Brian H. Review of *The Living Human Document: Revisioning Pastoral Counselling in a Hermeneutical Mode*, by Charles V. Gerkin. *The Princeton Seminary Bulletin* 6, 1 (1985): 52-54.
Elhard, Leland. Review of *Widening the Horizons: Pastoral Responses to a Fragmented Society*, by Charles V. Gerkin. *Trinity Seminary Review* 10 (Spring 1988): 6.
Fowler, Gene. Review of *Widening the Horizons: Pastoral Responses to a Fragmented Society*, by Charles V. Gerkin. *Princeton Studies* 8, 2 (1987): 81-83.
Houts, Donald C. Review of *Widening the Horizons: Pastoral Responses to a Fragmented Society*, by Charles V. Gerkin. *The Journal of Pastoral Care* 41, 2 (June 1987): 189-90.
Hunter, Rodney. Review of *The Living Human Document: Revisioning Pastoral Counselling in a Hermeneutical Mode*, by Charles V. Gerkin. *Theological Education* 25 (Autumn 1988): 80-82.
Jernigan, Homer L. Review of *Widening the Horizons: Pastoral Responses to a Fragmented Society*, by Charles V. Gerkin. *Pastoral Psychology* 36 (Summer 1988): 265-70.
Jones, J.P. Review of *Crisis Experience of Modern Life*, by Charles V. Gerkin. *The Journal of Pastoral Care* 33 (September 1979): 206-207.
Kraus, George. Review of *Widening the Horizons: Pastoral Responses to a Fragmented Society*, by Charles V. Gerkin. *Concordia Theological Quarterly* 51, 2-3 (April-July 1987): 223-24.
Lombarets, Herman. Review of *The Living Human Document: Revisioning Pastoral Counselling in a Hermeneutical Mode*, by Charles V. Gerkin. *Louvain Studies* 13, 1 (1988): 93-94.
Mills, L.O. Review of *Crisis Experience in Modern Life*, by Charles V. Gerkin. *Pastoral Psychology* 28 (Spring 1980): 209-11.
Mitchell, K.R. Review of *Crisis Experience in Modern Life*, by Charles V. Gerkin. *Theology Today* 37 (April 1980): 150-51.
_____. Review of *The Living Human Document: Revisioning Pastoral Counselling in a Hermeneutical Mode*, by Charles V. Gerkin. *The Journal of Pastoral Care* 38 (March 1984): 64-62.
Patton, John. Review of *Widening the Horizons: Pastoral Responses to a Fragmented Society*, by Charles V. Gerkin. *Saint Luke's Journal of Theology* 32 (December 1988): 61-62.
Prest, A.P.L. Review of *Crisis Experience in Modern Life*, by Charles V. Gerkin. *Saint Luke's Journal Of Theology* 23 (September 1980): 311-12.
Stroup, H.W. Review of *Crisis Experience in Modern Life*, by Charles V. Gerkin. *Dialog* 19 (Fall 1980): 314.
Switzer, D.K. Review of *Crisis Experience in Modern Life*, by Charles V. Gerkin. *Supervision and Training in Ministry* 3 (1980): 144-46.
Switzer, D.K. Review of *Crisis Experience In Modern Life*, by Charles V. Gerkin. *Religious Life* 49 (Summer 1980): 253-54.

Watermulder, D.B. Review of *Crisis Experience in Modern Life*, by Charles V. Gerkin. *The Christian Century* 97 (April 2, 1980): 385-86.
Wells, Donald. Review of *Widening the Horizons: Pastoral Responses to a Fragmented Society*, by Charles V. Gerkin. *The Christian Century* 104,11 (April 8, 1987): 338-39.
Wichern, F.B. Review of *The Living Human Document: Revisioning Pastoral Counselling in a Hermeneutical Mode*, by Charles V. Gerkin. *Bibliotheca Sacra* 41 (October-December 1984): 374.

**Clinical Pastoral Supervision, Pastoral Supervision and Clinical Pastoral Education**

Aalto, Kristi. "Pastoral Supervision in the Lutheran Church in Finland: Key to Professional Growth." *Journal of Supervision and Training in Ministry* 15 (1994): 110-16.
Adams, Henry Babcock. "Consultation: An Alternative to Supervision." *The Journal of Pastoral Care* 25, 3 (1971):157-64.
Adix, James. "Pastoral Authority: A Survival Issue." *Journal of Supervision and Training in Ministry* 2 (1979): 5-11.
Aist, Clark S. "Standards: A View from the Past and Prospects for the Future." *The Journal of Pastoral Care* 37 (March 1983): 60-67.
_____. "Professional Certification in the Clinical Pastoral Field." *Journal of Supervision and Training in Ministry* 3 (1980): 101-106.
Anderson, Herbert E. "The Spirituality of Learning to Care." *Journal of Supervision and Training in Ministry* 4 (1981): 21-36.
_____. "Incarnation and Pastoral Care." *Pastoral Psychology* 32, 4 (Summer 1984): 239-50.
_____. "Forming a Pastoral Habitus: A Rich Tapestry with Many Threads." *Journal of Supervision and Training in Ministry* 15 (1994): 231-42.
Anderson, Herbert, and Joan Scanlon. "Introduction: Supervision and Formation in Ministry." *Journal of Supervision and Training in Ministry* 15 (1994): 117-20.
Anderson, James A. "Goal Attainment Scaling Process in Education." *Journal of Supervision and Training in Ministry* 3 (1980): 29-38.
Anderson, John Gordon. "Education for Spirituality in CPE." *Journal of Pastoral Care* 32, 3 (September 1978): 155-60.
Ashbrook, James B. "Clinical Training–For What Kind of Ministry?" *Journal of Pastoral Care* 16, 2 (1962): 139-48.
Ashby Jr., Homer U. "Kohut's Contribution to Pastoral Care." *Journal of Supervision and Training in Ministry* 5 (1982): 149-56.
Asquith, Glen H. "Pastoral Supervision and Theology: An Integrative Approach." *Journal of Supervision and Training in Ministry* 13 (1991): 165-79.
_____. "Case Study Method." In Rodney Hunter et al., *Dictionary of Pastoral Care and Counselling*. Nashville: Abingdon Press, 1990, 123-26.
Augspurger, Richard E., and Roger D. Fallot. "Introduction: Philosophies of Pastoral Counselling Supervision." *Journal of Supervision and Training in Ministry* 8 (1986): 52-58.

Auten, Darryl J. "Supervision Training: Holistic Educational Model." DMin. dissertation, St. Stephen's College, Edmonton, 1982.

Avery, William. "Enhancing Supervision Using Fowler's Developmental Theory." *Journal of Supervision and Training in Ministry* 10 (1988): 3-18.

Avery, William O., and Norma S. Wood. "The Faded Intern/Supervisor Relationship." *The Journal of Pastoral Care* 48, 3 (1994): 267-71.

Baldridge, William E.M., and John J. Gleason. "A Theological Framework for Pastoral Care." *The Journal of Pastoral Care* 32, 4 (1978): 232-38.

Barnes, Ronald M. "Dreams in Spiritual Direction: Help or Distraction?" *Review for Religious* 45, 3 (May/June 1986): 402-20.

_____. "Psychology and Spirituality: Meeting at the Boundaries." *The Way Supplement* 69 (Autumn 1990): 29-42.

Barry, Agnes W. "Creating for Learning: Verbatim Alternatives." *Journal of Supervision and Training in Ministry* 6 (1983): 56-61.

_____. "The Sounds of Supervision: New Music for Models." *Journal of Supervision and Training in Ministry* 7 (1984-85): 68-70.

Barton, Clarence, and Amanda W. Ragland. "Transference and Countertransference in Supervision." In David Steere, ed., *The Supervision of Pastoral Care*, Louisville: Westminster/John Knox, 1989, 193-205.

Beck, James R. "The Pastoral Dimension of Supervision: A Study in Identification and Rapprochement." *Journal of Supervision and Training in Ministry* 9 (1987): 18-28.

Becker, Arthur H. "Transplanting CPE to the South African Scene." *The Journal of Pastoral Care* 32, 3 (1978): 184-90.

Beech, Lawrence A. "Supervision in Pastoral Care and Counselling: A Prerequisite for Effective Ministry." *The Journal of Pastoral Care* 24, 4 (1970): 227-32.

Bell, Perry D. "Issues in Pastoral Supervision of Interns." *Journal of Supervision and Training in Ministry* 11 (1989): 37-45.

Bench, J. Russell. "Images and Expectations of CPE." *Journal of Supervision and Training in Ministry* 9 (1987): 51-74.

Bennett, George. "Preparing Yourself for Supervision." In David Steere, ed., *The Supervision of Pastoral Care*. Louisville: Westminster/John Knox, 1989, 90-98.

Bergstrom, Shelley, Patricia L. Guilbeault and George Fitchett. "Factors Affecting the Choice of a CPE Center." *Journal of Supervision and Training in Ministry* 17 (1996): 112-21.

Bickel, Arthur O. "Theology/Spirituality Seminars." *Journal of Supervision and Training in Ministry* 2 (1979): 30-39.

Blackmore, Gershon. "Shepherding Moses and Aaron: A View of Pastoral Counselling Supervision." *Journal of Supervision and Training in Ministry* 17 (1996): 185-23.

Blanchette, Melvin C. "Interpretation and Resistance." In Barry K. Estadt et al., eds., *The Art of Clinical Supervision: A Pastoral Counselling Perspective*. New York: Paulist Press, 1987, 66-82.

_____. "Transference and Countertransference." In Barry K. Estadt et al., eds., *The Art of Clinical Supervision: A Pastoral Counselling Perspective*. New York: Paulist Press, 1987, 83-96.

_____. "Termination: The Creative Summing Up of the Counselling Relationship and the Learning Alliance." In Barry K. Estadt et al., eds., *The Art of Clinical Supervision: A Pastoral Counselling Perspective*. New York: Paulist Press, 1987, 97-110.

Bogia, Benjamin Preston. "Group Supervision versus Group Psychotherapy: Similarities and Differences for Clinical Pastoral Education." *The Journal of Pastoral Care* 41, 4 (September 1987): 252-57.

_____. "Supervision of CPE Students in Mid-Life Transition." *Journal of Supervision and Training in Ministry* 7 (1984-85): 6-14.

_____. "Supervision and Stress." *Journal of Supervision and Training in Ministry* 5 (1982): 55-60.

Boisen, Anton T. *The Exploration of the Inner World*. New York: Harper and Brothers, 1936.

_____. *Religion in Crisis and Custom*. New York: Harper and Brothers, 1945.

Bollinger, Richard A. "Clinical Pastoral Supervision: Tom Klink's Contribution," *Journal of Supervision and Training in Ministry* 11 (1989): 242-50.

Bonacker, Ralph D. "Clinical Training for the Pastoral Ministry: Purposes and Methods." *The Journal of Pastoral Care* 14, 1 (1960): 1-12.

Britton, Donald Lee. "The Role of Supervision/Consultation in Enabling and Enhancing Ministry." DMin Thesis, Wesley Theological Seminary, 1984.

Browning, Don. "Method in Religious Living and Clinical Education." *The Journal of Pastoral Care* 29, 2 (1975): 157-67.

_____. "Pastoral Care and Models of Training in Counselling." *Journal of Supervision and Training in Ministry* 2 (1979): 98-106.

_____. "Response to Hunter, Patton and Hall." *Journal of Supervision and Training in Ministry* 2 (1979): 115-18.

_____. "Mapping the Terrain of Pastoral Theology: Toward a Practical Theology of Care." *Pastoral Psychology* 36, 1 (Fall 1987): 10-28.

_____. "Pastoral Theology in a Pluralistic Age." *Pastoral Psychology* 29, 1 (Fall 1980): 24-35.

_____, ed. *Practical Theology*. San Francisco: Harper and Row, 1983.

_____. "Introduction." In Don Browning, ed. *Practical Theology*. San Francisco: Harper and Row, 1983.

_____. "The Pastoral Counselor as Ethicist: What Difference Do We Make?" *The Journal of Pastoral Care* 42, 4 (Winter 1988): 283-98.

Bruder, Ernest E. "Clinical Pastoral Training in Preparation for the Pastoral Ministry." *The Journal of Pastoral Care* 15, 1 (1961): 25-33.

_____. "An Overview of Clinical Pastoral Education." *Pastoral Psychology* (May 1965): 13-20.

Burbank, Beth. "Reflecting Upon Stories as a Way of Doing Theology in CPE." *Journal of Supervision and Training in Ministry* 9 (1987): 147-56.

_____. "Vignette: The Blessing of the Wrestler." *Journal of Supervision and Training in Ministry* 9 (1987) 198- 200.

Burbank, Beth, and Gerald C. Johnson. "Introduction: Story Theology and Ministry Supervision." *Journal of Supervision and Training in Ministry* 9 (1987): 131-34

Burck, Russell. "Therapeutic and Proclamatory Pastoral Care in Germany." *Journal of Supervision and Training in Ministry* 2 (1979): 82-97.

_____. "Pastoral Expressionism: Verbatims In the Pastoral Paradigm." *Journal of Supervision and Training in Ministry* 3 (1980): 39-56.

_____. "Images and Expectations of CPE." *Journal of Supervision and Training in Ministry* 9 (1987): 51-74.

Cain, David. "A Way of God's Theodicy: Honesty, Presence, Adventure." *The Journal of Pastoral Care* 32, 4 (1978): 239.

Callaghan, Rachel. "Religious Issues." In Barry K. Estadt et al., eds., *The Art of Clinical Supervision: A Pastoral Counselling Perspective*, 241-49.

_____, and Robert F. Davenport. "Group Counselling: A Model For Teaching and Supervision." In Barry K. Estadt et als., eds., *The Art of Clinical Supervision: A Pastoral Counselling Perspective*, 149-59.

Canadian Association for Pastoral Practice and Education (CAPPE). *Accreditation Standards Procedures and Guidelines for the Canadian Association of Pastoral Education.* Toronto, ON: CAPPE, 1996.

_____. *Certification Standards Procedures and Guidelines for the Canadian Association of Pastoral Education.* Toronto, ON: CAPPE, 1996.

Capps, Donald. *Life Cycle Theory and Pastoral Care.* Philadelphia: Fortress Press, 1983

_____. *Pastoral Care and Hermeneutics.* Philadelphia: Fortress Press, 1984.

_____. *Deadly Sins and Saving Virtues.* Philadelphia: Fortress Press, 1987.

_____. *Reframing: A New Method in Pastoral Care.* Philadelphia: Fortress Press, 1990.

Cedarleaf, J. Lennart. "An Early Certification Experience." *Journal of Supervision and Training in Ministry* 3 (1980): 113-18.

Cheston, Sharon. "Short Term Counselling." In Barry K. Estadt et al., eds., *The Art of Clinical Supervision: A Pastoral Counselling Perspective*, 111-21.

Christenson, Carl M., J. Holland and C.A. Wise. "Some Aspects of Training Pastoral Counselors." *The Journal of Pastoral Care* 22, 4 (1968): 212-22.

Christenson, Carl M. "Psychiatric Supervision of Pastoral Therapists." *Journal of Supervision and Training in Ministry* 1 (1978): 50-57.

Ciarrocchi, Joseph. "Addiction Counselling." In Barry K. Estadt et al., eds., *The Art of Clinical Supervision: A Pastoral Counselling Perspective*, 212-24.

Clark, Maurice. "Self-Disclosure: Supervisor as Model." *Journal of Supervision and Training in Ministry* 9 (1987): 119.

Clebsch, William, and Charles R. Jaekle. *Pastoral Care in Historical Perspective.* New York: Jason Aronson, 1975.

Clift, Jean Danky. "Theory and Practice of Clinical Supervision In Pastoral Counselling." *Journal of Supervision and Training in Ministry* 10 (1988): 36-58.

Clinebell, Charlotte. *Counselling for Liberation.* Philadelphia: Fortress Press, 1976.

Clinebell, Howard. *Basic Types of Pastoral Care and Counselling: Resources for the Ministry of Healing and Growth.* (rev.) Nashville: Abingdon Press, 1984.

_____. *Contemporary Growth Therapies: Resources for Actualizing Human Wholeness.* Nashville: Abingdon Press, 1981.

_____. *Growth Counselling: Hope-Centred Methods of Actualizing Human Wholeness.* Nashville: Abingdon Press, 1979.

_____. *Basic Types of Pastoral Care and Counselling.* Nashville: Abingdon Press, 1966.

Compton, John R. "The Supervisory Learning Contract." In Barry K. Estadt et al., eds., *The Art of Clinical Supervision: A Pastoral Counselling Perspective,* 41-52.

_____. "Supervisory Formats and Evaluation Procedures." In Barry K. Estadt et al., eds., *The Art of Clinical Supervision: A Pastoral Counselling Perspective,* 53-65.

Corrigan, James. "When a CPE Group Becomes a 'Toxic Brew'." *Journal of Supervision and Training in Ministry* 17 (1996): 78-87.

Cordner, G. Michael. "The Relevance of the Shadow for Pastoral Training." *Journal of Supervision and Training in Ministry,* 7 (1984-85): 182-87.

Couture, Pamela, and Rodney Hunter, eds. *Pastoral Care and Social Conflict.* Nashville: Abingdon Press, 1995.

Crossan, John Dominic. "Response: Pattern and Particularity in Suffering and Story." *Journal of Supervision and Training in Ministry* 9 (1987): 211-16.

Cunningham, Agnes, and C. John Weborg. "Formation for Life in the Middle." *Journal of Supervision and Training in Ministry* 15 (1994): 144-55.

Cunningham, Madonna Marie. "Consultation, Collaboration and Referral." In Robert Wicks et al., eds., *Clinical Handbook of Pastoral Counselling.* New York: Paulist Press, 1985, 162-70.

Dale, Kenneth. "Supervision and Training in Japan." *Journal of Supervision and Training in Ministry* 12 (1990): 81-82.

Danella, Francis W. "Theological Reflection: The Context of Pastoral Supervision." *Journal of Supervision and Training in Ministry* 13 (1991): 154-64.

Davenport, Robert F. "Ethical Issues in Supervision." In Barry K. Estadt et al., eds., *The Art of Clinical Supervision: A Pastoral Counselling Perspective,* 250-61.

Davis, Kathleen Ogden. "Working with Clinical Materials." In David Steere, ed., *The Supervision of Pastoral Care.* Louisville: Westminster/John Knox, 99-113.

Dawson, Caroline. "The Contributions and Limitations of CPE and Action Training for Theological Field Education." DMin Thesis, Toronto School of Theology and University of St. Michael's College, 1985.

Dayringer, Richard. "Goals in Clinical Pastoral Education." *Pastoral Psychology* (April 1971): 5-10.

Daugherty, James D. "Clinical Theology: A Dialogical Foundation for Clinical Pastoral Education." *Journal of Supervision and Training in Ministry* 15 (1994): 33-41.

DeArment, Daniel C. "How My Heart Has Changed." *Journal of Supervision and Training in Ministry* 6 (1983): 153-58.

Debner, Wendell R. "Supervision of Interns." DMin Thesis, Minnesota Consortium of Theological Schools, 1990.

de Jong, Jan. "Supervision and Theology in CPE." *Journal of Supervision and Training in Ministry* 1 (1978): 10-16.

Denys, Josef. "My Understanding of Ministry and Pastoral Supervision in Clinical Pastoral Education." *Pastoral Sciences* 9 (1990): 5-16.

Derrickson, Paul. "What Does CPE Contribute to Pastoral Competence?" *Journal of Supervision and Training in Ministry* 16 (1995), 137-44.

DeSobe, Gerald J. "A Model for Education and Supervision in Pastoral Counselling Training." *Journal of Supervision and Training in Ministry* 8 (1986): 182-89.

DeVoogd, Albert. "A Supervision Model for Training in Interpersonal Relationship Counselling." DMin Thesis, Western Theological Seminary, 1982.

Dickerson, Paul E. "Supervisory Training: A Consortium Model." *Journal of Supervision and Training in Ministry* 10 (1988): 19-28.

Donnenwirth, Richard A., Georgann Hilbert and Barbara Sheehan. "CPE Training Module on Gender, Sexuality and Collegiality." *Journal of Supervision and Training in Ministry* 6 (1983): 141-52.

Duffy, Regis. *A Roman Catholic Theology of Pastoral Care*. Philadelphia: Fortress Press, 1983.

Duncombe, David. "Binocular Rivalry as an Indicator of Spiritual Growth in CPE." *The Journal of Pastoral Care* 31, 1 (1977):18-21.

_____. "The Trivial Nature of Clinical Pastoral Education." *The Journal of Pastoral Care* 42, 1 (Spring 1988): 45-56.

_____."Street Ministry CPE: An Experiment in the Haight-Ashbury." *The Journal of Pastoral Care* 42, 4 (Winter 1988): 339-48.

Durston, Derek. "Self-Awareness and Cross-Cultural Ministry: Guiding Images for CPE in the Nineties." *Journal of Supervision and Training in Ministry* 14 (1992-93): 233-40.

Edgerton, Jarvis J. "Clinical Pastoral Education: A Model for Fleshing Out the Word." *Journal of Supervision and Training in Ministry* 6 (1983): 109-21.

Edson, Cynthia J. "Male and Female, He Created Them: An Encounter of Sex-Role Stereotypes in CPE." *The Journal of Pastoral Care* 27, 2 (1973): 158-71.

Estadt, Barry K. *Pastoral Counselling*. Englewood Cliffs, New Jersey: Prentice-Hall, 1983.

_____, Melvin Blanchette, and John Compton. eds., *The Art of Clinical Supervision: A Pastoral Counselling Perspective*. Engelwood Cliffs, New Jersey: Prentice-Hall, 1987.

_____. "Supervision: From Technician to Artist." In Barry K. Estadt, *Pastoral Counselling*. Englewood Cliffs, New Jersey: Prentice-Hall, 1983, 50-63.

_____. "Toward Professional Integration." In Barry K. Estadt et al., eds., *The Art of Clinical Supervision: A Pastoral Counselling Perspective*, 5-12.

_____. "The Core Process of Supervision" In Barry K. Estadt et al., eds., *The Art of Clinical Supervision: A Pastoral Counselling Perspective,* 13-40.

Everett, Craig A., and Anthony W. Seaton-Johnson. "An Analysis of Pastoral Counselling Supervisors: Their Identities, Roles and Resources." *The Journal of Pastoral Care* 37, 1 (March 1983): 50-59.

Ewing, James W. "The American Association of Pastoral Counselors (AAPC)." In Rodney Hunter et al., eds., *Dictionary of Pastoral Care and Counselling.* Nashville: Abingdon Press, 1991, 24.

_____. "Supervision in Long Term Psychotherapy." In Barry K. Estadt et al., eds., *The Art of Clinical Supervision: A Pastoral Counselling Perspective,* 122-34.

Fallot, Roger D. "Metaphors and Change in the Supervision of Psychotherapy and Pastoral Counselling." *Journal of Supervision and Training in Ministry* 6 (1983): 23-32.

Farley, Edward. "Symposium: The Reform of Theological Education as a Theological Task." *Journal of Supervision and Training in Ministry* 4 (1981): 83-107.

Fitchett, George. "Introduction to Religion and Self Psychology Memorial Symposium." *Journal of Supervision and Training in Ministry* 5 (1982): 91-95.

_____. "A Coherent Theory of Education Relevant for CPE." *Journal of Supervision and Training in Ministry* 6 (1983) 73-108.

_____. "The Paradoxical Nature of CPE." *Journal of Supervision and Training in Ministry* 3 (1980): 57-71.

_____, and George T. Gray. "Evaluating the Outcome of Clinical Pastoral Education: A Test of the Clinical Assessment Ministry Profile." *Journal of Supervision and Training in Ministry* 15 (1994): 3-22.

Fite, Robert Cotton. "Theory and Practice of Supervision of Pastoral Psychotherapists." *Journal of Supervision and Training in Ministry* 9 (1987): 100-17.

_____. "Ethical Dimensions of Gender Issues in Supervision." *Journal of Supervision and Training in Ministry* 12 (1990): 145-52.

Fontentot, Nancy. "Passivity in Supervision." In David Steere, ed., *The Supervision of Pastoral Care,* 206-21.

Foskett, John. "Seeing is Believing." *The Journal of Pastoral Care* 48, 4 (Winter 1994): 363-69.

Foskett, John, and David Lyall. *Helping the Helpers: Supervision and Pastoral Care.* London: SPCK, 1988.

Foy, Janet O. "Women in Pastoral Counselling: the Clients, the Therapist and the Supervisor." *Journal of Supervision and Training in Ministry* 6 (1983): 175-86.

Frazier, Richard. "The Use of One's Story in CPE." *Journal of Supervision and Training in Ministry* 1 (1978): 17-28.

_____. "How People Change in Pastoral Counselling and Supervision: Reflections on Empathy and Authority." *Journal of Supervision and Training in Ministry* 8 (1986): 34-44.

French, Porter. "Innocents Aboard: Clinical Training in the Early Days." *The Journal of Pastoral Care* 29, 1 (1975): 7-10.

Gardner, Marvin. "The Supervision of Pastoral Psychotherapy: A Developmental Model." *Journal of Supervision and Training in Ministry* 14 (1992-93): 125-37.

Gardner, Marvin. "Integrating the Pastoral Dimension into Pastoral Counselling Training Programs." *The Journal of Pastoral Care* 47, 1 (Spring 1993): 56-64.

Gaventa, William C. "Singing the Lord's Song in a Foreign Land: A Theoretical Foundation for Growth and Education in the CPE Process." *Journal of Supervision and Training in Ministry* 8 (1986): 21-32.

Geary, Thomas F. "Personal Growth in CPE." *The Journal of Pastoral Care* 31, 1 (1977): 12-17.

Gerber, Richard J. Response to "When a CPE Group Becomes a 'Toxic Brew,' or Is Something Else Going On Here?" *Journal of Supervision and Training in Ministry* 17 (1996): 91-94.

Gessell, John M. "What the Theological Schools Might Expect from Clinical Pastoral Education."*The Journal of Pastoral Care* 17, 2 (1963): 148-53.

Gibbons, James L., and David C. Myler, Jr. "Research as a Curricular Component of CPE." *Journal of Supervision and Training in Ministry* 1 (1978): 36-49.

Giblin, Paul, and Mona Christenson Barg. "Master's Level Pastoral Counselling Training: Skills and Competencies." *Pastoral Psychology*. 42, 1 (Spring 1993): 21-43.

Gillespie, Joseph P. "A Well Grounded Flight of Fancy." *Journal of Supervision and Training in Ministry* 9 (1987): 183.

Glaz, Maxine. "Theological Rigor and Covenantal: Foundations for Pastoral Supervision." *Journal of Supervision and Training in Ministry* 13 (1991): 244-56.

_____. "A New Pastoral Understanding of Women." In M. Glaz and J. Moessner, eds., *Women in Travail and Transition: A New Pastoral Care*, 11-32.

_____, and Jeanne Stevenson Moessner. "The Psychology of Women and Pastoral Care." In M. Glaz and J. Moessner, eds., *Women in Transition and Travail: A New Pastoral Care*, 33-62.

_____, and Jeanne Stevenson Moessner, eds. *Women in Transition and Travail: A New Pastoral Care*. Minneapolis: Fortress Press, 1991.

Glebe, Delton. "Law and Gospel in Pastoral Counselling." *Pastoral Psychology* (December 1965): 45-50.

Glendon, Lowell M. "Spiritual Direction: A Model for Group Supervision." In Barry K. Estadt et al., eds., *The Art of Clinical Supervision: A Pastoral Counselling Perspective*, 225-40.

_____. "Theological and Pastoral Integration." In Barry K. Estadt et al., eds., *The Art of Clinical Supervision: A Pastoral Counselling Perspective*, 275-86.

Graham, Larry Kent. "A Psychosystemic Approach to Supervision in Pastoral Psychotherapy." *Journal of Supervision and Training in Ministry* 12 (1990): 39-55.

_____. "Toward a Social and Political Theory of Pastoral Care and Counselling." *Journal of Supervision and Training in Ministry* 7 (1984-85): 83-101.

Grant, Brian W. "Supervision: The Formative Relationship for a Pastoral Psychotherapist." *Journal of Supervision and Training in Ministry* 8 (1986): 72-81.

Grant, Gerry. "An Objective Evaluation of an Eleven-week Supervised Pastoral Education Program." *The Journal of Pastoral Care* 29, 4 (1975): 254-61.

Greiner, Lyel B., and Robert Bendiksen "Conceptual Learning in Clinical Pastoral Education Supervisory Training: A Focus-Group Research Project with Recommendations." *The Journal of Pastoral Care* 48, 3 (Fall 1994): 245-56.

Guider, Margaret E. "Theological Education and Ministerial Formation: Coming to Terms with the Hidden Curriculum." *Journal of Supervision of Training and Ministry* 11 (1989): 54-64.

Guldner, Claude, and Thomas St. James O'Connor. "The Alf Group: A Model of Group Therapy with Children." *Journal of Group Psychotherapy, Psychodrama and Sociometry* 43, 4 (Winter 1991): 184-90.

Haight, Emily. "Paravision: A Model for Pastoral Supervision." *Journal of Supervision and Training in Ministry* 15 (1994): 86-95.

_____. "What Is Pastoral about Pastoral Supervision?" *Journal of Supervision and Training in Ministry* 16 (1995): 155-59.

Haines, Denise. "The Power to Lead: Forming Women for Ministry." *Journal of Supervision and Training in Ministry* 15 (1994): 190-99.

Hall, Charles E. "A Gift of Understanding." *Journal of Supervision and Training in Ministry* 11 (1989): 223-29.

_____. "Hall Response to Browning." *Journal of Supervision and Training in Ministry* 2 (1979): 111-15.

_____. "New Thrusts for the Association for Clinical Pastoral Education." *The Journal of Pastoral Care* 22, 4 (1968): 203-205.

Halstead, James. "Boundary Issues in Formation and Supervision: Objectives, Roles and Responsibilities." *Journal of Supervision and Training in Ministry* 15 (1994): 223-30.

Hammett, Hugh. "The Historical Context of the Origins of CPE." *The Journal of Pastoral Care* 29, 1 (1975): 76-85.

Hammett, Jenny Yates. "A Second Drink at the Well: Theological and Philosophical Context of CPE." *The Journal of Pastoral Care* 29, 1 (1975): 86-89.

Hand, Quentin L. "AAPC Constitution Revision: A Challenge to Integrate Function and Form." *The Journal of Pastoral Care* 30, 4 (1976): 320-24.

Harmon, Michelle. "The Clinical Pastoral Counselor and the Dialectic of Human Experience." *The Journal of Pastoral Care* 29, 2 (1975): 168-75.

Harris, J. Edward. "Supervision: A Biblical Metaphor." *Journal of Supervision and Training in Ministry* 2 (1979): 12-21.

_____. "Theological Education and Ministerial Formation in the Caribbean Context." *Journal of Supervision and Training in Ministry* 15 (1994): 166-76.

Hartung, Bruce M.. "The Capacity to Enter Latency in Learning Pastoral Psychotherapy." *Journal of Supervision and Training in Ministry* 2 (1979): 46-59.

_____. "Issues in Supervision During a Training Year." *The Journal of Pastoral Care* 31, 3 (September 1977): 172-77.

Hasty, Grace. "A Mutual Struggle to Accept Grace." *Journal of Supervision and Training in Ministry* 17 (1996): 4-15.

Heim, Joseph. "The Social Justice Issues in Supervision." In Estadt et al., eds., *The Art of Clinical Supervision: A Pastoral Counselling Perspective*, 262-74.

Hemenway, Joan E. "Position Paper on CPE Supervision and Learning." *The Journal of Pastoral Care* 36, 3 (September 1982): 194-202.

Hempel, Joel. "Group Practicum: A Model for Developing Pastoral Care Skills." *The Journal of Pastoral Care* 49, 3 (Fall 1995): 228-29.

Hilsman, Gordon J. "Grafting Clinical Pastoral Education: Teaching Competencies for the New Spiritual Care Work." *The Journal of Pastoral Care* 51, 1 (Spring 1997): 37-48.

Hiltner, Seward. "The Debt of Clinical Pastoral Education to Anton Boisen." *The Journal of Pastoral Care* 20, 3 (September 1966): 129-35.
_____. "Fifty Years of CPE." *The Journal of Pastoral Care* 29, 2 (1975): 90-98.
_____. "Pastoral Counselling and the Church." *The Journal of Pastoral Care* 31, 3 (1977): 194-209.
_____. "A Descriptive Appraisal, 1935-1980." *Pastoral Psychology* 29, 2 (Winter 1980): 86-98.
_____. "The Contributions of Liberals to Pastoral Care." In James Luther Adams and Seward Hiltner, eds., *Pastoral Care in the Liberal Churches*. Nashville: Abingdon Press, 1970.
_____. "Judgment and Appraisal in Pastoral Care." *Pastoral Psychology* (December 1965): 41-47.
_____. *Pastoral Counselling*. Nashville: Abingdon Press, 1949.
_____. *Preface to Pastoral Theology*. Nashville: Abingdon Press, 1958.
_____. *The Christian Shepherd*. Nashville: Abingdon Press, 1959.
Hinkle, John E. "Is the PhD Necessary for Pastoral Counselling?" *Journal of Supervision and Training in Ministry* 4 (1981): 69-80.
Hockley, Robert E. "Parallel Processes and the Like in CPE." *Journal of Supervision and Training in Ministry* 5 (1982): 77-87.
_____. "Clinical Pastoral Supervision: A Rationale." *Journal of Christian Education Papers* 60 (November 1977): 5-13.
Holifield, E. Brooks. *History of Pastoral Care in America*. Nashville: Abingdon Press, 1983.
_____. "History and Selfhood: An Historian's View." *The Journal of Pastoral Care* 28, 3 (1974):147-51.
Hommes, Tjaard G. "Supervision as Theological Method." *The Journal of Pastoral Care* 31, 3 (September 1987): 150-57.
Hoover, Edwin A. "Pastoral Supervision as an Interpersonal Experience." *The Journal of Pastoral Care* 31 (September 1971): 164-71.
_____. "The Distinction Between Adequate and Excellent Supervision: A Wholistic Perspective." *The Journal of Pastoral Care* 34, 4 (September 1980): 190-96.
Houts, Donald C. "Consultation Teams: A Supervisory Alternative." *Journal of Supervision and Training in Ministry* 3 (1980): 9-20.
_____. "Pastoral Care for Pastors: Toward a Church Strategy." *Pastoral Psychology* 25, 3 (Spring 1977): 186-96.
Howard, Judson D. "Interpersonal Group Seminar: A Training Method in the Pastoral Care of Groups." *The Journal of Pastoral Care* 14, 3 (1960): 160-66.
Hug, William F. "Beyond Theory and Technique: Reflections on the Process of Becoming." In Barry K. Estadt et al., eds., *Pastoral Counselling*. Englewood Cliffs, NJ: Prentice-Hall, 1983, 64-84.
Hughes-MacIntyre, Mary Francis. "Theory of Supervision in Pastoral Counselling." *Journal of Supervision and Training in Ministry* 13 (1991): 63-74.
Hughes-Tremper, Sherron L., Susan Kline and JoAnne O'Reilley. "Convinced of Collegiality." *Journal of Supervision and Training in Ministry,* 6 (1983): 109-21.

Hulme, W.E. "Lutheran Pastoral Care." In Hunter et al., eds., *Dictionary of Pastoral Care and Counselling.* Nashville: Abingdon Press, 1991, 670-72.
Humphries, John M. "Reflections by an Interim Supervisor." *Journal of Supervision and Training in Ministry* 4 (1981): 57-60.
Hunter, George I. "Hunter: Response to Browning." *Journal of Supervision and Training in Ministry* 2 (1979): 106-108.
Hunter, Rodney, H. Newton Malony, Liston O. Mills and John Patton, eds., *Dictionary of Pastoral Care and Counselling.* Nashville: Abingdon Press, 1990.
_____. "Moralizing." In Hunter et al., eds. *Dictionary of Pastoral Care and Counselling,* 758.
_____."The Future of Pastoral Theology." *Pastoral Psychology* 29, 1 (Fall 1980): 58-69.
_____. "The Therapeutic Tradition of Pastoral Care and Counselling." In Couture and Hunter, eds., *Pastoral Care and Social Conflict.* Nashville: Abingdon Press, 1995, 17-31.
_____, and John Patton. "The Therapeutic Tradition's Theological and Ethical Commitments Viewed through Its Pedagogical Practices: A Tradition in Transition." In Couture and Hunter, eds., *Pastoral Care and Social Conflict,* 32-42.
Ikenye, Ndung'u J.B. "Training and Supervision for Ministry in Kenya." *Journal of Supervision and Training in Ministry* 14 (1992-93): 139-46.
Jackson, Gordon E. "Response to Farley." *Journal of Supervision and Training in Ministry* 4 (1981): 109-13.
Jensen, Mark. "Life Histories and Narrative Theology." In David Steere, ed., *The Supervision of Pastoral Care,* 114-28.
Jernigan, H.L. "Models in Psychological and Pastoral Theory." In Hunter et al., eds., *Dictionary of Pastoral Care and Counselling,* 746-47.
Jewett, Julia, and Emily Haight. "The Emergence of Feminine Consciousness in Supervision." *Journal of Supervision and Training in Ministry* 6 (1983): 164-74.
Johanson, Gregory J. "The Parish Revisited: Reflections on How CPE Helped and Hindered a Return to Parish Ministry After Training." *The Journal of Pastoral Care* 32, 3 (September 1978): 147-54.
Johnson, Gerald Cowing. "Parable: The Bridge Between Theology and Psychology in Supervision." *Journal of Supervision and Training in Ministry* 9 (1987): 188-97.
Johnson, Paul E. "Clinical Pastoral Training at the Crossroads." *The Journal of Pastoral Care* 16, 2 (1962): 65-71.
_____. "Fifty Years of Clinical Pastoral Education." *The Journal of Pastoral Care* 22 (1968): 223-31.
Johnson, Richard. "Theory Paper of the Year." *Journal of Supervision and Training in Ministry* 4 (1981): 61-67.
Jones, Harold D. "CPE as Liturgical Encounter: An Interpersonal Theory of Learning." *Journal of Supervision and Training in Ministry* 9 (1988): 62-81.
Jordan, Merle. "Utilizing Helplessness With Students." *Journal of Supervision and Training in Ministry* 2 (1979): 73-81.
Jorjorian, Armen. "Some Reflections on the Future of the Summer Quarter of Clinical Pastoral Training." *The Journal of Pastoral Care* 13 (1960): 155-59.

_____. "The Meaning and Character of Supervisory Acts." *The Journal of Pastoral Care* 25, 3 (1971): 148-56.

Kae-Je, Bert. "Psychologist or Theologian? Pastoral Counselling, Supervision and Professional Identity." *The Journal of Pastoral Care* 47, 1 (Spring 1993): 65-72.

Karl, John C. "Forming the Inner Cup: The Ministry of Supervision with Pastoral Counselors." *Journal of Supervision and Training in Ministry* 7 (1984-85): 15-22.

Kestenbaum, Israel. " 'Mitzvah' and 'Talchlis': Jewish Paradigms for Pastoral Supervision." *Journal of Supervision and Training in Ministry* 15 (1994): 72.

Kilbourn, Elizabeth. "Canadian Association for Pastoral Education." In Hunter et al., eds., *Dictionary of Pastoral Care and Counselling*, 116-17.

King, S.D. "Southern Baptist Association for Clinical Pastoral Education." In Hunter et al., eds., *Dictionary of Pastoral Care and Counselling*, 1204-05.

Kline, Susan J. "Theory Paper of the Year: Making Space to Make Sense." *Journal of Supervision and Training in Ministry* 5 (1982): 25-33.

Klink, Thomas. "Issues in Learning Through Supervision." *The Journal of Pastoral Care* 17, 2 (1963): 61-72.

_____. "Supervision." *Journal of Supervision and Training in Ministry* 11 (1989): 161-203.

Knights, Ward, and Sanchalak Swarmi Krishanand Tirth. "Hindu/Christian Convergence in Clinical Pastoral Education: Some Reflections." *The Journal of Pastoral Care* 51, 2 (Summer 1997): 177-86.

Kriesel, H. Terry. "Training in Basic Pastoral Counselling Skills: A Comparison of a Microtraining Approach with a Skills Practice Approach." *The Journal of Pastoral Care* 31 (1977): 125-33.

Kropp, Calvin, Carol Pitts, Timothy Thomas, Sam Sligar, Kathryn Sandifer and Richard Hester: Georgia Association for Pastoral Counselling, Inc. "A Critique from a Relational Perspective: A Response to 'A Case Gone Wrong'." *Journal of Supervision and Training in Ministry* 17(1996): 48-58.

Lambourne, R.A. "The Theological Strategy of a British Pastoral Training Course." *The Journal of Pastoral Care* 24, 4 (1970): 227-32.

Lentz, John. "Supervising the Counselling Relationship." In Steere, ed., *The Supervision of Pastoral Care*, 161-71.

Lindsey, Carolyn. "Some Aspects of Live Supervision." In Steere, ed., *The Supervision of Pastoral Care*, 183-92.

Linnan, John E. "Spiritual Formation in the Roman Catholic Church: An Historical Sketch." *Journal of Supervision and Training in Ministry* 15 (1994): 121-32.

Loringer, Richard, and August Lageman. "Supervision and the Intern Ministry." *Journal of Supervision and Training in Ministry* 11 (1989): 46-58.

Luecke, David. "Counselling With Couples." In Estadt et al., eds., *The Art of Clinical Supervision: A Pastoral Counselling Perspective*, 135-48.

Lyall, David, and John Foskett. *Helping the Helpers: Supervision and Pastoral Care*. London: SPCK, 1989.

MacLachlan, Archie. "Canadian Pastoral Care Movement." In Hunter et al., eds., *Dictionary of Pastoral Care and Counselling*, 118-20.

Maguire, Max. "A Case of Transference." *Journal of Supervision and Training in Ministry* 7 (1984-85): 75-76.

Malarkey, Lucy, and Rea McDonnell. "Epilogue: Approaching Mystery." In Estadt et al., eds., *The Art of Clinical Supervision: A Pastoral Counselling Perspective,* 287-96.

Maloney, Dorothy, and Richard Miller-Tod. "Responses To 'Theological and Philosophical Reflections on the Training of Pastoral Counselors' by J. Jeffrey Means et al." *Journal of Supervision and Training in Ministry* 8 (1986): 82-101.

Mann, John D. "Use of the CPE Model in Developing Congregational Campus Ministry." *The Journal of Pastoral Care* 32 (1978): 232-38.

Manzella, Margaret. "A Journey into Irrationality: Some Reflections from a CPE Program." *The Journal of Pastoral Care* 31 (1977): 4-11.

Marutle, Daniel D.T. "Supervision and Training for Ministry in South Africa." *Journal of Supervision and Training in Ministry* 14 (1992-93): 147-52.

Mason, Randall C. "Open Agenda Conferences: Purpose and Method." *Journal of Supervision and Training in Ministry* 2 (1979): 22-30.

_____. "Role Models, Training and the Parish." *Journal of Supervision and Training in Ministry* 1 (1978): 70-84.

Matthews, Penelope J. "Deepening in Grace: A Theological Framework for Understanding Supervision as a Process of Spiritual Formation." *Journal of Supervision and Training in Ministry* 16 (1995): 196-216.

Mauney, J. Luther. "Recognizing Resistance in Supervision: A Course for Parish Ministers." DMin Thesis, Lutheran Theological Southern Seminary, 1982.

_____. "Analysis of Supervisory Impasse." *Journal of Supervision and Training in Ministry* 3 (1980): 21-28.

May, William F. "Response to Edward Farley's 'The Reform of Theological Education as a Theological Task'." *Journal of Supervision and Training in Ministry* 4 (1981): 121-34.

Mayse, Marilyn, and Paula Jeanne Teague. "Women Supervised by Men." *Journal of Supervision and Training in Ministry* 9 (1987): 35-41.

McCarthy, Marie. "Discerning the Ethical Commitments Implicit in Models of Supervision." *Journal of Supervision and Training in Ministry* 12 (1990): 132-44.

McCarthy, Marie, and David B. McCurdy. "Symposium: Supervision and Training as an Ethical Endeavor." *Journal of Supervision and Training in Ministry* 12 (1990): 106-10.

McCord, James I. "Seward Hiltner's Contributions to the Life of the Churches and to Professional Theological Education." *Pastoral Psychology* 29, 1 (Fall 1980): 13-16.

McWilliams, Frances C. "Voices Crying in the Wilderness: Prophetic Ministry in Clinical Pastoral Education." *The Journal of Pastoral Care* 51, 1 (Spring 1997): 37-48.

Meakes, Elizabeth, and Thomas St. James O'Connor. "Miriam Dancing and With Leprosy: Women's Experience of Supervision in CAPE." *Pastoral Sciences* 12 (1993): 25-39.

Means, Jeffrey, Ellery Duke, Pamela Holliman and H. Eileen Burtle. "Theological and Philosophical Reflection on the Training of Pastoral Counselors." *Journal of Supervision and Training in Ministry* 8 (1986): 82-101.

Means, Jeffrey. "Formation for Pastoral Counselling." *Journal of Supervision and Training in Ministry* 15 (1994): 200-209.

Melchert, Ernest J. "A Look at an Extended Quarter of CPE." *The Journal of Pastoral Care* 29, 1 (1975): 42-44.

Merwald, A.A. "Supervision of the Psychological Self in Pastoral Education." *Journal of Supervision and Training in Ministry* 5 (1982): 167-80.

Meyer, David C. "Resistance to Clinical Learning: Four Biblical Types." *Journal of Supervision and Training in Ministry* 2 (1979): 60-72.

Meyer, Lauree Hersch. "Response ... Struggling Is Like Wrestling With God." *Journal of Supervision and Training in Ministry* 9 (1987): 201-10.

Mills, Liston O. "Seward Hiltner's Contributions to Pastoral Care and Counseling." *Pastoral Psychology* 29, 1 (Fall 1980): 8-12.

Mitchell, Kenneth R. "Ethical Issues in Supervision: Justice, Authority, Equality." *Journal of Supervision and Training in Ministry* 12 (1990): 153-61.

_____. "Thomas Klink: An Overview." *Journal of Supervision and Training in Ministry* 11 (1989): 151-61.

_____. "Response to Edward Farley's 'The Reform of Theological Education as a Theological Task.'" *Journal of Supervision and Training in Ministry* 4 (1981): 115-19.

_____. "Response to Carl Christensen 'Psychiatric Supervision of Pastoral Therapists.'" *Journal of Supervision and Training in Ministry* 1 (1978): 85-87.

_____. "The Views of Three Critics: Editor's Comments." *Journal of Supervision and Training in Ministry* 11 (1989): 220-22.

Moore, Mary Kennderick, and Shirley B. Moore. "The Experience of Joint Placement in Clinical Pastoral Education: From Homelessness Back to Home." *Journal of Supervision and Training in Ministry* 9 (1987): 42-50.

Morris, Robert R. "Authority Issues in Cross-Gender Clinical Pastoral Education Supervision." DMin Thesis, Columbia Theological Seminary, 1990.

Murtagh, Lawrence J. "The Supervisor as Servant of the Word." *Journal of Supervision and Training in Ministry* 7 (1984-85): 65-66.

Nelson, William. "A Narrative Approach to Theological Reflection." *Journal of Supervision and Training in Ministry* 9 (1987): 157-82.

Niswander, Bonnie J. "The Ministry of Clinical Supervision of Pastoral Psychotherapy: A Process of Professional Formation." *Journal of Supervision and Training in Ministry* 9 (1987): 75-99.

_____. "Response: Back to the Future." *Journal of Supervision and Training in Ministry* 11 (1989): 215-19.

Nyomi, Setriakor Kobla. "Towards Pastoral Integration of an Issue: Reflections of a Ghanaian in CPE." *Journal of Supervision and Training in Ministry* 14 (1992-93): 225-32.

O'Connor, Thomas St. James. "Les Miserables and the Lepers, Tragedy and Fairy Tale: The Paradox of Salvation." *Consensus* 16, 1 (1990): 105-108.

_____. "Ministry Without a Future: A Pastoral Care Approach to Patients with Senile Dementia." *The Journal of Pastoral Care* 46, 1 (Spring 1992): 5-12.

_____. "Take What You Can and Dance: Adult Education and Pastoral Supervision." *Journal of Supervision and Training in Ministry* 15 (1994): 50-62.

O'Connor, Thomas St. James, and Claude Guldner. "The Alf Group: A Model of Group Therapy with Children." *Journal of Group Psychotherapy, Psychodrama and Sociometry* 43, 4 (Winter 1991): 184-90.

_____, and Elizabeth Huss. "The Broken Balloon: A Metaphor for Divorce." *Journal of Divorce and Separation* (Winter 1995): 211-23.

_____, and Elizabeth Meakes. "Miriam Dancing and With Leprosy: Women's Experience of Supervision in CAPE." *Pastoral Sciences* 12 (1993): 25-39.

_____, Elizabeth Meakes, Marlene Bourdeau, Maria Papp and Pam McCarroll-Butler. "Diversity in the Pastoral Relationship: An Evaluation of the Helping Styles Inventory." *The Journal of Pastoral Care* 49, 4 (Winter 1995): 365-74.

_____, Elizabeth Meakes, Karen Ann Fox, Kathleen O'Neill and Glenn Empey. "Quantitative and Qualitative Research on a Regional Basic SPE Program." *The Journal of Pastoral Care* 51, 2 (Spring 1997): 37-48.

_____, Pam McCarroll-Butler, Shannon Gadowsky, Kathleen O'Neill and Elizabeth Meakes. "Making the Most and Making Sense: Ethnographic Research on Spirituality in Palliative Care." *The Journal of Pastoral Care* 51, 1 (Spring 1997): 25-36.

_____, Ruth Pickering, Martha Schuman and Elizabeth Meakes. "On the Right Track: Client Experience of Narrative Therapies." *Contemporary Family Therapy* 19, 4 (December 1997): 479-95.

_____, and Elizabeth Meakes. "Hope in the Midst of Challenge: Evidence-based Pastoral Care" (in press). *The Journal of Pastoral Care* 52, 2 (Spring 1998).

Oates, Wayne E. "Pastoral Supervision Today." *Pastoral Psychology* 24 (Fall 1975): 17-29.

_____. "The Contribution of Paul Tillich to Pastoral Psychology." *Pastoral Psychology* (February 1968): 11-16.

Oden, Thomas. *Pastoral Counselling*. Classic Pastoral Care Series, Volume 3. New York: Crossroad, 1987.

_____. *The Care of Souls in the Classic Tradition*. Philadelphia: Fortress Press, 1984.

_____. *Game Free: A Guide to the Meaning of Intimacy*. San Francisco: Harper and Row, 1974.

O'Reilly, JoAnn. "Crossing the Threshold into the Supervisory Process." *Journal of Supervision and Training in Ministry* 11 (1989): 133-36.

O'Shea, Ann. "The Emmaus Story: A Model for Pastoral Supervision." *Journal of Supervision and Training in Ministry* 9 (1987): 29-34.

Pangrazzi, Arnaldo. "The Artistic Process in Clinical Pastoral Education." *Journal of Supervision and Training in Ministry* 5 (1982): 35-43.

Parker, Duane. "Consumer Protection Issues in CPE." *The Journal of Pastoral Care* 29 (1975): 50-54.

_____. "Student-Directed CPE." *The Journal of Pastoral Care* 32, 3 (1978): 161-69.

Parker, G. Keith. "Problems and Possibilities of Cross-Cultural Supervision." *Pastoral Psychology* 26, 4 (Summer 1978): 263-76.

Patton, John. *Pastoral Care in Context: An Introduction to Pastoral Care.* Louisville: Westminster/John Knox Press, 1993.

———. "Pastoral Counselling." In Hunter et al., eds., *Dictionary of Pastoral Care and Counselling,* 851.

———. "Supervision, Pastoral." In Hunter et al., eds., *Dictionary of Pastoral Care and Counselling,* 1239-43.

———. "The 'Holy Complexity' of the Clinical: Some Reflections on Pastoral Supervision." *Journal of Supervision and Training in Ministry* 13 (1991): 243-53.

———. "Tom Klink's Continuing Contribution to Pastoral Supervision and Professional Education for Ministry." *Journal of Supervision and Training in Ministry* 11 (1989): 230-41.

———. "Pastoral Supervision and Theology." *Journal of Supervision and Training in Ministry* 8 (1986): 59-71.

———. "Theological Integration of Pastoral Supervision." In W.B. Oglesby, ed., *New Shape of Pastoral Theology: Seward Hiltner.* New York: Paulist Press, 1969, 234-47.

———. "Patton: Response to Browning." *Journal of Supervision and Training in Ministry* 2 (1979): 108-11.

Patton, John, and John Warkentin. "A Dialogue on Supervision and Consultation." *The Journal of Pastoral Care* 25, 3 (1971): 165-74.

Pattison, E. Mansell. "Systems Pastoral Care." *The Journal of Pastoral Care* 26, 1 (1972): 2-14.

———. *Pastor and Parish: A Systems Approach.* Philadelphia: Fortress Press, 1977.

Petering, Carl. "Theological Integration Seminar." *Journal of Supervision and Training in Ministry* 9 (1987): 135-46.

Peterson, John H. "Wilderness and Covenant: A Theory of Learning for CPE." *Journal of Supervision and Training in Ministry* 7 (1984-85): 39-49.

Plummer, Stuart A. "Reflections on Supervisory Work with Women Students: Some Issues and Opportunities." *Journal of Supervision and Training in Ministry* 6 (1983): 159-63.

Pohly, Kenneth. *Transforming the Rough Places: The Ministry of Supervision.* Dayton, OH: Whaleprints, 1993.

Poling, James N. "Beginning Thoughts on a Theological Method for Ministry." *Pastoral Psychology* 30, 4 (Summer 1982): 163-70.

Potts, M.D. "The Extended Unit: A Viable Alternative." *Journal of Supervision and Training in Ministry* 4 (1981): 49-56.

Powell, Robert C. *CPE: Fifty Years of Learning Through Supervised Encounter with Living Human Documents.* New York: Association for Clinical Pastoral Education, 1975.

———. "Mrs. Ethel Phelps Stokes Hoyt (1887-1952) and the Joint Committee on Religion and Medicine (1923-1936): A Brief Sketch." *The Journal of Pastoral Care* 29, 1 (1975): 99-105.

Powell, Robert Z. "Peership with the Supervisor as a Criterion for Advanced CPE." *The Journal of Pastoral Care* 29, 1 (1975): 45- 49.

Pruett, James W. "My Theory and Practice of Clinical Supervision with Pastoral Counselling Trainees." *Journal of Supervision and Training in Ministry* 11 (1989): 74-90.

Pruyser, Paul. *Minister as Diagnostician.* Philadelphia: Westminster Press, 1976.

_____. "Response (to Christensen)." *Journal of Supervision and Training in Ministry* 1 (1978): 38-60.

Rader, Blaine B. "Supervision of Pastoral Psychotherapy." *The Journal of Pastoral Care* 31, 3 (September 1977): 178-85.

_____. "The Organizational Context of Supervision and Training." *Journal of Supervision and Training in Ministry* 3 (1980): 87-89.

Rafford, Robert L. "Androgogy and Supervision." *Journal of Supervision and Training in Ministry* 5 (1982): 69-75.

Ramsay, Nancy. "Pastoral Supervision: A Theological Resource for Ministry." *Journal of Supervision and Training in Ministry* 13 (1991): 190-205.

Randall, Frances. "Black Africa–A Pioneer Venture." *Journal of Supervision and Training in Ministry* 12 (1990): 76-80.

Randall, Martha. "A Study of Black Students' Experiences in Clinical Pastoral Education." *Journal of Supervision and Training in Ministry* 14 (1992-93): 213-24.

Ray, Peter. "The Gift and the Challenge: Reflections on the Cross-Cultural Supervision of Pastoral Counselling Trainees." *Journal of Supervision and Training in Ministry* 14 (1992-93): 181-200.

Redcliffe, Gary. "Post-Liberal Foundations for Pastoral Care." In Adrian M. Visscher, ed., *Pastoral Studies in the University Setting*, 211-21.

Reed, James. "Anglican Pastoral Care." In Hunter et al., eds., *Dictionary of Pastoral Care and Counselling*, 42-43.

Rieder, Keith. "Supervision of Pastors in Training: A Clinical Model." *Journal of Supervision and Training in Ministry* 14 (1992-93): 53-60.

Ring, Roger. "Cycles of Transformation: A Slightly Different Person." *Journal of Supervision and Training in Ministry* 7 (1984-85): 50-62.

Sanderson, Paul D. "Key Issues in the Pastoral Supervisory Relationship." *Pastoral Psychology* 26, 4 (Summer 1978): 240-52.

Schaufelberger, Kent A. "Adoption as Grace, Faith and Story: A Metaphor of Process Education." *Journal of Supervision and Training in Ministry* 17 (1996): 136-63.

Schenfler, Lowell W. "The Sounding Board: A Model for Pastoral Supervision in the Church." DMin Thesis, United Theological Seminary (Dayton), 1981.

Schlauch, Chris. "Functioning as an Ethicist in Pastoral Supervision: Casting the Questions." *Journal of Supervision and Training in Ministry* 12 (1990): 111-31.

Schmuker, Frederick. "The Interpretation of Tongues." *Journal of Supervision and Training in Ministry* 5 (1982): 61-67.

Schurman, Paul G. "Supervising the Pastoral Counselor." *Journal of Supervision and Training in Ministry* 1 (1978): 63-69.

Schwartz, Julie. "Shall We Dance? Dialogue, Relationship, and Challenge in Supervision." *Journal of Supervision and Training in Ministry* 17 (1996): 224-40.

Seabright, Russell F. "Supervision and Training for Ministry in Indonesia." *Journal of Supervision and Training in Ministry* 12 (1990): 83-86.

———. "Response: How Time Has Altered our Perceptions." *Journal of Supervision and Training in Ministry* 11 (1989): 211-14.

Seaton-Johnson, Anthony W., and Craig A. Everett. "An Analysis of Clinical Pastoral Education Supervisors: Their Identities, Roles, and Resources." *The Journal of Pastoral Care* 34, 3 (September 1980): 148-58.

Shea, John. "Response: Hosting the Uninvited." *Journal of Supervision and Training in Ministry* 9 (1987): 217-26.

Sheehan, Barbara. "Gender Issues in Supervision." In Steere, ed., *The Supervision of Pastoral Care* 222-35.

Sheehan, Mary Ellen. "Theological Reflection and Theory-Praxis Integration–An Experience with the Case Study Method." *Pastoral Sciences* 3 (1984): 25-38.

Silberman, Jefferey M. "Covenant–A Relational Theory of Education for CPE." *Journal of Supervision and Training in Ministry* 11 (1989): 93-103.

Skaggs, Bruce. "Group Supervision." In Steere, ed., *The Supervision of Pastoral Care*, 172-82.

Smith, Alexa. "Student Responses to Clinical Pastoral Education." In Steere, ed., *The Supervision of Pastoral Care*, 129-45.

Somers-Clarke, Carol, and Logan Jones. "The Clinical Rhombus Revisited: Learning Through Resistance and Change." *The Journal of Pastoral Care* 47, 3 (Fall 1993): 207-15.

Southard, Samuel. "Criteria for Evaluating Supervisors-in-Training." *The Journal of Pastoral Care* 17 (1963): 193-202.

St. Clair, Robert James. "Toward a Social Field Theory of Supervision." *The Journal of Pastoral Care* 23, 3 (1963): 142-52.

Stair, M. Jean. "A Systemic Comment: A Call to Partnership. Response to 'Problematic Supervision in Seminary Field Education'." *Journal of Supervision and Training in Ministry* 17 (1996): 65-70.

Stalfa, Frank J. "Vocation as Autobiography: Family of Origin Influence on the Caregiving Role in Ministry." *The Journal of Pastoral Care* 48, 4 (Winter 1994): 370-80.

Steere, David. "Clinical Supervision in Pastoral Care." In Steere, ed., *The Supervision of Pastoral Care*, 15-38.

———. "Supervision Among the Helping Professions." In Steere, ed., *The Supervision of Pastoral Care*, 39-64.

———. "A Model for Supervision." In Steere, ed., *The Supervision of Pastoral Care*, 65-89.

———. "An Experiment in Training Supervisors for Field Education." In Steere, ed., *The Supervision of Pastoral Care*, 262-84.

———. "Preface." In Steere, ed., *The Supervision of Pastoral Care*, 9-13.

———. "An Experiment in Supervisory Training." *The Journal of Pastoral Care* 23 (1969): 202-17.

Steinhoff-Smith, Roy. "The Tragedy of Clinical Pastoral Education." *Pastoral Psychology* 41, 1 (1992): 45-54.

Stevens, R. Paul. "Systemic Equipping: Beyond the Packaged Lay Training Program." *Pastoral Sciences* 10 (1991): 61-75.

Stewart, Charles W. "The Ministry of Supervision." In Orlo Strunk, ed., *Dynamic Interpersonalism for Ministry*. New York: Paulist Press, 1973, 227-36.
_____. "Training Pastoral Supervision for Seminary Field Education." *The Journal of Pastoral Care* 25, 1 (1971): 24-32.
_____. "Living Issues in CPE: A Dialogue." *The Journal of Pastoral Care* 29, 3 (1975): 148-56.
Stockwell, Foster, and Douglas E. Wingeier. "The Training of Religious Leaders in China." *Journal of Supervision and Training in Ministry* 17 (1996), 224-40.
Stokes, Allison. *Ministry After Freud*. New York: Pilgrim Press, 1985.
Stone, Howard. "Briefly Noted: Training the Pastoral Counselor." *Journal of Supervision and Training in Ministry* 5 (1982): 7-12.
_____. "Religious Beliefs in Pastoral Care." *Journal of Supervision and Training in Ministry* 15 (1994): 63-69.
Strunk, Orlo. "Emanuel Movement." In Hunter et al., eds., *Dictionary of Pastoral Care and Counselling*, 350.
_____. "Training of Empathic Abilities: A Note." *The Journal of Pastoral Care* 12, 4 (1975): 222-25.
Summers, Thomas. "Story Day in CPE." *Journal of Supervision and Training in Ministry* 4 (1981): 37-48.
_____. "Pastoral Certification from a Developmental Perspective." *Journal of Supervision and Training in Ministry* 3 (1980): 73-85.
Taylor, David M. "Clinical Pastoral Training." *The Journal of Pastoral Care* 15, 1 (1961): 34-40.
Teague, Paula Jeanne. "Weighty Friend and Clearness Committee: Metaphors for Pastoral Supervision." *Journal of Supervision and Training in Ministry* 12 (1990): 58-72.
Thomas, Jack L. "A Theory of Education Relevant for CPE." *Journal of Supervision and Training in Ministry* 5 (1982): 15-23.
Thomas, John Rea. "Evaluations of Clinical Pastoral Training and 'Part-Time' Training in a General Hospital." *The Journal of Pastoral Care* 13 (1959): 28-38.
Thomas, Sandra M. "The Ministry of Pastoral Care: Guiding the Care-Giving Work of the Large Congregation." DMin Thesis, Lancaster Theological Seminary, 1991.
Thornton, Edward E. "Clinical Pastoral Education (CPE)." In Hunter et al., *Dictionary of Pastoral Care and Counselling*, 180.
_____. *Professional Education for Ministry*. Nashville: Abingdon Press, 1970.
_____. "Some Hard Questions for Clinical Pastoral Educators." *The Journal of Pastoral Care* 22, 4 (1968): 194-202.
Tiller, Daryl J. "The Self as Instrument." In Steere, ed., *The Supervision of Pastoral Care*, 146-60.
Tollerud, Toni R. "Clinical Pastoral Education: A Layperson's Journey." *Journal of Supervision and Training in Ministry* 11 (1989): 59-72.
Tracy, David. "Revisionist Practical Theology and the Meaning of Public Discourse." *Pastoral Psychology* 26, 2 (Winter 1977): 83-94.
Tucker, Grayson L. "The Supervision of Church Volunteers in the Local Congregation." In Steere, ed., *The Supervision of Pastoral Care*, 236-49.

Ulanov, Ann Belford. "The Feminine and the World of CPE." *The Journal of Pastoral Care* 29, 1 (1975): 11-22.

van Arkel, Jan T. de Jongh. "Teaching Pastoral Care and Counselling in an African Context: A Problem of Contextual Relevance." *The Journal of Pastoral Care* 49, 2 (Summer 1995): 189-99.

VandeCreek, Larry. *A Research Primer for Pastoral Care and Counselling.* Decatur, GA: The Journal Of Pastoral Care Publications, 1988.

_____, Hilary Bender and Merle R. Jordan *Research in Pastoral Care and Counselling: Quantitative and Qualitative Approaches* Decatur, GA: Journal of Pastoral Care Publications, Inc, 1988

_____. "A Statistical Profile of the American Association of Pastoral Counselors and the Association for Clinical Pastoral Education." *Pastoral Psychology* 31, 3 (Spring 1983): 170-78.

_____. "The Measurement of Student Learning During Clinical Pastoral Education: The Clinical Ministry Assessment Profile and the Q-sort Technique." *Pastoral Sciences* 8 (1989): 17-30.

_____, and Michael R. Sexton. "ACPE Consultation Experience: Feedback from Basic and Advanced Students." *The Journal of Pastoral Care* 48, 1 (Spring 1994): 55-63.

_____, and Loren Connell. "Evaluation of the Hospital Chaplain's Pastoral Care: Catholic and Protestant Differences." *The Journal of Pastoral Care* 45, 3 (1991): 289-96.

_____, and John Valentino. "Affective and Cognitive Changes in First-Unit Clinical Pastoral Education Students." *The Journal of Pastoral Care* 45, 4 (1991): 375-88.

VanKatwyk, Peter. "A Grief Observed: A Theological and Family Systems Approach to Grief." *The Journal of Pastoral Care* 47, 2 (Summer 1993): 141-47.

_____. "The Helping Styles Inventory: A Tool for Supervised Pastoral Education." *The Journal of Pastoral Care* 42, 4 (Winter 1988): 319-29.

_____. "The Helping Styles Inventory: An Update." *The Journal of Pastoral Care* 49, 4 (Winter 1995): 375-83.

_____. "Healing Through Differentiation: A Pastoral Care and Counselling Perspective." *The Journal of Pastoral Care* 51, 3 (Fall 1997): 283-92.

Van den Blink, A.J., and James N. Poling. "Theology and Supervision." *Journal of Supervision and Training in Ministry* 13 (1991): 257-73.

_____. "Reflections on Supervision of Pastoral Psychotherapy." *Journal of Supervision and Training in Ministry* 17 (1996), 95-111.

Van Wagner, Charles A. "Supervision of Lay Pastoral Care." *The Journal of Pastoral Care* 31, 3 (September 1977): 158-63.

Vignaud, Davelyn L. "The Place of Worship in Pastoral Care." *Pastoral Psychology* 29, 2 (Winter 1980): 99-108.

Voss, Richard W. "Crisis Intervention: Critical Issues in Supervision." In Estadt et al., eds., *The Art of Clinical Supervision: A Pastoral Counselling Perspective*, 160-94.

_____. "Family Counselling." In Estadt et al. eds., *The Art of Clinical Supervision: A Pastoral Counselling Perspective*, 195-211.

Wagenhofer, John P. "Foundations for a Supervisor Certification Program." *Journal of Supervision and Training in Ministry* 14 (1992-93): 61-68.
Wallace, H. Mae. "Fast Serves and Hard Volleys." *Journal of Supervision and Training in Ministry* 7 (1984-85): 66-67.
Weeks, Louis. "Supervising Teachers in a Christian Education Program." In Divid Steere, ed., *The Supervision of Pastoral Care*, 250-61.
Weston, John H. "Gender Politics (and Another Matter) in a Residents Group." *Journal of Supervision and Training in Ministry* 11 (1989): 25-36.
Williams, Dean M. "CPE Graduation Sermon." *Journal of Supervision and Training in Ministry* 1 (1978): 46-50.
Wilson-Robinson, Patricia. "Something Within Reaches Out: Multicultural Dialogues." *Journal of Supervision and Training in Ministry* 16 (1995):170.
Wimberly, Edward P. "Indigenous Theological Reflection on Pastoral Supervision: An African-American Perspective." *Journal of Supervision and Training in Ministry* 13 (1991): 180-89.
Wingeier, Douglas E. "Pastoral Selection in Samoa: Procedures and Criteria." *Journal of Supervision and Training in Ministry* 16 (1995): 217-23.
Wise, Carroll. "The Supervisory Alliance in Pastoral Psychotherapy." *The Journal of Pastoral Care* 30, 1 (September 1977): 186-93.
_____. *The Meaning of Pastoral Care*. New York: Harper and Row, 1966.
_____. "Relationship between Clinical Training and Field Work Supervision." *The Journal of Pastoral Care* 8, 4 (1954): 189-94.
_____. *Pastoral Counselling: Its Theory and Practice*. New York: Harper and Brothers, 1951.
Woodruff, C. Roy. "Theological Reflection in the Supervisory Process." *The Journal of Pastoral Care* 34, 4 (1980): 197-203.
Wright, Shirley B. et al. "An Experiment in Tandem Care." *Journal of Supervision and Training in Ministry* 10 (1988): 29-35.
Young, James H. "A Process Model of Supervision in Ministry in the Context of Cross-Cultural Social Group Interaction." *Journal of Supervision and Training* 14 (1992-93): 167-74.
Young, Robert A. "Witchdoctoring in Supervision." *Journal of Supervision and Training in Ministry* 7 (1984-85): 70-71.

**Works by Systematic Theologians**

Braaten, Carl E. "The Person of Jesus Christ." In Carl Braaten and R. Jensen, eds., *Christian Dogmatics,* Vol. 1. Philadelphia: Fortress Press, 1984, 469-557.
Clarkson, John F., ed. *Church Teaches: Documents of the Church in English Translation*. Rockford, IL: Tan Books, 1973.
Hodgson, Peter. *Revisioning the Church: Ecclesial Freedom in the New Paradigm*. Philadelphia: Fortress Press, 1989.
Kline, C.B. "Theological Anthropology, Discipline of." In Hunter et al., *Dictionary of Pastoral Care and Counselling*, 1259.
McBrien, Richard. *Catholicism,* Vols. 1 and 2. Minneapolis: Winston/Seabury Press, 1980.

Tracy, David. "Practical Theology in the Situation of Global Pluralism." In Mudge and Poling, eds., *Formation and Reflection*, 139-54.
_____. *Blessed Rage for Order*. Minneapolis: Seabury Press, 1975.
_____. *The Analogical Imagination: Christian Theology and the Culture of Pluralism*. New York: Crossroad, 1981.
_____. *Plurality and Ambiguity*. New York: Harper and Row, 1987.
_____. "The Role of Theology in Public Life: Some Reflections." *Word and World: Theology of Christian Ministry* 4 (Summer 1984): 230-39.
_____. "The Foundations of Practical Theology." In Browning, ed., *Practical Theology*. New York: Harper and Row, 1983, 61-82.
_____. "Theoria and Praxis: A Partial Response." *Theological Education* 17 (Spring 1981): 167-74.
_____. "Defending the Public Character of Theology: How My Mind Has Changed." *The Christian Century* 98 (April 1, 1981): 350-56.
_____. "Revisionist Practical Theology and the Meaning of Public Discourse." *Pastoral Psychology* 26, 2 (Winter 1977): 83-94.

**Practical Theologians and Other Influences on Charles Gerkin's Theology**

Browning, Don. *A Fundamental Practical Theology* Minneapolis: Fortress Press, 1991.
_____. "Methods and Foundations for Pastoral Studies in the University." *Pastoral Studies in the University*. Ottawa: St. Paul's, 1989, 49-65.
_____. "Introduction to Pastoral Counselling." In Wicks et al., eds., *Clinical Handbook of Pastoral Counselling*, 5-13.
_____. *Religious Ethics and Pastoral Care*. Philadelphia: Fortress Press, 1983.
Gadamer, Hans-Georg. *Philosophical Hermeneutics*. Berkeley: University of California Press, 1976.
_____. *Reason in the Age of Science*. Cambridge: MIT Press, 1981.
_____. *Truth and Method*. New York: Crossroad, 1982.
Meier, Augustine. "The Applications of Hermeneutics to Psychotherapy Practice, Theory and Research." *Pastoral Studies in the University*. Ottawa: St. Paul's, 1989, 109-35.
Moltmann, Jurgen. *The Church in the Power of the Spirit*. New York: Harper and Row, 1977.
_____. *The Crucified God*. New York: Harper and Row, 1974.
_____. *The Trinity and the Kingdom*. San Francisco: Harper and Row, 1981.
Niebuhr, H. Richard. *The Meaning of Revelation*. New York: MacMillan, 1941.
_____. *The Responsible Self*. New York: Harper and Row, 1963.
Ricoeur, Paul. *The Rule of Metaphor: Multi-disciplinary Studies of the Creation of Meaning of Language*. Toronto: University of Toronto Press, 1975.
_____. *Essays in Biblical Interpretation*. Philadelphia: Fortress Press, 1980.
_____. *Interpretation Theory: Discourse and the Surplus of Meaning*. Fort Worth: Texas Christian University Press, 1976.
_____. *Time and Narrative,* Vol. 1. Chicago: University of Chicago Press, 1984.
_____. *Time and Narrative,* Vol. 2. Chicago: University of Chicago Press, 1985.
_____. *Time and Narrative,* Vol. 3. Chicago: University of Chicago Press, 1988.

Tillich, Paul. *Love, Power and Justice.* New York: Oxford University Press, 1980.
_____. *The Protestant Era.* Chicago: University of Chicago Press, 1957.
_____. *The Courage to Be.* Chicago: University of Chicago Press, 1952.
_____. *Systematic Theology*, Vols. 1 and 2. Chicago: University of Chicago Press, 1951.
Winquist, Charles. *Practical Hermeneutics.* Cico, CA: Scholars Press, 1981.

**Clinical Supervision in Other Professional Disciplines and Other Related Works**

Bardill, Donald R., and Benjamin Saunders. "Marriage and Family Therapy and Graduate Social Work Education." In Howard Liddle et al., eds., *Handbook of Family Therapy Training and Supervision.* New York: Guilford Press, 1988, 316-30.
Beavers, W.R. "Family Therapy Supervision: An Introduction and Consumer's Guide." *Journal of Family Psychotherapy,* 1, 4 (1986): 15-24.
Berger, Michael. "Academic Psychology and Family Therapy Training." In Liddle et al., eds., *Handbook of Family Therapy Training and Supervision,* 303-15.
Bischoff, Richard J. "Themes in Therapist Development During the First Three Months of Clinical Experience." *Contemporary Family Therapy* 19 4(1997): 563-80.
Bordin, E. "A Working Alliance Based Model of Supervision." *The Consulting Psychologist* 11, 1 (1983): 5-12.
Bower, Gordon H., and Ernest R. Hilgard. *Theories of Learning.* Englewood Cliffs, NJ: Prentice-Hall, 1981.
Breunlin, Douglas C., Howard Liddle and Richard C. Schwartz. "Concurrent Training of Supervisors and Therapists." In Liddle et al., *Handbook of Family Therapy Training and Supervision,* 207-24.
Breunlin, Douglas C., et al. "Cybernetics of Videotape Supervision." *Handbook of Family Therapy Training and Supervision,* 194-206.
Brundage, Don, and Dorothy MacKeracher. *Theories of Learning.* Toronto: OISE, 1981.
Caldwell, Karen, Dorothy S. Becvar, Robert Bertolino and Doris Diamond. "A Postmodern Analysis of a Course on Clinical Supervision." *Contemporary Family Therapy* 19, 2(1997): 269-88.
Colapinto, Jorge. "Teaching the Structural Way." In Liddle et al., *Handbook of Family Therapy Training and Supervision,* 17-37.
Constantine, J., Fred Piercy and D. Sprenkle. "Live Supervision-of-Supervision in Family Therapy." *Journal of Marital and Family Therapy* 10, 1 (1984): 95-98.
Caust, B., J. Libow and P. Raskin. "Challenges and Promises of Training Women as Family Systems Therapists." *Family Process* 20, 4 (1981): 439-48.
Duhl, B. "Toward Cognitive-Behavioral Integration in Training Systems Therapists: An Interactive Approach to Training in Generic Systems Thinking." *Journal of Psychotherapy and the Family* 1, 4 (1989): 91-108.
Ekstein, Rudolph, and Robert Wallerstein. *The Teaching and Learning of Psychotherapy,* 2nd ed. New York: International Universities Press, 1972.

Erikson, Erik. *Identity and the Life Cycle.* New York: W.W. Norton, 1980.
Falicov, Celia Jaes. "Learning to Think Culturally" In Liddle et al., *Handbook of Family Therapy Training and Supervision,* 335-57.
Fisch, Richard. "Training in the Brief Therapy Model." In Liddle et al., *Handbook of Family Therapy Training and Supervision,* 78-92.
Haley, Jay. "Reflections on Supervision." In Liddle et al., *Handbook of Family Therapy Training and Supervision,* 358-67.
_____. *Learning and Teaching Therapy.* New York: Guilford Press, 1996.
Jacobs, Daniel, Paul David and Donald Meyer. *The Supervisory Encounter.* London: Yale University Press, 1995.
Kadushin, Alfred. *Supervision in Social Work* New York: Columbia University Press, 1976.
Kane, Corrine M. "An Experiential Approach to Family-Of-Origin Work with Marital and Family Therapy Trainees" *Journal of Marital and Family Therapy* 22,4 (1996): 481-488.
Kaslow, Florence. *Supervision, Consultation and Staff Training in the Helping Professions.* San Francisco: Jossey-Bass, 1977.
Kaslow, F.W. "Marital Therapy Supervision and Consultation." *The American Journal of Family Therapy* 19, 2 (1991): 84-92.
Kaufman, Barbara. "Training Tales in Family Therapy: Exploring 'The Alexandria Quartet'." *Journal of Marital and Family Therapy* 21,1 (1995): 67-76.
Kniskern, David P., and Alan Gurman. "Research." In Liddle et al., *Handbook of Family Therapy Training and Supervision,* 368-77.
Knowles, Malcolm. *The Modern Practice of Adult Education: From Pedagogy to Andragogy.* New York: Cambridge Adult Education, 1980.
Kolb, David. *Experiential Learning.* Englewood Cliffs, NJ: Prentice-Hall, 1984.
Kushnir, Talma. "Live Supervision in Family Therapy and Social Facilitation Effects: A Case Study with Physiological Measures." *Contemporary Family Therapy* 19, 4(1997): 553-62.
Latz, Martha. "On an Exercise for Training Beginning Marital and Family Therapists in Language Skills" *Journal of Marital and Family Therapy* 22,1 (1996): 121-126.
Lee, Robert E., Shirley Emerson and Patricia B. Kochka. "Using the Michigan State University Family Therapy Questionnaire for Training." *Contemporary Family Therapy* 19, 2(1997): 289-304.
Liddle, Howard, Douglas C. Breunlin and Richard C. Schwartz. "Family Therapy Training and Supervision: An Introduction." In Liddle et al., *Handbook of Family Therapy Training and Supervision,* 3-10.
_____. "Redefining the Mission of Family Therapy Training: Can Our Differentness Make a Difference?" *The Clinical Supervisor* 2, 2 (1986): 109-24.
_____, and G. Saba. "Teaching Family Therapy at the Introductory Level: A Model Emphasizing a Pattern which Connects Training and Therapy." *Journal of Marital and Family Therapy* 8 (1982): 63-72.
_____. "Family Therapy Training and Supervision: Current Issues and Future Trends." *International Journal of Family Therapy* 4 (1982): 81-97.
_____. "On Teaching a Contextual or Systemic Therapy: Training Content, Goals and Methods." *American Journal of Family Therapy* 8 (1980): 55-69.

_____, and B. Tucker. "Intra- and Interpersonal Process in the Group Supervision of Beginning Family Therapists." *Family Therapy* 5, 1 (1978): 13-28.

_____, B. Tucker and G. Hart. "Supervision in Family Therapy: A Developmental Perspective." *Journal of Marriage and Family Counselling* 2 (1976): 269-76.

_____, Gail S. Davidson and Mary Jo Barrett. "Outcomes of Live Supervision: Trainee Perspectives." In Liddle et al., *Handbook of Family Therapy Training and Supervision*, 386-98.

Long, Janie K., John J. Lawless and Diamond R. Dotson. "Supervisory Styles Index: Examining Supervisees' Perceptions of Supervisory Style" *Contemporary Family Therapy* 18, 4 (1996): 589-606.

Lyman, Bobbie J., Cheryl Storm and Charles York. "Rethinking Assumptions about Trainess' Life Experience" *Journal of Marital and Family Therapy* 21,2 (1995): 193-203.

Mazza, Judith. "Training Strategic Therapists: The Use of Indirect Techniques." In Liddle et al., *Handbook of Family Therapy Training and Supervision*, 93-109.

McCollum, Eric E., and Joseph L. Wetchler. "In Defense of Case Consultation: Maybe 'Dead' Supervision Isn't Dead After All." *Journal of Marital and Family Therapy* 21,2 (1995): 155-166.

McDaniel, S., T. Weber and J. McKeever. "Multiple Theoretical Approaches to Supervision: Choices in Family Therapy Training." *Family Process* 22, 4 (1983): 491-500.

McGoldrick, Monica, John K. Pearce and Joseph Giordano, eds. *Ethnicity and Family Therapy.* New York: Guilford Press, 1982.

Mueller, William S., and Bill L. Kell. *Coping with Conflict: Supervising Counselors and Psychotherapists.* New York: Appleton-Century-Crofts, 1972.

Myers-Briggs, I. *The Myers-Briggs Type Indicator Manual.* Princeton, NJ: Educational Testing Service, 1962.

Nichols, W. "An Integrative Psychodynamic and Systems Approach." In Liddle et al., *Handbook of Family Therapy Training and Supervision*, 110-27.

Papero, D. "Training in Bowen Theory." In Liddle et al., *Handbook of Family Therapy Training and Supervision*, 62-77.

Pirrotta, Sergio, and Gianfranco Cecchin. "The Milan Training Program." In Liddle et al., *Handbook of Family Therapy Training and Supervision*, 38-61.

Schwartz, Richard, Howard Liddle and Douglas C. Breunlin. "Muddles in Live Supervision." In Liddle et al., *Handbook of Family Therapy Training and Supervision*, 183-93.

Schwartz, Richard. "The Trainer-Trainee Relationship in Family Therapy Training." In Liddle et al., *Handbook of Family Therapy Training and Supervision*, 172-82.

Touliatos, John, Byron W. Lindholm and William C. Nichols. "The Shaping of Family Therapy Education: An Update." *Contemporary Family Therapy* 19, 3(1997): 391-408.

Wheeler, D., J. Myers Avis, L. Miller and S. Chaney. "Rethinking Family Therapy Education and Supervision: A Feminist Model." *Journal of Family Psychotherapy* 1, 4 (1986): 53-72.

Whipple, Vicky. "Developing an Identity as a Feminist Family Therapist: Implications for Training." *Journal of Marital and Family Therapy* 22,3 (1996): 381-396.

Williams, Anthony. *Visual and Active Supervision.* New York: Norton and Co., 1995.

Yalom, Irvin D. *The Theory and Practice of Group Psychotherapy.* New York: Basic Books, 1975.

# Index

absolutism, 3, 68
abstract theology, 1
adequate praxis, 1, 3, 4, 5, 88-96
advocacy, 64
Alfred, case of, 72, 79, 86-87
alienation, 67
American Association for Marriage and Family Therapy (AAMFT), 2
American Association for Pastoral Counselling (AAPC), 2, 13
analogical, 3, 4, 46, 75, 100
anthropology, theological, 6, 30
applied theology, 1, 103
Approach vs. Model, 19
Approach, clinical pastoral supervision, 20-22
Association for Clinical Pastoral Education (ACPE), 9-13
assumptions, theological, 1
Attachment theory, 47

behaviour, 67-68
behaviouralist, supervision, 18, 56
beneficence, ethics, 32
Bible, 16, 47, 67
Bill, case of, 7, 15, 21-2, 81
Boisen, Anton, 1, 8, 9, 10, 43-47
Boston approach (Institute for Pastoral Care), 11, 79
boundary, supervision, 19
  theology, 1
Bower, Gordon, 18
Bowlby, John, 47
branches, clinical training, 9
Brechenridge, Jack, 12
Browning, Don, 29, 47
Bruner, Jerome, 18
Buber, Martin, 42

Cabot, Richard, 2, 10
call in ministry, 88
Canadian Association for Pastoral Practice and Education (CAPPE), formerly CAPE, 4, 9, 12, 13
Canadian Council for Supervised Pastoral Education (CCSPE), 12
Capps, Don, 29, 38
care, 5, 64
cases, 5
case studies, 2, 3, 39, 49-50
Centreton, case, 62
centrifugal, 48, 82
centripetal, 48, 82
Chedoke campus, HHSC, 12
Christian fact, 29-30, 44-47
  interpretation, 3
Christology, from below, 25, 41-42, 45
circular, 5
Clark, Susan, case of, 50, 52, 58
clinical method, 2, 8, 15
Clinical Pastoral Education (CPE), 1, 2, 9-11
clinical pastoral supervision, 1, 3, 4,
  and clinical supervision, 20-22
  and pastoral supervision, 15
  assumptions, 22
  contribution to Gerkin, 77-87
  definition, 7-9, 103
  distinctive elements, 22-23
  source of, 22-23
clinical rhombus, 17
clinical supervision, 2, 6, 20-22, 103
  and family therapy, 21-22
Code of Ethics, 13
common sense, ethics, 53-61
competence, 5, 13, 28, 88, 94
complexity, supervision, 4, 7
concrete, theology, 1
congregation and supervision, 13-14
congruence in ministry, 13
constructed theology, 44
consulting team, family therapy, 20
context as educator, 94
Council for Clinical Training, 10

crisis experience, 42-43
criteria, analysis of texts, 23
critical incident, 49-50
cross, theology, 63
Crossan, Dominic, 47

definition, clinical pastoral supervision, 7-9
developmental supervision, 18, 92
    tasks, 7
Dewey, John, 18
dialectical outcome, supervision, 4, 5, 46, 103
differences, supervision, 4-6
diplomat, AAPC, 2
distinctive, 1, 4, 57, 97-99
diversity, learning styles, 7
document, living human, 2, 8, 32
doing, theology, 1, 77
dreams, in supervision, 36
dual relationships, 19
Dulles, Avery, 84
Dunbar, Helen, 2, 10, 11
dyadic supervision, 35
dynamics, supervisee, 8

Early writings, Gerkin (1954-79), 44, 47
ecclesial, status, 34
ecclesiology, 84
ecumenical, 5
education, adult, 7-8, 74
ego, 4, 5, 48, 54
Ekstein, Rudolph, 16-17, 21
Emanuel Episcopal Church, Boston, 10
Emmanuel Movement, 1, 10-11
empowerment, supervision, 34
end point, theology, 9
equipper of saints, 14-15
Erikson, Erik, 15, 25, 47
eschatological, identity, 53
ethics, 13, 32-33
ethnicity, 8, 35-37
ethnographic, 34
explanation, 4

faith, 6, 51
family of origin, 93
family, systems, 47
feeling, 67-8
field education and supervision, 14
field, supervision, 1, 5
Fitchett, George, 16-18, 75-76
Four characteristics, Gerkin's theology, 44-56
Freud, Sigmund, 48
Fromm, Eric, 48
Frye, Northrop, 48
fusion, horizon, 3-4, 43-44, 75-76, 87, 104
    and Gerkin's incarnational theology, 43-44

Gadamer, Hans-Georg, 3, 48
gender, 4, 8, 34-35
Georgia Association for Pastoral Counselling, Inc, 26
Gerkin, Charles V., 2, 6, 33-34, 39
    contribution to clinical pastoral supervision, 72-77
    four characteristics, 44-56
    history, 44
    incarnational theology, 3, 5-6, 42f.
goal, clinical pastoral supervision, 7
    supervisee, 88
good taste, 53-54
grace, 5
grace and judgment, 109n.8
group supervision, 13, 36
Guiles, Philip, 11

Haight, Emily, 35
Hamilton Health Sciences Corporation, 12
Hartung, Bruce, 24
Helping Styles Inventory (HSI), 24
hermeneutic, circle, 51
    detours, 50
    interdisciplinary, 29
    of supervision, 38, 55
    pastoral, 29

retrieval, 55
suspicion, 55
theory, 3, 54-55, 67-68, 57
hermeneutical approach, 5, 29-34, 733, 104
   play, 56
Hilgard, Ernest, 18
Hiltner, Seward, 11, 47
Hommes, Tjaard, 30
hope, 6, 60, 62-3
horizon of interpreter, 5
   text, 104
horizon of meaning, 3
horizons, fusion, 4, 5
human experience, source of theology, 39
humanistic supervision, 18
Hunter, Rodney, 21

identical fusion, 4, 104
identity, 66
Immanence, God, 26
Incarnation, 3
incarnational theology, 3, 6, 38, 41f.
   Gerkin, 42-43, 66
   Protestant, 42-43
   Roman Catholic, 41-42
   Wise, Carroll, 42
individual supervision, 13
Indonesia, 35
insight, 68
institutional, 7
integrate, 9
interdisciplinary, 3
interpretation, 2, 3, 66
   as dialogical game, 55-56
interpreter and text, 3
invitation of grace, 4
isomorphic supervision, 20
I-Thou, 42

Japan, 35
Jensen, Mark, 31
Jewett, Julia, 35
joining and baptism, 26
   and grace, 26
Jones, Logan, 25

Journal of Supervision and Training in Ministry, 5, 34
journals, kinds, 5
justice, 33

Kell, Bill, 17
Keller, William, 2, 10
Kenya, 35
Klink, Thomas, 41
Knowles, Malcolm, 18, 38
Kohut, Heinz, 26, 38
Kolb, David, 38
Kort, Wesley, 48

language of force and meaning, 50-51, 52-53, 60-61
   and hermeneutics, 52
later writings, Gerkin (1980-1984), 48-49
Laura, case of, 60, 64, 97
lay supervision, 34
learner-centred approach, 35
learning contract, 8, 35
learning difficulties, supervision, 17
Learning Styles, 8, 88
Liddle, Howard, 19
limitations of research, 100-101
living human document, 8, 39
Lutheran, 5, 11

MacKnight, Earle, 12
MacLachlan, Archie, 12
marginalization, 34
marriage and family therapy, 2
Mary, case of, 88-97
McCardy, David, 32-33
McCarthy, Marie, 32-33
McClelland, David, 83
Meakes, Elizabeth, 34-35
meaning, 3, 81-82, 111n.11
meaninglessness, 61, 68
medicine, 2
Merwald, Alfred, 26
method in theology, 1, 5, 49-52, 57, 99-100
   classical and reductionism, 49

Methodism, 44, 62
    catholicity of grace, 46
Mike, care of, 41, 51-52, 58-59, 97
minister, what to do, who am I, 8
Minuchin, Salvator, 41
Moltmann, Jurgen, 38, 47
moralizing, 32
Mountain Sanitorium, Hamilton, 12
Mueller, William, 17
multidisciplinary and multilingual, 47-49
Myers-Briggs, 38, 88
mystery, 4, 104
narrative and hermeutics, 52-56, 74-75, 109n.17
    and ethics, 53
    and story, 104
    Christian story, 53
    identity, 53
narrative hermeneutical theology, 31, 89
neo-Freudanism, 48-49
New York approach, 11, 79
Niebuhr, Richard, 38, 54

Oates, Wayne, 12
object relations theory, 47-49, 60, 65
O'Connor, Thomas, 34-35
Oden, Thomas, 47
orthopraxis, 29
overseer, 15
oversight of minister, 14-15

Papero, Daniel, 17
parabolic teacher, 14
parallel process, 16
partners, conversation, 1, 8
pastor, 3
pastoral care, 2
pastoral counselling, 2, 3,
    centre, 7
Pastoral Counselling Education, 11, 35
Pastoral Psychology, 5
pastoral relationship, 8
Pastoral Sciences, 5
pastoral skills, 7

pastoral supervision, 2, 7
    contemporary, 13
    definition, 11, 104
    history of, 10-12
    Middle Ages, 13
    N.T., 13
    O.T., 13
    theological images of, 13-15
pastoral theologian, 4
pastoral theology, 104
Patton, John, 14-15
personal dynamics, 8
personal identity, 8, 13
personality, 8
philosophical concern, 1
plurality, truth, 29
    interpretation, 41
Pohly, Ken, 13-14, 31
Poling, James, 61
power, 46-47, 82-83
powerlessness, 76, 82-83
practical theology, 1, 81, 105
practice of supervisee, 9, 77, 89
practices of ministry, 105
praxis, 1, 4, 6, 105
    five areas, 90-95
praxis/theory/praxis, 4, 6, 49, 51, 66, 75-76, 77, 105
problems about learning, 17
professional and personal growth, 105
    chapter 1, n.3
professional associations, 7, 12, 13
professional identity, 8, 12
professions, 1
Protestant practical theology, 42-43
    principle, 44
providence, 61
psychiatry, 2, 7
psychodynamic tradition, 21-22
psychology, 2, 7, 12

questions and answer approach, 50
questions, three, 1, 2, 4, 97-102
    Gerkin's contribution, 56-59, 69-71

Randall, Frances, 36
redemption, 26, 60-61
reductionism, 29
reflecting teams, family therapy, 20
revisionist practical theologians, 34
rhombus, clinical, 17, 25
Ricoeur, Paul, 50, 52-55, 74
Rogers, Carl, 18, 38, 57
Roman Catholic, 5
    practical theology, 41-44

sacraments, place of, 84-85
Sager, Cliff, 48
Sally, case of, 23, 28, 39-40, 97
schemata and figures, 50
Schlauch, Chris, 32-33
scientific supervision, 18
Scripture, 10
Seabright, Russell, 36
self, 6
self-awareness, 8
self-directed learning, 8
service in ministry, 28
similarities, 5
sin, 5, 60-62
social science approach, 5, 24-29, 57, 73-74, 79, 85, 105, 108n.5
    identical correlation, 25, 72
    language of, 25
    theological method, 25
    values and assumptions, 24-28
social work, 7, 18-19
sociology, 11
Somers, Clark, Carole, 25
soul, life of, 60-64, 77
sound judgment, 53
sources, for theology, 2, 28, 33, 37-38
    for clinical pastoral supervision, 2
special interest approach, 5, 34-38, 72, 105
    and gender, 34-35
    ethnicity, 35-37
    lay, 37
Split ACPE and AAPC, 10-11

standpoint, Christian fact, 44-47
standpoint, multiple, 34
Steere, David, 13-14
Stokes, Allison, 10
structural systems theory, 41
Supervised Pastoral Education (SPE), 12, 34-35, 107n.16
supervisee, 7-8, 91
supervision, 4
    and education, 8
    and support, 18
    and therapy, 19, 107n.31
synoptic view and Christology, 46
systemic, 19
systems theory, 48, 65

Table 1, 24
teachers, Christian education, 37
text, 1, 7
*The Journal of Pastoral Care*, 5
theologian, 2
theological anthropology, 6, 30
    Gerkin's standpoint in Christian fact, 60-64
    multidisciplinary, 64-65
    narrative and hermenutics, 67-69
    praxis, 66
theologizing, 3-4
theology, 1
theory, 1, 6
therapy and supervision, 19, 107n.31
thesis, 4
thinking, 1
Thomas, Jack, 27
three questions, 1, 4, 57-59, 70-71, 88-96, 97-100
Tillich, Paul, 38, 44
    and Protestant principle, 44-45
Time, in Gerkin, 46
Toronto, 12
Tracy, David, 1, 47
Tradition, 10
transformed praxis, 1, 6, 82, 88-96
transformation, 1, 46, 49
    definition, 95-96

Tucker, Grayson, 37
two source theology, 2, 28, 33

uncertain approach, 24
understanding/explanation/understanding, 50, 68, 105
understanding, postmodern, 3
United Methodist, 3, 44

validation in supervision, 35
VanKatwyk, Peter, 25
Van Wagner, Charles, 37
verbatims, 3, 9, 50
vignettes, 3
visit, pastoral, 9
volunteers and supervision, 37
Voss, Richard, 25

Wallerstein, Robert, 16-17, 25
Weeks, Louis, 37
Wise, Carroll, 42, 47
women's experiences of supervision, 34-35

Yalom, Irvine, 17

# Series Published by Wilfrid Laurier University Press for the Canadian Corporation for Studies in Religion / Corporation Canadienne des Sciences Religieuses

## Editions SR

1. *La langue de Ya'udi : description et classement de l'ancien parler de Zencircli dans le cadre des langues sémitiques du nord-ouest*
   Paul-Eugène Dion, O.P.
   1974 / viii + 511 p. / OUT OF PRINT
2. *The Conception of Punishment in Early Indian Literature*
   Terence P. Day
   1982 / iv + 328 pp.
3. *Traditions in Contact and Change: Selected Proceedings of the XIVth Congress of the International Association for the History of Religions*
   Edited by Peter Slater and Donald Wiebe with Maurice Boutin and Harold Coward
   1983 / x + 758 pp. / OUT OF PRINT
4. *Le messianisme de Louis Riel*
   Gilles Martel
   1984 / xviii + 483 p.
5. *Mythologies and Philosophies of Salvation in the Theistic Traditions of India*
   Klaus K. Klostermaier
   1984 / xvi + 549 pp. / OUT OF PRINT
6. *Averroes' Doctrine of Immortality: A Matter of Controversy*
   Ovey N. Mohammed
   1984 / vi + 202 pp. / OUT OF PRINT
7. *L'étude des religions dans les écoles : l'expérience américaine, anglaise et canadienne*
   Fernand Ouellet
   1985 / xvi + 666 p.
8. *Of God and Maxim Guns: Presbyterianism in Nigeria, 1846-1966*
   Geoffrey Johnston
   1988 / iv + 322 pp.
9. *A Victorian Missionary and Canadian Indian Policy: Cultural Synthesis vs Cultural Replacement*
   David A. Nock
   1988 / x + 194 pp. / OUT OF PRINT
10. *Prometheus Rebound: The Irony of Atheism*
    Joseph C. McLelland
    1988 / xvi + 366 pp.
11. *Competition in Religious Life*
    Jay Newman
    1989 / viii + 237 pp.
12. *The Huguenots and French Opinion, 1685-1787: The Enlightenment Debate on Toleration*
    Geoffrey Adams
    1991 / xiv + 335 pp.
13. *Religion in History: The Word, the Idea, the Reality / La religion dans l'histoire : le mot, l'idée, la réalité*
    Edited by/Sous la direction de Michel Despland and/et Gérard Vallée
    1992 / x + 252 pp.
14. *Sharing Without Reckoning: Imperfect Right and the Norms of Reciprocity*
    Millard Schumaker
    1992 / xiv + 112 pp.
15. *Love and the Soul: Psychological Interpretations of the Eros and Psyche Myth*
    James Gollnick
    1992 / viii + 174 pp.

16. *The Promise of Critical Theology: Essays in Honour of Charles Davis*
    Edited by Marc P. Lalonde
    1995 / xii + 146 pp.
17. *The Five Aggregates: Understanding Theravāda Psychology and Soteriology*
    Mathieu Boisvert
    1995 / xii + 166 pp.
18. *Mysticism and Vocation*
    James R. Horne
    1996 / vi + 110 pp.
19. *Memory and Hope: Strands of Canadian Baptist History*
    Edited by David T. Priestley
    1996 / viii + 211 pp.
20. *The Concept of Equity in Calvin's Ethics**
    Guenther H. Haas
    1997 / xii + 205 pp.
    * Available in the United Kingdom and Europe from Paternoster Press.
21. *The Call of Conscience: French Protestant Responses to the Algeria War, 1954-1962*
    Geoffrey Adams
    1998 / 320 pp. est.
22. *Clinical Pastoral Supervision and the Theology of Charles Gerkin*
    Thomas St. James O'Connor
    1998 / x + 152 pp.

# Comparative Ethics Series /
# Collection d'Éthique Comparée

1. *Muslim Ethics and Modernity: A Comparative Study of the Ethical Thought of Sayyid Ahmad Khan and Mawlana Mawdudi*
   Sheila McDonough
   1984 / x + 130 pp. / OUT OF PRINT
2. *Methodist Education in Peru: Social Gospel, Politics, and American Ideological and Economic Penetration, 1888-1930*
   Rosa del Carmen Bruno-Jofré
   1988 / xiv + 223 pp.
3. *Prophets, Pastors and Public Choices: Canadian Churches and the Mackenzie Valley Pipeline Debate*
   Roger Hutchinson
   1992 / xiv + 142 pp. / OUT OF PRINT
4. *In Good Faith: Canadian Churches Against Apartheid*
   Renate Pratt
   1997 / xii + 366 pp.

# Dissertations SR

1. *The Social Setting of the Ministry as Reflected in the Writings of Hermas, Clement and Ignatius*
   Harry O. Maier
   1991 / viii + 230 pp. / OUT OF PRINT
2. *Literature as Pulpit: The Christian Social Activism of Nellie L. McClung*
   Randi R. Warne
   1993 / viii + 236 pp.

# Studies in Christianity and Judaism /
# Études sur le christianisme et le judaïsme

1. *A Study in Anti-Gnostic Polemics: Irenaeus, Hippolytus, and Epiphanius*
   Gérard Vallée
   1981 / xii + 114 pp. / OUT OF PRINT
2. *Anti-Judaism in Early Christianity*
   Vol. 1, *Paul and the Gospels*, edited by Peter Richardson with David Granskou
   1986 / x + 232 pp.
   Vol. 2, *Separation and Polemic*
   Edited by Stephen G. Wilson
   1986 / xii + 185 pp.

3. *Society, the Sacred, and Scripture in Ancient Judaism: A Sociology of Knowledge*
   Jack N. Lightstone
   1988 / xiv + 126 pp.
4. *Law in Religious Communities in the Roman Period: The Debate Over* **Torah** *and* **Nomos** *in Post-Biblical Judaism and Early Christianity*
   Peter Richardson and Stephen Westerholm with A. I. Baumgarten, Michael Pettem and Cecilia Wassén
   1991 / x + 164 pp.
5. *Dangerous Food: 1 Corinthians 8-10 in Its Context*
   Peter D. Gooch
   1993 / xviii + 178 pp.
6. *The Rhetoric of the Babylonian Talmud, Its Social Meaning and Context*
   Jack N. Lightstone
   1994 / xiv + 317 pp.
7. *Whose Historical Jesus?*
   Edited by William E. Arnal and Michel Desjardins
   1997 / vi + 337 pp.

# The Study of Religion in Canada / Sciences Religieuses au Canada

1. *Religious Studies in Alberta: A State-of-the-Art Review*
   Ronald W. Neufeldt
   1983 / xiv + 145 pp.
2. *Les sciences religieuses au Québec depuis 1972*
   Louis Rousseau et Michel Despland
   1988 / 158 p.
3. *Religious Studies in Ontario: A State-of-the-Art Review*
   Harold Remus, William Closson James and Daniel Fraikin
   1992 / xviii + 422 pp.
4. *Religious Studies in Manitoba and Saskatchewan: A State-of-the-Art Review*
   John M. Badertscher, Gordon Harland and Roland E. Miller
   1993 / vi + 166 pp.
5. *The Study of Religion in British Columbia: A State-of-the-Art Review*
   Brian J. Fraser
   1995 / x + 127 pp.

# Studies in Women and Religion / Études sur les femmes et la religion

1. *Femmes et religions\**
   Sous la direction de Denise Veillette
   1995 / xviii + 466 p.
   \* Only available from Les Presses de l'Université Laval
2. *The Work of Their Hands: Mennonite Women's Societies in Canada*
   Gloria Neufeld Redekop
   1996 / xvi + 172 pp.
3. *Profiles of Anabaptist Women: Sixteenth-Century Reforming Pioneers*
   Edited by C. Arnold Snyder and Linda A. Huebert Hecht
   1996 / xxii + 438 pp.
4. *Voices and Echoes: Canadian Women's Spirituality*
   Edited by Jo-Anne Elder and Colin O'Connell
   1997 / xxviii + 237 pp.

# SR Supplements

1. *Footnotes to a Theology: The Karl Barth Colloquium of 1972*
   Edited and Introduced by Martin Rumscheidt
   1974 / viii + 151 pp. / OUT OF PRINT
2. *Martin Heidegger's Philosophy of Religion*
   John R. Williams
   1977 / x + 190 pp. / OUT OF PRINT

3. *Mystics and Scholars: The Calgary Conference on Mysticism 1976*
   Edited by Harold Coward and Terence Penelhum
   1977 / viii + 121 pp. / OUT OF PRINT
4. *God's Intention for Man: Essays in Christian Anthropology*
   William O. Fennell
   1977 / xii + 56 pp. / OUT OF PRINT
5. *"Language" in Indian Philosophy and Religion*
   Edited and Introduced by Harold G. Coward
   1978 / x + 98 pp. / OUT OF PRINT
6. *Beyond Mysticism*
   James R. Horne
   1978 / vi + 158 pp. / OUT OF PRINT
7. *The Religious Dimension of Socrates' Thought*
   James Beckman
   1979 / xii + 276 pp. / OUT OF PRINT
8. *Native Religious Traditions*
   Edited by Earle H. Waugh and K. Dad Prithipaul
   1979 / xii + 244 pp. / OUT OF PRINT
9. *Developments in Buddhist Thought: Canadian Contributions to Buddhist Studies*
   Edited by Roy C. Amore
   1979 / iv + 196 pp.
10. *The Bodhisattva Doctrine in Buddhism*
    Edited and Introduced by Leslie S. Kawamura
    1981 / xxii + 274 pp. / OUT OF PRINT
11. *Political Theology in the Canadian Context*
    Edited by Benjamin G. Smillie
    1982 / xii + 260 pp.
12. *Truth and Compassion: Essays on Judaism and Religion in Memory of Rabbi Dr. Solomon Frank*
    Edited by Howard Joseph, Jack N. Lightstone and Michael D. Oppenheim
    1983 / vi + 217 pp. / OUT OF PRINT
13. *Craving and Salvation: A Study in Buddhist Soteriology*
    Bruce Matthews
    1983 / xiv + 138 pp. / OUT OF PRINT
14. *The Moral Mystic*
    James R. Horne
    1983 / x + 134 pp.
15. *Ignatian Spirituality in a Secular Age*
    Edited by George P. Schner
    1984 / viii + 128 pp. / OUT OF PRINT
16. *Studies in the Book of Job*
    Edited by Walter E. Aufrecht
    1985 / xii + 76 pp. / OUT OF PRINT
17. *Christ and Modernity: Christian Self-Understanding in a Technological Age*
    David J. Hawkin
    1985 / x + 181 pp.
18. *Young Man Shinran: A Reappraisal of Shinran's Life*
    Takamichi Takahatake
    1987 / xvi + 228 pp. / OUT OF PRINT
19. *Modernity and Religion*
    Edited by William Nicholls
    1987 / vi + 191 pp.
20. *The Social Uplifters: Presbyterian Progressives and the Social Gospel in Canada, 1875-1915*
    Brian J. Fraser
    1988 / xvi + 212 pp. / OUT OF PRINT

Available from:
# WILFRID LAURIER UNIVERSITY PRESS
Waterloo, Ontario, Canada   N2L 3C5